アイテップ
iTEP公認
プラクティスガイド

iTEP International 著

IBCパブリッシング

まえがき

　アメリカ合衆国カリフォルニア州にあるiTEP Internationalが開発・販売するiTEP Academic、iTEP SLATE（Secondary Level Assessment Test of English）は、コンピューターベースで気軽に受験でき、そのスコアを使ってアメリカの1,000校を超える大学や高校に正規留学する道を開く、いままでにない簡便かつ画期的なテストです。

　そして、そのようなテスト制作の経験をもとに、ビジネス関係者の総合的な英語力を、同じくコンピューターベースで受けられるのがiTEP Businessとなります。

　iTEPテストは10年近く前から、日本にも上陸していました。しかし、日本はバブル経済がはじけた後、長い間、留学生の数も減り続け、それと並行するように日本の国際競争力や日本人の英語でのコミュニケーション力の劣化が問われていました。教育業界でも、より会話やコミュニケーションを重んじた英語教育の必要性が問われながらも、大学受験のありかたについての疑問が今でも投げかけられています。

　しかし、もっと大切なことは、世界の就職マーケットについて、日本人があまりにも情報を持っていないということです。一般的には、日本人は高校を卒業すれば日本の大学に入学し、その後、国内の企業に就職というおきまりのルートで人生設計を考えてきました。しかし世の中のAI化やパンデミックなどによる環境の変化の中で、そうしたルートが必ずしも一生を保証するものではないということが、語られるようになってきています。

　であれば、もっと世界に目を向けた人生の「サステナビリティー」を考えるべきなのではと思っている人も多いのではないでしょうか。

　そんな需要に応える最初の一歩はいうまでもなく留学です。そして、留学を通して海外で自分の力量を試してみる多様な可能性を見つけられれば、人生設計そのものがより広い機会に向けて開かれてゆくはずです。

　そんな留学を目指す人には、本書で紹介するiTEP AcademicやiTEP SLATEはその可能性に最も身近で、いつでもチャレンジできるテストとなるはずです。

英語の４技能を考えてみたとき、日本人が一番苦手なのはスピーキング、そして次がライティングかもしれません。一部の検定テストで、コミュニケーション力を測る上で最も大切なこの２つの技能が測定できないままに大学や職場での英語を使う現場に放り込まれ、苦しんでいる人も多いはずです。そうした意味では、iTEP Internationalが提供するもう一つのテストiTEP Businessは他の２つのテストのビジネス版として活用できる総合的な英語力を査定するテストとして日本でも需要が高まるのではないかと期待されています。

　さらに、留学という高いハードルに挑戦するのはまだまだと思う人も、自らの英語力の現状を改めて認識して、将来に備えるためにiTEPを受けることも可能です。

　アメリカの大学への留学は、iTEP Academicのスコアでいえば、４点以上をとることができれば多くの大学が受け入れてくれます。そんな目標を頭において、何度でも受験できるこのテストに挑戦すれば、知らないうちに英語の全ての技能での実力がついてくるはずです。

　変化する社会と国際環境──そして国際環境の影響を受けて、さらに波紋を広げる日本のビジネス環境や学術環境を思えば、我々は今もっと役に立つ英語を通して世界の情報を集め、交流しなければならないことはいうまでもないことです。

　iTEP Internationalの３つのテストを通して、そうした未来への挑戦の緒を掴んでいただければ幸いです。

iTEP Japan代表

賀川　洋

本書の構成

　『iTEP公認プラクティスガイド』で対象としているテストは、iTEP Academic Core、Academic Plus、SLATE (Secondary Level Assessment Test of English) Core、SLATE Plus、Business Core、Business Plusです。4技能（リスニング、リーディング、ライティング、スピーキング）＋文法の全5章と、付録（リスニング・パートのスクリプト及び各章の練習問題の解答）で構成されています。

　各章に用意された演習問題を解きながら、iTEPテストで出題されるさまざまなタイプの設問を詳しく分析していきます。

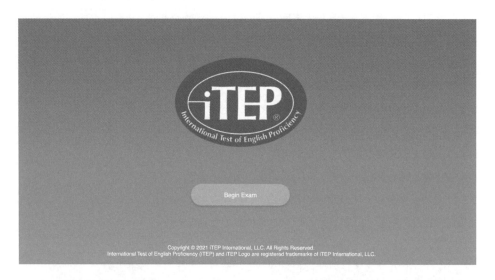

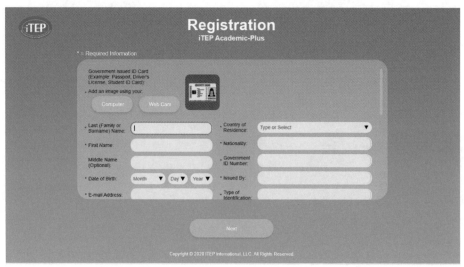

　また本ガイドには、iTEPの試験に取り組むための戦略やヒントだけでなく、英語学習全般に役立つ戦略も示されています。ライティング、スピーキング問題にどう取り組み、いかに解答を形成していくかについての知識は、iTEPテストだけでなく、ほかの検定テストでも大いに役立つ内容です。日々の英語学習にぜひご活用ください。

　「文法」のユニットでは、文法上のポイントや重要文法項目を一通り詳しく見ていきます。いずれの項目もiTEP Academic、SLATE、Businessのテストで取り扱われます。個々の文法事項は、それに対応する設問のタイプと結び付いていて、各「文法」の章の冒頭で四角く囲って強調してあります。

　「リスニング」のユニットでは、さまざまなタイプの問題を詳しく紹介しています。いずれの問題形式もiTEP Academic、SLATE、Businessのリスニング・セクションで採用されているものです。まず、短い対話とそれに関する設問の例が示されます。続いて、長めの対話や講義の例が、練習問題や各問いの解説とともに提示されます。全てのリスニングの練習問題は音声化されているので、まず音を聞いてから設問に解答し、それから解説を読んでください。
リスニングの練習問題は、以下のiTEPのウェブサイトで入手できます。

　　　　https://itepexamjapan.com/practiceguide

　「リーディング」のユニットで紹介するのは、iTEP Academic、SLATE、Businessのリーディング・セクションに見られるさまざまなタイプの問題です。ここでは、短いパッセージを繰り返し提示し、多様な問題の種類を分析します。これによって、リーディングパッセージの内容やいろいろな分析方法、取り組み方に的を絞ることができます。長めのパッセージや練習用テスト問題も提示され、また詳しい解法が紹介されます。

　「ライティング」のユニットでは、受験者による解答例と採点者の講評を見ていきます。また、このユニットでは、iTEP Academic、SLATE、Businessで出題されるいろいろなタイプのライティング問題について解説しています。時間的制約の下で英文を書く練習やそのための方策が紹介され、またワークシートに沿って書くことで、自分の意見やその表現方法について考えることができます。フォーマルな文章や学術論文の書き方が紹介され、さらに、フォーマルな文章のさまざまな構成についても説明されています。

　「スピーキング」のユニットでは、大局的かつ戦略的な方法で、iTEP Academic、SLATE、Businessのスピーキング・セクションに見られるさまざまなタイプの問題について解説しています。解答例や、スピーキング・セクションの攻略方法が提示されます。

　ぜひ、このプラクティス・ガイドをご活用ください！　必ずや、これが試験対策の目標達成とともに、総合的な語学力の向上に役立つことを実感していただけるはずです。

iTEP 公式テストの受験方法

■申し込み方法

以下のiTEP Japanウェブサイトから申し込みを行ってください。自宅受験、テストセンターでの受験の2種類があります。

    https://itepexamjapan.com

■受験場所

自宅、または全国のテストセンター（*iTEP Business-Plusは自宅受験のみ）の中から選びます。テストセンター一覧はこちらです。

    https://itepexamjapan.com/testcenter

■試験日

自宅受験の場合：24時間365日いつでも受験可能です。

テストセンター受験の場合：申し込みの際に受験希望日を選択します。希望日に基づき、iTEP Japan事務局がテストセンターの予約を行います。

■受験に必要なもの

自宅受験の場合：

- ・PC（Windows OS 8.1/10以降または、Mac OS X）
- ・キーボード、マウス
- ・PC内蔵カメラ、またはウェブカメラ
- ・Google Chromeブラウザ
- ・マイク付きヘッドセットまたは、マイク付きイヤホン（有線のみ可）
- ・YouTubeを快適に見ることができる程度のネット回線速度
  （ダウンロード：1 Mbps以上推奨　アップロード：250 kbps以上推奨）
- ・雑音が入らない静かな部屋（雑音が入ったり、背後に人が映るとスコアが無効となります）
- ・写真付きの身分証明書

テストセンター受験の場合：

- ・本人確認ができる、写真付きの身分証明書を持参する。

■スコアレポートの送付

・スコアレポートは受験終了後、最短1営業日でeメールで送付されます。

・スコアを送付する留学先の学校は、受験時のレジストレーション画面で、選択します。

・留学先の学校へは、採点終了後、自動的にスコアが送付されます。

■試験内容

テクニカルチェック・受験者情報登録：10分

試験時間：80分

　*テスト会場での受験の場合は、試験当日は、時間に余裕をもって会場に行ってください。

■受験の流れ

自宅受験の場合：

①ウェブサイトより受験の申し込み、受験料金の支払いをします。

②同日中に、受験IDとPWが記載されたメールが発行されます。

③受験環境・マニュアルの確認をします。詳細は

　　　https://itepexamjapan.com/archives/blog/1464

④いつでも好きなタイミングで受験できます（24時間365日）。

⑤受験開始（受験時のレジストレーション画面で、スコア送付先の学校を選択します）

⑥採点終了後、スコア送付先の学校には自動的にスコアが送付されます。

⑦受験後、最短1営業日で、メールでスコアレポートが送付されます。

テストセンター受験の場合：

①ウェブサイトより受験の申し込みをします。

②希望するテストセンターと受験日を選択し、受験料金の支払いをします。

③iTEP Japan事務局がテストセンターの予約・確保を行います。

④テストセンター予約完了後、事務局より通知メールが届きます。（通常1-2営業日以内）

⑤試験当日、テストセンターで受験をします。

　　（受験時のレジストレーション画面で、スコア送付先の学校を選択します）

⑥採点終了後、留学先には自動的にスコアが送付されます。

⑦受験後、最短1営業日で、eメールでスコアレポートが送付されます。

目 次

Unit 1 GRAMMAR   1

Unit 2 LISTENING 81

Unit 3 READING 105

Unit 4 WRITING 171

Unit 5 SPEAKING　　　　　　　　　　　　　　　　　　　261

Appendix　　　　　　　　　　　　　　　　　　　　　　　287

UNIT 1
GRAMMAR

Introduction to GRAMMAR

iTEPの文法セクションは、25問の多肢選択問題で構成されており、各設問は受験者がどれだけ英語の構造面での重要な特徴に習熟しているかを測るものです。このセクションでは、単純なものから複雑なものまで幅広い構文の問題が取り扱われるとともに、初級レベル・上級レベル両方の語彙が問われます。それぞれのタイプの設問を解く前に、画面に例題が示されます。

iTEPの文法セクションでは、空所補充問題と誤文訂正問題の2種類が出題されます。空所補充問題で受験者が求められるのは、正解を選んで文中の空所を正しく埋めることです。誤文訂正問題では、受験者は文中の下線部から文法的に誤っているものを選ぶよう求められます。

出題構成

このセクションでは次のような項目に関する問題が出題されます

- **動詞の形**
- **構文**
- **接続詞**
- **品詞**
- **冠詞と前置詞**
- **分量の表現**
- **代名詞**

試験時間：**10分間**

レベル：**CEFR A〜C**

パート1
空欄補充問題

いくつかの選択肢の中から下線部にあてはまる語句を選ぶ問題
全13問

パート2
誤文訂正問題

英文の間違っている箇所を選択肢の中から選ぶ問題
全12問

問題例

Part 1. Complete the Sentence

Yesterday we _____ the new public library.

      A. visit

      B. visited

      C. will visit

      D. visiting

Part 2. Error Correction

Rehearsals for the school play began next week, and the first performance will be the week after.

      A. the

      B. began

      C. first

      D. after

Grammar

Listening

Reading

Writing

Speaking

Appendix

Chapter 1　動詞の形

時の表現

　文法セクションで最も頻出するタイプの設問は、文中の時間関係の表現を根拠にして動詞の正しい形を判断するよう求めるものです。それ以外にも、iTEP の設問には、動詞の形が誤っており、この誤用を正解として指摘しなければならないようなものもあります。

　最も頻出する時間関係の表現は、習慣的（あるいは日常的に発生すること）、特定の過去、不特定な過去、今起こっていることなどを表すと考えられるものです。通例、こうした表現に応じて、動詞の形が変わります。こうした表現を見極める力があれば、iTEP の文法セクションで正解を選べるはずです。

> このチャプターでは太字になっている項目についてテストします
>
> - **動詞の形**
> - **構文**
> - 接続詞
> - **品詞**
> - 冠詞と前置詞
> - 分量の表現
> - 代名詞

　以下の表を見て、こうした時の区分に対応する時間表現の典型例を確認してください。

	習慣的	特定の過去	不特定の過去	今起こっていること
表現の例	every day sometimes every on Wednesdays in the spring every year	last week yesterday two years ago last year in 1996 on Wednesday	since 1999 for 25 years	now right now currently at this time
動詞の時制	現在形	過去形	現在完了形	現在進行形
動詞の活用形	take / takes read / reads drive / drives talk / talks study / studies	took read drove talked studied	has taken / have taken has read / have read has driven / have driven has talked / have talked has studied / have studied	am taking is taking are taking am reading is reading are reading
文例	*"She studies medicine."*	*"She studied chemistry last year."*	*"She has studied medicine for three years."*	*"She is studying for a test she will take tomorrow."*

Grammar

> **TIP** 習慣的な時間を表現するには、動詞の現在形を用いる。
> 特定の過去の時間を表現するには、動詞の過去形を用いる。
> 不特定な過去の時間を表現するには、動詞の現在完了形を用いる。
> 今起こっていることを表現するには、動詞の現在進行形を用いる。

習慣的

習慣的な時間を表す表現と動詞の形を見てみましょう。

例題1 **Complete the Sentence**

Mrs. Brown _____ her children to school by car every day.

    A. taking

    B. is taken

    C. takes

    D. has taken

　この例題の正解は**C**です。この文からは、子どもたちを学校へ連れて行くという行動がブラウン夫人にとって習慣的なものであることが読み取れます。それは彼女の習慣です。Aが誤りなのは、動詞の形として不完全だからです。Aは、iTEPにおける非常に典型的な誤答の例なので、これが誤りである理由をきちんと認識し、こうした選択肢を正解と取り違えないようにしなければなりません。Aを成り立たせるためには、直前に何らかの補助的な動詞の形を加える必要があり、それが選択肢か文中に示されていなければなりません。例えば、もしAが**is taking**であれば、動詞の形は完全なものとなります。とはいえ、依然として誤答です。理由は、文の最後の２語にあります。**every day**という時間の表現は、明らかに**C**が正解であることを示しています。

　Bが誤答なのは、受動態だからです。また、Dが誤りなのは、現在完了形だからです。

例題2 **Error Correction**

Mrs. Brown <u>is taking</u> her children <u>to</u> school <u>by</u> car every <u>day</u>.

    A. is taking

    B. to

    C. by

    D. day

　この文では、誤っている語句を指摘しようとしているわけですから、正解は**A**です。この行動

Grammar

Listening

Reading

Writing

Speaking

Appendix

は今進行しているものではなく、習慣的なものなので、現在形のtakesが用いられるべきです。is takingのような現在進行形ではありません。

複数形の主語と動詞の形の一致

次に文の主語が複数形になる例を見てみましょう。

例題3　**Complete the Sentence**

The parents ＿＿＿＿＿＿ their children to school by car every day.

    A. take

    B. were taken

    C. taking

    D. takes

複数形の主語と動詞の形との一致は、iTEPでは非常に高頻度で問われる文法事項です。まず、この例題の文の主語が複数形であることに気づく必要があります。つまり、ここで求められる動詞の形はtakeです。従って、**A**が正解です。Dが誤答なのは、単数を表す主語を受けるものだからです。Bが誤答なのは、受動態だからです。Cが誤りなのは、動詞の形として不完全だからです。

特定の過去

以下に、動詞の形と時間の表現に関する別の例題を示します。

例題4　**Complete the Sentence**

Last week, the president of the company ＿＿＿＿＿＿ that the company's offices would be moving.

    A. announced

    B. has announced

    C. had announced

    D. was announcing

この例題の正解は**A**です。特定の過去を表す時間の表現last weekがあるので、ある行動が過去の特定の時点で取られたことが分かります。従って、動詞の過去形を使えばこの文が正しく完成

Grammar

します。Bは現在完了形なので、このような特定の過去を表すには不適当です。Cは過去完了形なので、単純な過去を表す文では不適当です。Dは過去進行形で、これが使えるのは何らかの別の過去を表す節を伴った場合だけです。

不特定な過去

文によっては、何かが過去に起きたことを表していながら、厳密な時が特定されないことがあります。その場合、伝えられる重要な事実は、出来事の発生そのもの、あるいは誰かがそのような出来事を経験したこと自体です。以下に、その種の文の例を示します。

例題5 **Complete the Sentence**

Mrs. Johnson _____ in this neighborhood for 30 years.

  A. lives

  B. living

  C. is living

  D. has lived

正解は**D**です。ここで鍵になる時間の表現は for 30 years（30年にわたって）です。他の選択肢が誤りなのは、for 30 years という時間表現が現在完了形を導くものだからです。仮にこの文にfor 30 years という表現が含まれていなければ、AもCも正解となり得ます。Bは、動詞の形として不完全です。

複数形との一致

この場合も、常に複数形・単数形との一致に目を向けられるようにしておく必要があります。次の例題の誤りを見つけられますか。

例題6 **Error Correction**

Mrs. Brown and her husband has lived in this neighborhood for 30 years.

  A. her

  B. has

  C. this

  D. for

正解は**B**ですが、これは文の主語Mrs. Brown and her husbandが複数を表しているので、複数に対応する動詞の形——have livedを用いる必要があるからです。**B**のhasが誤りとなります。

今起こっていること

今起こっていることを表す時間表現と動詞の形の例を、以下に示します。

例題7 **Complete the Sentence**

We _____ any more applications at this time.

      A. are not taken

      B. have not taken

      C. are not taking

      D. do not taking

この問題の正解は**C**です。この例題の鍵となる時間の表現はat this time（今のところ、現時点では）です。**A**が誤りなのは受動態だからです。**B**が誤答なのは現在完了形だからです。**D**が間違いなのは、do notにtakingという-ing形を続けるのが不適切だからです。

"Error Correction" の解答法

4つの時間表現——習慣的、特定の過去、不特定な過去、今起こっていること——の例題を使って、誤った箇所をどう見つければいいか、見てみましょう。

［習慣的］

例題8 **Error Correction**

Every Saturday morning, <u>the</u> soccer team <u>was training</u> in the university gym, and it <u>is closed</u> to all <u>other</u> students.

正解は**was training**です。時間の表現Every Saturday morningがあるので、習慣的な行為を表すtrainsが正しい形です。

Grammar

[特定の過去]

例題9　**Error Correction**

Last year, <u>the</u> city council <u>creating</u> a new park <u>in</u> the center <u>of town</u>.

正解は **creating** です。 created と修正すれば、時間の表現 last year と一致します。

[不特定な過去]

例題10　**Error Correction**

My wife <u>and</u> I <u>live</u> <u>next to</u> the police station for 25 <u>years</u>.

　正解は **live** です。 for 25 years という時間の表現があるので、習慣を表す現在形は誤りです。 修正するには、 have lived または lived とします。 have lived と lived の違いに注意してください。 have lived という句を使うと、この夫婦が今でも警察署に隣に住んでいることになります。 動詞 lived なら、夫婦はもう警察著の隣に住んではいませんが、かつて25年間住んでいたことを意味します。

[今起こっていること]

例題11　**Error Correction**

The <u>theater company</u> is currently <u>hold</u> auditions for the new production <u>that</u> it <u>plans</u> to stage.

　正解は **hold** です。 正しくは holding とすべきで、それによって is という be 動詞とともに現在進行形が作られます。

EXERCISE

Part 1. Complete the Sentence

1. On Mondays, my sister _____ her bike to school before she meets up with her friends for coffee.

   A. rides

   B. riding

   C. is riding

   D. has ridden

2. Right now, I _____ an essay on Marianne Moore; she is my new favorite poet.

   A. is writing

   B. am writing

   C. have written

   D. has written

3. The *Mona Lisa* is a classic painting, and there _____ a print hanging in my grandmother's living room.

   A. is

   B. are

   C. were

   D. am

4. Back in 2001, I _____ all the way from San Francisco to Los Angeles.

   A. am bicycling

   B. have bicycled

   C. bicycled

   D. bicycling

5. For 100 years the Daughters of American War Veterans _____ been donating time to service people.

   A. have

   B. having

   C. will have

   D. is

6. Two years ago, both Mike and Nick _____ from the university with the best grades.

   A. graduate

   B. graduated

   C. are graduating

   D. will graduate

7. Since her tenth birthday, she _____ been practicing her flute daily.

   A. has

   B. having

   C. have

   D. was

Grammar

Listening

Reading

Writing

Speaking

Appendix

Grammar

Part 2. Error Correction

8. Every night, Kara reading to her daughter as she rocks her to sleep after dinner.

   A. night
   B. reading
   C. her
   D. after

9. This morning I started a music class; now I is learning piano.

   A. This
   B. I started
   C. now
   D. is

10. We did visited the local farmers market several times this year.

    A. We did
    B. the local
    C. several
    D. this year

11. Yesterday after school, she walks to the library all by herself.

    A. after
    B. walks
    C. all
    D. herself

12. Occasionally, the rain fell for hours, keeping everyone inside where they watch movies until the rain stops.

    A. fell
    B. everyone
    C. where
    D. until

13. My job is hiring new staff, so now they have giving me fewer hours.

    A. My
    B. is hiring
    C. so now
    D. have

14. When she was in the fifth grade, Tina win the spelling competition.

    A. When
    B. she
    C. fifth
    D. win

15. Every year, my family is watching the fireworks that explode in the sky on Memorial Day.

    A. my
    B. is watching
    C. that
    D. on

Grammar

Listening

Reading

Writing

Speaking

Appendix

Chapter 2 論理的なつながりを表す語句

内容を結び付ける

論理的なつながりを表す語句が用いられるのは、一文中で意味上の関係がある2つの部分を結び付ける場合です。こうした文中の2つの部分の間にある意味上の関係は、次の4つに分けられます：時間、因果関係、反意、条件です。これらの各意味分野においては、さまざまな方法を使って文中の2つの部分を結び付けることができます。こうした結び付きを実現するには、副詞節を導く接続表現、等位接続詞のたぐい、前置詞・群前置詞、その他の表現が用いられます。意味上の関係や、結合方法によって、どのような動詞の形を使えばいいかが決まります。iTEPの試験で出題される多くの文法問題は、受験者がこの表現の仕組みを左右する規則を見抜けるかどうかを測るものです。

> このチャプターでは太字になっている項目についてテストします
>
> - 動詞の形
> - **構文**
> - **接続詞**
> - 品詞
> - 冠詞と前置詞
> - 分量の表現
> - 代名詞

以下の表を見て、こうした時の区分に対応する時間表現の典型例を確認してください。

	時間	因果関係	反意	条件
副詞節を導く接続表現	until after before when while since once whenever as soon as	because as since now that as long as so that in order that	even though although though while whereas where	if unless even if provided (that) providing (that) in case whether or not only if
等位接続詞のたぐい	and then	so	but yet	or (else)
前置詞・群前置詞	during after before since until upon	because of due to	despite in spite of	

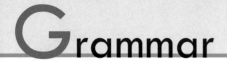

Grammar

その他の表現	then next after that following that before that afterwards meanwhile beforehand	therefore consequently	however nonetheless nevertheless on the other hand in contrast on the contrary	otherwise

Group A

- The soccer team lost the match **because** many of the players became sick the night before.
- **Because** many of the players became sick the night before, the soccer team lost the match.
- Many of the players became sick the night before, **so** the soccer team lost the match.
- The soccer team lost the match **due to** the sickness that many players had the night before.
- **Because** of the sickness that many of the players had the night before, the soccer team lost the match.
- Many of the players got sick the night before. **Therefore**, the soccer team lost the match.

Group B

- **Even though** many of the players were sick, the soccer team still won the match.
- The soccer team still won the match **though** many of the players were sick.
- Many of the players were sick, **but** the soccer team still won the match.
- **Despite** the terrible sickness they had gotten the night before, the soccer team won the match.
- The soccer team won the match **despite** the sickness that many of the players had.
- Many of the players got sick the night before. **Nonetheless**, they still won the match the next day.

Group C

- **After** the soccer team had won the game, they were greeted by their fans outside the stadium.

- The soccer team members were greeted by their fans outside the stadium **after** they had won the game.
- The soccer team members were greeted by their fans outside the stadium **after** winning the game.
- **After** winning the game, the soccer team members were greeted by their fans outside the stadium.
- The soccer team won the game. **Then**, they were greeted by their fans outside the stadium.

Group D

- **If** the provincial government does not fund the new road project, traffic will continue to get worse in this area.
- Traffic will continue to get worse in this area **if** the provincial government does not fund the new road project.
- The provincial government will fund the new road project, **or else** traffic will continue to get worse in this area.
- The provincial government will fund the new road project. **Otherwise**, traffic will continue to get worse in this area.

　前出の表やグループ分けした例文を見ると、英語の節同士を関連付ける仕組みは複雑に感じられるかもしれません。しかし、実際には、この仕組みには規則があるので予測が可能です。一旦この規則を覚えれば、それに基づいてiTEPの文法セクションで答えを判断できるのです。身近な教師に尋ねれば、表の内容や節同士を結び付ける方法についてさらに学ぶ手助けをしてもらえるかもしれません。以下に、いくつかiTEPが判定する際に用いる可能性がある方法を紹介します。

　一般に、類似の意味を表すさまざまな異なる形があり得ることを覚えておく必要があるでしょう。多くの場合、iTEPの文法問題では、小さな違いが正答か誤答かを判断する要因となり得ます。

複文中で時間を判断する

　時間の表現だけが、文中で時の概念を伝えるものではありません。英語には、時を表す方法がたくさんあります。あるいは、より正確には、ある出来事が別の出来事の前だったのか後だったのかを表す方法、ということです。主に、iTEPの試験では、文中の時間関係を

Grammar
Listening
Reading
Writing
Speaking
Appendix

Grammar

判断した上で、正解を選ぶことが求められます。たいていは、動詞の形が時間関係を適切に表現する役割を担っています。多くの場合、iTEP の文法セクションで試されるのが、動詞の正しい形を文中の他の情報を基に判断する力です。この種の文では、往々にして2つの節が、before や after のような副詞節を導く語句を挟んで隔てられています。

　以下の文を検討してみましょう。各文に、下線部が2つずつあります。どちらの出来事が先で、どちらが後でしょうか。

1. The teacher will give the students homework before the class finishes.
2. Before the class finishes, the teacher will give the students homework.
3. The host and hostess of the party relaxed after the last guests had left.
4. After the last guests had left, the host and hostess of the party relaxed.

例題1　Complete the Sentence

Timothy passed a written test and a road test _____ getting his driver's license.

　　A. because
　　B. only if
　　C. during
　　D. before

　正解は D です。A と B が誤りなのは、これらの語句が別の節を導くものだからです。つまり、空所の後に主語が必要です。選択肢 C が誤りなのは、during という前置詞が getting のような動名詞を従えることができないからです。そのような構文は論理的に意味をなしません。

例題2　Error Correction

So the city built the neighborhood park, there was nowhere for the children to play.

　　A. So
　　B. built
　　C. there
　　D. for

　正解は A です。もし2つの節の順序が逆であれば、so でも構いません。built the neighborhood park が2つの出来事のうちの後の方に当たるので、so を before に代えれば正しい文になります。

14

Grammar
Listening
Reading
Writing
Speaking
Appendix

so、because、because of、due to、therefore の違いを知る

　iTEPの文法問題では、英語で因果関係を説明する際に用いられる構文間の違いを見極める力が試されることがあります。文中の部分間にこの種の関係を持たせる方法は、いろいろあります。先述のGroup Aの文を参照すれば、さまざまな構文を用いて同じ事柄を表現できることが分かるでしょう。こうした例文から、どのような形を見つければiTEPの文法セクションで正解を選べるかが分かります。以下の文はGroup Aのもので、それらにさらに詳しい説明や助言を付け加えてあります。

副詞節を導く語句

　下記の最初の2文では、副詞節を導く語becauseが用いられており、それが原因と結果を結び付けています。この場合、文中に2つの節があるので、主語と動詞が2つずつ見つかるはずです。節には主語と動詞の両方が備わっている、ということを覚えておいてください。そして、2つの節を持つ文は複文と呼ばれます

Form 1: 副詞節を導く語句が文の中間にある場合

The soccer team lost the match because many of the players became sick the night
　　　　主語＋動詞　　　　　　副詞節を導く語　　　　　　主語＋動詞
before.
注意：この構文ではカンマが使われない。

Form 2: 副詞節を導く語句が文頭にある場合

Because many of the players became sick the night before, the soccer team lost
副詞節を導く語　　　　　　主語＋動詞　　　　　　　　　　　　　　主語＋動詞
the match.
注意：この構文ではカンマが必要。

Form 3: 等位接続詞

Many of the players became sick the night before, so the soccer team lost the
　　　　主語＋動詞　　　　　　　　　　　　等位接続詞＋主語＋動詞
match.
注意：この構文ではカンマが必要。

Grammar

Form 4: 群前置詞が文頭にある場合

<u>Because of</u> the <u>sickness</u> that many of the players had the night before,
　　　　　　群前置詞＋目的語

<u>the soccer team</u> <u>lost</u> the match.
　　　　　　主語＋動詞

注意：Form 1 と Form 4 の違いに着目。よく似ているが、Form 4 では節が 1 つしかない。because
of は群前置詞で、副詞節を導くものではない点を覚えておきたい。

Form 5: 群前置詞が文の中間にある場合

The <u>soccer team</u> <u>lost</u> the match <u>due to</u> the <u>sickness</u> that many players had the night
　　　主語＋動詞　　　　　　　群前置詞＋目的語

before.

注意：この構文ではカンマが使われない。

Form 6: 文をつなぐ表現が使われる場合、文が 2 つある場合

Many of the <u>players</u> <u>got</u> sick the night before. <u>Therefore</u>, the <u>soccer team</u> <u>lost</u>
　　　　　主語＋動詞　　　　　　　　　　　　　　文をつなぐ表現　　　　　主語＋動詞

the match.

注意：therefore が文頭で使われる場合、直後にカンマが置かれる。

例題3　Complete the Sentence

The computer is infected with spyware _____ it does not have up-to-date
antivirus protection.

     A. once

     B. until

     C. because

     D. after

正解は **C** です。この文には主語と動詞を備えた節が 2 つあり、副詞節を導く because が意味上、
最も適切です。

例題4　Error Correction

<u>During</u> it is the middle <u>of</u> August, <u>you can</u> expect the <u>temperature</u> outside to be 100
degrees.

     A. During

     B. of

Grammar

Listening

Reading

Writing

Speaking

Appendix

　　　C. you can

　　　D. temperature

　この文は前置詞を含む句で始まっていますが、during it isという組み合わせは誤りです。従っ
て、正解は**A**です。正しくはbecauseかsinceです。

despite と in spite of や、even though、although、 though の違いを知る

　文中の概念を結び付ける語句にはいろいろあり、混同してしまうこともあります。例え
ば、前置詞despiteと群前置詞in spite ofや、副詞節を導くeven though、although、
thoughなどです。以下で、再度Group Bの文を見てみましょう。

Form 1: 副詞節を導く語句が文頭にある場合

Even though many of the players were sick, the soccer team still won the match.

副詞節を導く句＋　　　　　　　　主語＋動詞　　　　　　　　　主語＋動詞

注意：この構文ではカンマが必要。

Form 2: 副詞節を導く語句が文の中間にある場合

The soccer team still won the match though many of the players were sick.

　　　　　主語＋動詞＋　　　　　　　副詞節を導く語　　　　主語＋動詞

注意：この構文ではカンマが使われない。

Form 3: 前置詞が文頭にある場合

Despite the terrible sickness they had gotten the night before, the soccer team won

前置詞＋　　　　　　　　目的語　　　　　　　　　　　　　　　　　　　主語＋動詞

the match.

注意：この構文ではカンマが必要。

Form 4: 前置詞が文の中間にある場合

The soccer team won the match despite the sickness that many of the players had.

　　　主語＋動詞＋　　　　　前置詞　　　　＋目的語

注意：この構文ではカンマが不要。

Grammar

Complete the Sentence

Katie would like to ride racehorses competitively for a living _____ her mother strongly disapproves.

    A. though

    B. despite

    C. so that

    D. in spite of

　正解は**A**です。選択肢**B**と**D**が誤りなのは、直後に動名詞disapprovingを従える必要があるからです。選択肢**C**が誤答なのは、これに続く節の動詞にwould disapproveという仮定法かwill disapproveという未来表現を用いる必要があるからです。

例題6　**Error Correction**

We <u>decided</u> to stay at <u>the</u> park <u>although</u> the rain that was <u>getting</u> us wet.

    A. decided

    B. the

    C. although

    D. getting

　正解は**C**です。この接続詞が不適切なのは、関係代名詞のthatが続いているからです。もしthatがこの文になければ、**C**は適切です。ここでは、thatが削除の対象となる選択肢ではないので、**C**をin spite ofに修正する必要があります。

during と while の違いを知る

　ご承知のとおり、文や節をつなぐ語句の違いが分かっていることは、英語をうまく書いたり話したりする上で大変重要です。また、iTEPの試験の文法セクションでも役立つ知識です。もう一つ、よく混同しやすいのが、duringとwhileです。duringは前置詞であるのに対して、whileは副詞節を導く接続詞です。

> **TIP** 　節を導く接続詞whileには、通例、主語と動詞が続きます。duringは普通、名詞または名詞句を従えます。

Grammar

Listening

Reading

Writing

Speaking

Appendix

> **Form 1: 副詞節を導く語句が文頭にある場合**
>
> <u>While</u> he <u>was running</u> the race, <u>he</u> <u>felt</u> a pain growing
>
> 副詞節を導く語＋主語＋動詞　　　　　　主語＋動詞
>
> in his knees.
>
> 注意：この構文ではカンマが必要。
>
> **Form 2: 前置詞が文頭にある場合**
>
> <u>During</u> the <u>race</u>, <u>he</u> <u>felt</u> a pain growing in his knees.
>
> 前置詞＋　　　目的語　主語＋動詞
>
> 注意：この構文ではカンマが必要。

例題7 **Complete the Sentence**

The older couple fell asleep ＿＿＿＿＿＿ the final act of the play.

    A. during

    B. while

    C. because

    D. despite

　正解は**A**です。the final act of the playの部分には動詞がないので、これは前置詞に導かれる句であるはずです。duringが選択肢の中で唯一の前置詞です。他の選択肢が誤りなのは、どれも主語と動詞を備えた節を導くものだからです。

例題7 **Error Correction**

<u>During</u> the man <u>who</u> drove the red car <u>was telling</u> his side of the story, the driver of <u>the</u> other car involved in the accident left the scene.

    A. During

    B. who

    C. was telling

    D. the

　正解は**A**です。2つの節があり、同時に発生する2つの出来事を表現しているので、副詞節を導く語whileが必要です。前置詞のduringは使えません。

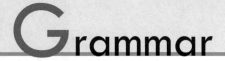

Grammar

EXERCISE

Part 1. Complete the Sentence

1. _____ it's raining, the children will not be able to go outside and play.
   A. As long as
   B. During
   C. Before
   D. Upon

2. Megan is going to major in science _____ she wants to become a physicist.
   A. whereas
   B. during
   C. as
   D. after

3. Vehicle damage will continue _____ the state does not repair the many potholes on local streets and highways.
   A. if
   B. unless
   C. even if
   D. once

4. Martha prefers to watch jazz and tap dancing performances _____ her husband prefers a classic ballet production.
   A. as soon as
   B. as long as
   C. whereas
   D. whenever

5. My family likes to begin Christmas shopping early, _____ no major unexpected bills pop up.
   A. since
   B. in case
   C. now that
   D. provided

6. Wait until you hear from me _____ you complete the application for the student loan.
   A. until
   B. during
   C. before
   D. since

7. _____ David Hockney is nearly 80 years old, he continues to create art in new ways using modern media and technology.
   A. After
   B. Whenever
   C. In case
   D. Even though

8. Wait _____ you save enough money for a down payment before you try to purchase a car.

   A. when

   B. because

   C. until

   D. if

Part 2. Error Correction

9. I will <u>leave</u> 20 minutes early <u>when</u> I arrive <u>on</u> time <u>even if</u> there is traffic.

   A. leave

   B. when

   C. on

   D. even if

10. <u>Where</u> my brother is <u>living</u> at home with <u>our</u> parents, <u>he'll</u> save money.

    A. Where

    B. living

    C. our

    D. he'll

11. The kids want <u>to go to</u> the zoo <u>after</u> school, <u>whereas</u> the snake exhibit <u>is open</u>.

    A. to go to

    B. after

    C. whereas

    D. is open

12. <u>You</u> can be happy <u>unless</u> you take the steps <u>to</u> make <u>yourself</u> so.

    A. You

    B. unless

    C. to

    D. yourself

13. Kathryn is willing to become an American citizen <u>in order</u> to marry the man <u>she</u> loves <u>by the time</u> she was raised <u>as a</u> Chinese citizen.

    A. in order

    B. she

    C. by the time

    D. as a

14. Introverted people <u>are said</u> to find renewed energy from spending time alone <u>before</u> extroverts recharge <u>in</u> the company <u>of</u> others.

    A. are said

    B. before

    C. in

    D. of

15. <u>Since</u> you eat all of the food <u>on your</u> plate, you <u>can</u> have ice cream <u>for</u> dessert.

    A. Since

    B. on your

    C. can

    D. for

Grammar

Listening

Reading

Writing

Speaking

Appendix

Grammar

Chapter 3 能動態と受動態

態を理解する

動詞の別の側面の１つに、態と呼ばれるものがあります。英語教師は、動詞には能動態と受動態があると説明します。話し言葉や書き言葉の大半で能動態が使われますが、iTEPの受験者は受動態を認識できなければなりません。加えて、能動態であれ受動態であれ、動詞に時制と相（アスペクト）という特性があることは変わりません。能動態、受動態の機能を決定づける根本的な問題は「誰が、あるいは何が行為者か」ということです。

動詞が能動態で用いられた文では、通例、誰が行為者かがはっきりしています。行為者が文の主語に一致するのが普通だからです。一方、受動態の文では、行為者が不明確なことが多く、全く述べられないこともあります。能動態、受動態で用いられた動詞のさまざまな形を見極められることは、iTEPの文法セクションで正しい解答を導く上で重要です。

例文を見る前に、次の表で能動態、受動態の文のさまざまな形の詳細を確認してください。この表では、driveという動詞を例に取っています。driveが不規則動詞である点に注意してください。受動態になると、過去分詞drivenが用いられます。

また、時制や相（アスペクト）がbe動詞によって明示される点にも注意してください。

> このチャプターでは太字になっている項目についてテストします
>
> - **動詞の形**
> - **構文**
> - 接続詞
> - **品詞**
> - 冠詞と前置詞
> - 分量の表現
> - 代名詞

時制／動詞の形	能動態	受動態
単純現在形	drive / drives	am / is / are driven
現在進行形	am / is / are driving	am / is / are being driven
単純過去形	drove	was / were driven
過去進行形	was driving	was / were being driven
現在完了形	have / has driven	have / has been driven
過去完了形	had driven	had been driven
未来表現	will drive	will be driven

仮定法過去	would drive	would be driven
仮定法過去完了	would have driven	would have been driven
to 不定詞	to drive	to be driven
完了不定詞	to have driven	to have been driven
現在分詞／動名詞	driving	being driven
完了分詞	having driven	having been driven

例題1　Complete the Sentence

The truck was _____ to the border and left there for several days.

　　A. driving
　　B. drove
　　C. driven
　　D. drives

　正解は **C** です。正しい受動態の形にするには、過去分詞が必要です。選択肢Cは過去分詞です。選択肢Aは一見正解に見えます。しかし、トラックを運転できるのは人間だけですから、この選択肢では不自然な意味になります。トラック「が」運転することはできません。選択肢BとDは、動詞の形が誤っています。

例題2　Error Correction

The car was <u>drive</u> into <u>the park</u> by two suspects <u>before</u> the police <u>stopped</u> them.

　　A. drive
　　B. the park
　　C. before
　　D. stopped

　正解は**A**です。The carで文が始まるので受動詞が必要であることがわかります。車は自ら運転できませんから、受動態でなければなりません。driveという形は受動態ではないので、drivenに訂正する必要があります。

Grammar

EXERCISE

Part 1. Complete the Sentence

1. The food _____ by the students in the cafeteria at lunch time every day.
   - A. was ate
   - B. is eaten
   - C. is eating
   - D. eating

2. The children _____ been taught the correct way to spell their first and last names.
   - A. has
   - B. have
   - C. are
   - D. will

3. The boxers _____ by experienced trainers every day of the week for four months.
   - A. is taught
   - B. was taught
   - C. will be taught
   - D. has taught

4. The driver has been _____ the directions to the soccer game in the village.
   - A. give
   - B. gives
   - C. given
   - D. gave

5. The homes _____ out of wood found in the surrounding area.
   - A. have being built
   - B. are being build
   - C. are been built
   - D. are being built

6. The answer would have been right, but there _____ no period at the end.
   - A. has
   - B. had
   - C. were
   - D. was

7. The food has to _____ shared evenly among all of the children in the morning class.
   - A. to be
   - B. be
   - C. been
   - D. being

8. The car _____ by a mechanic with 10 years of experience.
   - A. are being repaired
   - B. is being repaired
   - C. are repaired
   - D. have repaired

Part 2. Error Correction

9. <u>The</u> ball <u>has</u> hit by a bat in the
   <u>sports</u> of <u>both</u> cricket and baseball.
   A. The
   B. has
   C. in both
   D. sports

10. <u>Had</u> seen the crime <u>from</u> the
    window, <u>everybody</u> knew exactly
    where <u>they hid</u> the money.
    A. Had
    B. from
    C. everybody
    D. they hid

11. The <u>shoemaker</u> was being told
    exactly <u>which</u> repairs the little
    <u>boy's</u> brown shoes <u>needing</u>.
    A. shoemaker
    B. which
    C. boy's
    D. needing

12. <u>Before</u> having been <u>told</u> the rules,
    the <u>participants</u> are expected <u>to</u>
    <u>follow</u> them exactly.
    A. Before
    B. told
    C. participants
    D. to follow

13. <u>All</u> the soldiers are <u>been</u> told <u>what</u>
    to do <u>if they</u> encounter the enemy.
    A. All
    B. been
    C. what
    D. if they

14. The potato <u>was peeling</u> <u>using</u> a
    special type <u>of</u> knife called <u>a</u> potato
    peeler.
    A. was peeling
    B. using
    C. of
    D. a

Grammar

Listening

Reading

Writing

Speaking

Appendix

Grammar

Chapter 4 動名詞と不定詞

態を理解する

　iTEPの試験では、動名詞（動詞の-ing形）やto不定詞（to＋動詞の原形）を特定の動詞とともに使ってよいかどうかを識別する力がよく問われます。動詞と動名詞やto不定詞との間に目的語や副詞が入る場合もあります。こうした文は、大きく4種類の構文に分かれます。以下のページに挙げた動詞と一緒に、いつ、どのように動名詞やto不定詞が使われるのかを覚えれば、iTEPのさまざまな問題に解答しやすくなります。4つの構文、例文、それぞれの構文をとる動詞のリストを注意して見ていきましょう。他の生徒や先生と一緒に、それぞれの構文と動詞のリストを使って文を書いてみましょう。

> このチャプターでは太字になっている項目についてテストします
>
> - 動詞の形
> - **構文**
> - 接続詞
> - **品詞**
> - 冠詞と前置詞
> - **分量の表現**
> - 代名詞

動詞＋ to 不定詞

　以下の表中の動詞が動詞の活用形を従える場合、ふつうto不定詞（to＋動詞の原形、to speakなど）が用いられます。

to不定詞を従える動詞 She agreed to speak before the game.（彼女は試合の前にスピーチをすることに同意しました）				
agree	continue	hesitate	offer	start
aim	dare	hope	ought	stop
appear	decide	hurry	plan	strive
arrange	deserve	intend	prefer	swear
ask	detest	leave	prepare	threaten
attempt	dislike	like	proceed	try
be able	expect	long	promise	use
beg	fail	love	propose	wait
begin	forget	mean	refuse	want
care	get	neglect	remember	wish

Grammar

Listening

Reading

Writing

Speaking

Appendix

例題1 **Complete the Sentence**

The audience hesitated _____ at first because they did not know if the play was over or not.

    A. clapping

    B. clap

    C. to clap

    D. clapped

正解は **C** です。動詞 hesitate はふつう to 不定詞（この文では to clap）を従えます。

例題2 **Error Correction**

The suspect agreed coming out of the house after the police surrounded the property.

    A. The

    B. coming

    C. after

    D. surrounded

正解は **B** です。正しい文にするには、to come が必要です。

動詞＋目的語＋ to 不定詞

以下に掲げた動詞は、動詞と to 不定詞の間に目的語を取ります。

〈目的語＋to不定詞〉を従える動詞 Everyone expected her to win.（だれもが彼女が勝つと予想しました）				
advise	command	hire	order	require
allow	dare	instruct	pay	send
ask	direct	invite	permit	teach
beg	encourage	lead	persuade	tell
buy	expect	leave	prepare	urge
challenge	forbid	love	promise	want
choose	force	motivate	remind	warn

Grammar

例題3 **Complete the Sentence**

The officer commanded his troops _____ up the hill several times.

    A. charging

    B. charge

    C. to charge

    D. charged

　正解は **C** です。command という動詞は「目的語＋to不定詞」を従えるため to charge が必要です。

例題4 **Error Correction**

Catherine's father advised her <u>study</u> engineering <u>in college</u>, <u>not</u> literature.

    A. Catherine's

    B. study

    C. in college

    D. not

　正解は **B** です。ここでは to study が必要です。

動詞＋動名詞

　動詞の中には、後ろに動名詞（-ing形、例：speaking）を従えるものがあります。動名詞は名詞の働きをする場合が多いことに注意が必要です。これらは、以下の表に掲げた動詞の後で、動作の内容を表します。

後ろに動名詞を従える動詞および動詞句 They enjoyed working on the boat.（彼らはボートを漕いで楽しみました）				
admit	delay	finish	postpone	resume
advise	deny	forbid	practice	risk
appreciate	detest	get through	quit	spend (time)
avoid	dislike	imagine	recall	suggest
can't help	enjoy	mind	report	tolerate
complete	escape	miss	resent	waste (time)
consider	excuse	permit	resist	

Grammar

Listening

Reading

Writing

Speaking

Appendix

例題5　**Complete the Sentence**

Rita says she enjoys _____ for all her friends.

    A. cooking

    B. cook

    C. to cook

    D. cooked

　正解は**A**です。この文では、cookingが名詞の働きをしています。cookingは動作を表す動名詞です。他の選択肢は、正しい活用形ではありません。

例題6　**Error Correction**

The government asked the newspapers to postpone to make the story public until the president was able to leave the area.

    A. asked

    B. to make

    C. until

    D. was able

　正解は**B**です。動詞postponeの後に続くには、makingの形に直す必要があります。

動詞＋前置詞＋動名詞

　前置詞が続く動詞の中には、前置詞の後ろに名詞の働きをする動名詞を必要とするものがあります。

後ろに前置詞＋動名詞を従える動詞句 We concentrated on doing well.（私たちはうまくやることに集中しました）		
admit to	depend on	plan on
approve of	disapprove of	prevent (someone) from
argue about	discourage from	refrain from
believe in	dream about	succeed in
care about	feel like	talk about
complain about	forget about	think about
concentrate on	insist on	worry about
confess to	object to	

Grammar

例題7 **Complete the Sentence**

The president of the company made it clear that he did not approve of _____ more than $500.

      A. spend

      B. spent

      C. to spend

      D. spending

approve ofの後ろには、動名詞spendingが続く必要があります。したがって、**D**が正解です。

例題8 **Error Correction**

James's father discouraged him from <u>joined</u> the basketball team <u>because</u> James's grades <u>were</u> <u>too low</u>.

      A. joined

      B. because

      C. were

      D. too low

この誤文訂正問題では、joinedが誤りで、joiningに直さなければなりません。したがって、正解は**A**です。

EXERCISE

Part 1. Complete the Sentence

1. The administration agreed _____ a meeting with parents about next year's calendar.
   - A. to schedule
   - B. schedule
   - C. schedules
   - D. scheduling

2. The thief would not admit _____ stealing the sports car, so the police showed him the video footage, and then he admitted_____ it.
   - A. for
   - B. to
   - C. them
   - D. with

3. The school will _____ threatening or bullying behavior by any student; there is simply no tolerance for this.
   - A. an excuse
   - B. to excuse
   - C. not excuse
   - D. be excused

4. The girl's mother did not approve _____ the way she was dressing, so she changed into another outfit.
   - A. by
   - B. for
   - C. of
   - D. with

5. Our supervisor advised all the employees _____ all their reports completed prior to the meeting.
   - A. to have
   - B. have
   - C. had
   - D. having

6. The doctor advised _____ instead of taking the car in order to work some exercise into each day.
   - A. to walk
   - B. walk
   - C. walked
   - D. walking

7. Politicians will argue _____ anything, it seems, even when there is nothing for them to be arguing _____ .
   - A. before
   - B. after
   - C. between
   - D. about

Grammar

Listening

Reading

Writing

Speaking

Appendix

8. The new paintings at the art
   museum appear _____
   arriving sometime this fall.
   A. are
   B. to be
   C. for
   D. being

Part 2. Error Correction

9. Our congress will aim <u>focusing</u>
   their attention on <u>making</u> <u>our</u>
   country a <u>better</u> place.
   A. focusing
   B. making
   C. our
   D. better

10. <u>Once</u> we get <u>through looking</u> at all
    of these photos, we can <u>beginning</u>
    organizing <u>them</u>.
    A. Once
    B. through looking
    C. beginning
    D. them

11. News reporters like <u>to talk</u> <u>with</u>
    <u>what is</u> happening <u>all around</u> the
    world.
    A. to
    B. with
    C. what is
    D. all around

12. <u>We promised</u> ice cream to the kids
    <u>if they</u> wanted <u>working</u> for it after
    their chores <u>were done</u>.
    A. We promised
    B. if they
    C. working
    D. were done

13. <u>The</u> Athletic Department proposed
    to <u>starts</u> having concessions
    <u>on both</u> sides of the gym <u>by the</u>
    entrances.
    A. The
    B. starts
    C. on both
    D. by the

Grammar

Listening

Reading

Writing

Speaking

Appendix

Chapter 5 前置詞とその意味

前置詞を知る

iTEPの試験では、前置詞、そして英語の文中における適切な前置詞の用法を問う問題が多く出題されます。英語には多くの前置詞がありますが、iTEPの試験では約25個の前置詞しか用いられません。これらの前置詞の意味と使い方を知れば、iTEPの問題に正しく答えることができます。iTEPでは、正しい前置詞の選択を要求する空所補充問題がよく出題されます。iTEPで出題される前置詞の問題の例は以下のとおりです。

> このチャプターでは太字になっている項目についてテストします
>
> ● **動詞の形**
> ● **構文**
> ● 接続詞
> ● 品詞
> ● **冠詞と前置詞**
> ● 分量の表現
> ● 代名詞

例題1 Complete the Sentence

The truck driver went _____ the tunnel to make sure the items were delivered on time.

    A. among

    B. on

    C. at

    D. through

正解は**D**です。文のキーワードはtunnelですが、これは人が通り「抜ける」場所です。論理的に、人はトンネル「の間で」、「の上で」、「の一点で」運転することはできません。

例題2 Error Correction

<u>Because</u> of the heavy snow <u>that</u> was falling, we drove <u>with</u> the local streets, <u>not</u> the highway.

    A. Because

    B. that

    C. with

    D. not

Grammar

人は通り「とともに」運転することはできないため、この文で修正が必要なのは選択肢 **C** です。よく使われる前置詞については、以下の表をご参照ください。

よく使われる前置詞					
of	on	as	over	without	with
in	at	into	between	before	after
to	from	like	out	under	during
for	by	through	against	around	among

EXERCISE

Part 1. Complete the Sentence

1. Sporting events are much more fun when you go _____ a big crowd of your best friends.
   A. with
   B. from
   C. over
   D. during

2. My mom likes to keep her chocolate _____ the refrigerator so that it doesn't melt.
   A. into
   B. over
   C. in
   D. around

3. The CEO makes the big decisions since he is the head_____ the company, even though he is out of touch with the consumers.
   A. of
   B. about
   C. around
   D. from

4. It was a long trip, but we were glad we drove _____ the beach because the weather was so beautiful.
   A. in
   B. of
   C. to
   D. through

5. David wanted to impress Sarah, so he bought a very expensive, beautiful present _____ her.

   A. of

   B. for

   C. as

   D. about

6. The president of the United States lives in the White House, which is located _____ 1600 Pennsylvania Avenue in Washington, D.C.

   A. at

   B. in

   C. for

   D. through

7. Sarah is _____ Montreal originally, but now she lives in New York.

   A. from

   B. over

   C. on

   D. for

Part 2. Error Correction

8. The tall trees <u>in the</u> forest cast shade <u>from</u> the smaller plants, so plants <u>that</u> <u>grow</u> well in shade tend to grow best there.

   A. in the

   B. from

   C. that

   D. grow

9. North America is <u>in</u> the western hemisphere, and Europe is in <u>the</u> eastern hemisphere, <u>with</u> the Atlantic Ocean <u>like</u> them.

   A. in

   B. the

   C. with

   D. like

10. Cuckoo clocks <u>are</u> unique because they have <u>a little</u> bird <u>that</u> pops <u>between</u> and chirps every hour.

   A. are

   B. a little

   C. that

   D. between

11. Jo realized too late <u>that</u> she had a stain on the back <u>of her</u> dress, so she had to stand with her back <u>under</u> the wall all night <u>so that</u> no one could see it.

   A. that

   B. of her

   C. under

   D. so that

12. Oliver was enjoying <u>the</u> play very much, so he was <u>annoyed</u> when a baby started crying <u>on</u> the second half and <u>he</u> couldn't hear.

   A. the

   B. annoyed

   C. on

   D. he

13. When Kile wanted <u>to</u> lose weight, he <u>decided</u> to start drinking <u>his</u> coffee <u>during</u> cream or sugar in it.

   A. to

   B. decided

   C. his

   D. during

14. There were many <u>tests of</u> space flight, <u>like</u> sending a dog into space, <u>against</u> anyone would risk sending <u>a</u> human.

   A. tests of

   B. like

   C. against

   D. a

15. <u>Colleen's</u> apartment had <u>a</u> bakery <u>through</u> it, and she loved to smell the bread baking <u>on the</u> ground floor early every morning.

   A. Colleen's

   B. a

   C. through

   D. on the

Grammar
Listening
Reading
Writing
Speaking
Appendix

Chapter 6 冠詞と指示語

冠詞を理解する

　冠詞は、iTEPの試験でよく評価される文法項目です。冠詞の使用は英語学習上つまずきやすく、特に学習者の第一言語に類似の文法形式がない場合には困難です。冠詞に慣れるためには、定冠詞と不定冠詞の概念に習熟することが重要です。「定（definite）」とはたいてい、特定の人、場所、物が、話し手［書き手／聞き手／読み手］にとって既知であることを意味します。すでに紹介されていたり、よく知られていたりする人、場所、物は「定（definite）」です。英語の定冠詞はtheです。たとえばthe moonは、地球を周回する特定の月を表します。

　不定冠詞は、会話や文章の中でまだ紹介されていないなどの理由で、まだ特定されていないものに言及するために使われることがあります。不定冠詞 a と anは、不特定の単数のものを表すために使われます。aは子音で始まる名詞を導きます。an は、an elephantのように、母音で始まる名詞を表します。以下の 2 つの文について考えてみましょう。

> このチャプターでは太字になっている項目についてテストします
>
> ● 動詞の形
> ● 構文
> ● 接続詞
> ● 品詞
> ● **冠詞と前置詞**
> ● **分量の表現**
> ● 代名詞

Yesterday, <u>a car</u> went speeding past me on the highway. Later as I drove a little farther down the road, I noticed that <u>the car</u> had gotten into an accident.

注：この例文にはcarという単語が2回出てきます。1回目は、carという概念が新たに導入されたため、不定冠詞が必要になります。そのため、話者は車を指す冠詞として a を使っています。2回目のcarでは、話者と聞き手の両方にとってその車が既知のものとなったため、話者はthe carを使っています。

　不特定の名詞が複数形の場合は、someを使います。たとえばa bananaは複数形になるとsome bananasになります。someは、some riceや some milkのように、不可算名詞の不定冠詞としても使われます。以下の説明を見て、a、an、some、theのうちどの冠詞を使うべきかを考えてみましょう。

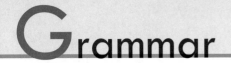

Grammar

パターン 1: a と an

可算名詞の単数形の前では a [an] を使います。
　　例：I had both <u>a banana</u> and <u>an apple</u> for breakfast today.

人の職業や性質を言うときには a [an] を使います。
　　例：Annie is <u>a nurse</u>; her mother is <u>an accountant</u>.

相手にとって既知ではないものについて話すときには a [an] を使います。
　　例：I went to visit <u>a museum</u> today. It was <u>an interesting place</u>.

パターン 2: the

述べている物事が他にない唯一のものであることを知っている場合は the を使います。
　　例：<u>The planet Mars</u> could hold a key to <u>the Earth's</u> past.

ある物事が相手にとって既知になったあとは the を使います。
　　例：<u>The store</u> I used to work at closed down this summer.

例題1　Complete the Sentence

To reduce the use of fossil fuels, we can use the power of _____ sun.

　　A. a
　　B. this
　　C. these
　　D. the

　太陽は1つしかないため、正解は D です。sun は特定のものであり不定冠詞を伴わないので、A は不正解です。複数の太陽のうちいずれかを選ぶということはできないので、B と C は不正解です。また、C は複数形の名詞を後ろに伴う必要があるので不正解です。

例題2　Complete the Sentence

Do you have _____ paperclip that I could use?

A. a

B. this

C. these

D. an

　正解は**A**です。話し手は特定のクリップを求めているわけではないため、不定冠詞が必要です。Dも不定冠詞ですが、paperclipは母音で始まらないため正しい選択肢ではありません。

例題3　**Error Correction**

They <u>want</u> to build <u>those</u> university <u>in</u> my <u>hometown</u>.

A. want

B. those

C. in

D. hometown

　正解は**B**です。この選択肢を修正しなければいけない理由は、universityが単数なのにthoseは後に複数形の名詞を要求するからです。

a と an の使用

　冠詞の a と anを選ぶ際には、母音字と子音字、そしてそれらの音に注意を払うことが大切です。母音字で始まる不特定の名詞は、ふつう不定冠詞anを前に置きます。一方、子音字で始まる不特定の名詞は、ふつう不定冠詞aを前に置きます。しかし、母音字で始まる単語の中にも、子音で始まるものがあります。これらの単語の前にはaを置きます。また、子音字で始まっても、最初の音が母音である単語もあります。これらの単語の前にはanを置きます。それぞれの不定冠詞の用例については、以下の表を参照してください。

Grammar

a 以下の語句は、〈子音字＋子音〉で始まります。		an 以下の語句は、〈母音字＋母音〉で始まります。	
a table	a fat cat	an orange	an eager student
a window	a cool evening	an elevator	an old woman
a computer	a slightly lazy man	an actress	an irate guest
最初の文字の音が重要！			
a 以下の語句は、〈母音字＋子音〉で始まります。		an 以下の語句は、〈子音字＋母音〉で始まります。	
a university (u の音は you と同様に子音 y の音を含むため、a が正しい冠詞です)		an hour (h が黙字でhourは母音で始まるため、anが正しい冠詞です)	
a usual thought (u の音は子音 y の音を含みます)		I got an F on the test. (ef「エフ」と発音)	
a European country (Euの音は子音 y の音を含みます)		Mark it with an X. (ex「エックス」と発音)	
a unique experience (u の音は子音 y の音を含みます)			
I got a one on the test. (oneはwonと同じ発音です)			

指示詞

　特定の人や場所、ものを導入する別の種類の語に「指示詞」があります。英語でよく使われる指示詞は、this、that、these、thoseの4つです。下の表を見て、これらの単語が単数／複数や距離によって意味が異なることを確認しましょう。

	接近した／近い	離れた／遠い
単数	this	that
複数	these	those

　iTEPの文法問題は、英語の文におけるこれらの語の適切な使用について理解しているかどうかを評価します。以下の例題を見てみましょう。

例題4 **Complete the Sentence**

Because it is too old to be used for anything, _____ building is marked for destruction.

    A. a

    B. this

    C. these

    D. an

B がこの例題の正解です。最初の節で建物が紹介されているので、どの建物が話題になっているのかは分かっています。したがって、不定冠詞は使われないこととなり、選択肢 A と D は不正解です。言及されている建物は 1 つだけなので、選択肢 C の複数を表す指示詞も不正解です。

例題5 **Error Correction**

The migration <u>of</u> the monarch butterfly is <u>an</u> amazing phenomenon in nature. <u>That</u> beautiful creatures <u>fly</u> thousands of miles during the trip.

    A. of

    B. an

    C. That

    D. fly

第 2 文では主語が creatures であるため、正しい指示詞は that ではなく these になります。したがって、正解は C です。

例題6 **Complete the Sentence**

The cars that were produced in our German factory were faster than _____ that were built in our American factory.

    A. that

    B. this

    C. these

    D. those

正解は **D** です。言及されている名詞は cars（自動車）であるため、比較の構文の後半において自動車を表すために、複数を表す指示詞を用いなければなりません。C の these は名詞のくり返しを避ける代名詞としての機能がないので誤りです。

Grammar

EXERCISE

Part 1. Complete the Sentence

1. The best time to wake up is just as _____ sun comes up.
   - A. an
   - B. the
   - C. these
   - D. those

2. The boys wanted to find out if _____ teammates would be at the party.
   - A. those
   - B. that
   - C. this
   - D. a

3. Because the play started late, _____ parts were canceled.
   - A. a
   - B. that
   - C. this
   - D. some

4. Jane never expected a gift from _____ person.
   - A. an
   - B. those
   - C. that
   - D. these

5. On the way to the park, pick up _____ hot dog.
   - A. these
   - B. those
   - C. an
   - D. a

6. _____ orange is a type of fruit that has to be peeled.
   - A. A
   - B. An
   - C. These
   - D. Some

7. The dentist said that _____ teeth needed to be pulled.
   - A. a
   - B. some
   - C. an
   - D. this

Part 2. Error Correction

8. It turns out that the bugs were just attracted to those light.
   - A. It
   - B. that
   - C. the
   - D. those

9. They decided to rescue a older dog from the shelter.

   A. to

   B. a

   C. from

   D. the

10. Taking this pictures will show those people where the boat is.

   A. this pictures

   B. show

   C. those people

   D. the boat

11. She took her phone to the store with to hope that it could be fixed.

   A. to the

   B. to hope

   C. it

   D. could be

12. Whenever we decide which of a cars we like, we will tell the children.

   A. of

   B. a cars

   C. will

   D. the children

13. Mistakes are easy to make when these TV is on.

   A. are easy

   B. to make

   C. these TV

   D. is on

Grammar

Listening

Reading

Writing

Speaking

Appendix

Grammar

Chapter 7 比較級と最上級

比較級の使用

　iTEPの文法セクションでは、比較の構文を認識したり、適切に構成したりする能力を評価する問題がよく出題されます。この種の文は、人や場所、物を比較するもので、しばしば more than や less than といった言い回しが使われます。これらの問題で正解するためには、比較級の形容詞と並列の文法構造の両方を理解している必要があります。比較文の並列構造を問う例題を以下に挙げます。

　まず、比較構文の最もシンプルな形は、形容詞の -er 形（比較級）に than という単語を加えたものです。この形が使用された例題を見てみましょう。

> このチャプターでは太字になっている項目についてテストします
>
> ● 動詞の形
> ● **構文**
> ● 接続詞
> ● **品詞**
> ● 冠詞と前置詞
> ● 分量の表現
> ● **代名詞**

例題1 **Complete the Sentence**

The total revenue for the company in 2013 was ＿＿＿＿＿＿ than the revenue in 2012.

    A. high
    B. highest
    C. higher
    D. more high

　正解は **C** です。この文では、higher が「2013年の総収入」と「2012年の総収入」の2点を比較しています。A は不正解です。high は比較級の形容詞ではありません。B は最上級の形容詞のため、不正解です。D は一見正解のようですが、比較級の形が誤っています。

例題2 **Error Correction**

The gross domestic product of the northern states was highest than that of the southern states.

    A. The

Grammar

Listening

Reading

Writing

Speaking

Appendix

B. of
C. highest
D. that

　正解は**C**です。この文では、比較級の形容詞 higher に修正する必要があります。指示詞that は、文中で前に使用された語句を置き換えることができます。この文中では、thatはthe gross domestic productを置き換えています。

moreを使用する比較級	例文
「y」以外で終わり、 かつ音節が2つある形容詞 ※例外あり	The apartment is more modern than the others we have seen. Tom is more helpful than Peter.
音節が3つ以上ある 全ての形容詞	Ella is more hardworking than Anne. Josh is more attractive than Adam.

形容詞の比較級

比較級のパターン

■音節が1つの語の場合		
	原級	比較級
「-er」を後ろに加える	long	longer
	short	shorter
	new	newer
	old	older
	strong	stronger
	weak	weaker
語尾が「e」で終わる語の場合は「-r」をつける	large	larger
	nice	nicer
短母音＋1子音字で終わる場合は子音字を重ねた後ろに「-er」をつける	big	bigger
	hot	hotter

Grammar

■音節が2つ以上の語の場合		
音節が2つあり、かつ「y」で終わる場合は末尾の「y」を「i」に変え、「-er」を加える	busy	busier
	easy	easier
	happy	happier
	heavy	heavier
	pretty	prettier
音節が2つ以上ある語の場合は直前に「more」を置く	beautiful	more beautiful
	dangerous	more dangerous
	difficult	more difficult
	exciting	more exciting
	interesting	more interesting
	popular	more popular
	understandng	more understanding

例外のパターン		
	good	better
	bad	worse
	little	less
	many	more
	far	father

形容詞の中には、「-er」の形に変化しないものもあることを覚えておきましょう。一般的には音節が2つ以上ある、長い形容詞です。これらの形容詞は、「more」という単語を使用して比較級を表現します。

例題3　Complete the Sentence

My husband listens to old jazz albums, but I prefer _____ music, like hip hop.

    A. modernest

    B. moderner

    C. more modern

    D. most modern

　正解は**C**です。modernは語尾に「-er」をつけられない形容詞の1つで、比較級にするには修飾語moreが必要です。

　また、名詞や名詞句が比較級形容詞の後に続く比較文もあります。この場合、比較級形容詞は名詞や名詞句を修飾しています。thanが比較級形容詞のすぐ後ろに来ず、少し分かりにくいため注意が必要です。

例題4　Complete the Sentence

The northern states had a _____ gross domestic product than the southern states, making it difficult for the southern states to purchase commodities.

    A. high

    B. highest

    C. higher

    D. more high

　正解は**C**です。gross domestic productがhigherとthanの間に入ることに注意しましょう。

　次は「as+形容詞+as」という形で表現される比較構文です。他の比較文と同じく、比較される2つの項目が同じ文法形式である必要があります。また、この構文では、否定の修飾語を用いるかどうかで、比較される2つの項目が同等であるかそうでないかが変わります。以下の2つの例文から、否定語notによって文の意味がどう変わるかを見てみましょう。

The fruit and vegetables grown in colder regions of the country are <u>as delicious as</u> those grown in the warmer southern regions.（寒い国で栽培された果物や野菜は、温暖な南部の地域で栽培されたものと<u>同じくらいおいしい</u>）

Grammar

The fruit and vegetables grown in colder regions of the country are <u>not as delicious as</u> those grown in the warmer southern regions.（寒い国で栽培された果物や野菜は、温暖な南部の地域で栽培されたもの<u>ほどおいしくない</u>）

　iTEPの試験では、この比較構文を識別する力があるかどうかを問う、様々な問題が出題されます。出題される問題の例は以下の通りです。

例題5　**Complete the Sentence**

The professor chose a textbook that was not ＿＿＿＿＿ as the textbook from last year's class.

　　　A. expensive

　　　B. too expensive

　　　C. as expensive

　　　D. most expensive

　この例題では、正解は **C** です。A は比較級ではないので不正解です。B は、これでこの文が終わるのであれば正解です。D は than ではなく as が使われているため、不正解です。

　次は副詞を使った比較構文です。2つの人、場所、物の動きや状態を比較します。この場合、「as ＋副詞＋ as」という構文が使われます。この構文の例は以下の通りです。

例題6　**Error Correction**

<u>The</u> team <u>lost</u> because they <u>did not move</u> the ball as <u>effective</u> as their competitors.

　　　A. The

　　　B. lost

　　　C. did not move

　　　D. effective

　正解は **D** です。この例題では、文を完成させるために副詞が必要です。動詞 move を修飾する副詞は、effectively です。

Grammar

Listening

Reading

Writing

Speaking

Appendix

形容詞の最上級

　形容詞の最上級は、iTEPの試験でもよく用いられます。このケースでは冠詞theの適切な使い方や、most、one ofなどの構文に注意する必要があります。最もシンプルな最上級の形は、形容詞の「-est」を末尾に加えたものです。以下の例文を見てみましょう。

例題7 **Complete the Sentence**

Tokyo is one of the _____ cities in world and is also one of the most densely populated.

        A. large

        B. largest

        C. most large

        D. most largest

　この文にはone of theが含まれているので、正しい答えは**B**です。選択肢**A**と**D**は、最上級ではないので不正解です。**C**は一見正解のようですが、形容詞largeの正しい最上級の形ではありません。それぞれの単語の最上級パターンは、下の表を見てみましょう。

■音節が1つのみ	■音節が2つ	■音節が3つ以上	■例外パターン
smallest	happiest	most beautiful	best/worst
tallest	most peaceful	most creative	least

例題8 **Error Correction**

The team <u>won</u> because they <u>had</u> the <u>quickly</u> runners in the competition.

        A. The

        B. won

        C. had

        D. quickly

　quicklyは副詞であり、名詞を修飾することができないので**D**が正解です。quicklyという単語を、最上級の形容詞quickestに置き換える必要があります。

Grammar

only と、最上級の形容詞に伴う the の使用

　前述したように、定冠詞theは人、場所、物、考え方などがあらかじめ特定されている場合や、話し手・書き手、聞き手・読み手の両者にとって既知である場合に使われます。ただし、それ以外でも定冠詞を使用する場合があります。名詞が biggest のような最上級で修飾されている場合は、この名詞は唯一のものなので、定冠詞が用いられます。また、文中の名詞が唯一のものであることが確認された場合にも、定冠詞が用いられます。これらのケースが実際に用いられている例文を見てみましょう。

例題9　Complete the Sentence

When he was out in the desert all alone, he felt like _____ loneliest man in the world.

    A. a

    B. an

    C. the

    D. some

　正解は C です。loneliestは最上級なので、文中のmanは唯一の人となり定冠詞が必要です。

例題10　Error Correction

It is said that Costa Rica has a most beautiful sunsets because of the way the light hits the waters of the ocean.

    A. is said

    B. a

    C. because

    D. hits

　正解は B です。mostは最上級なので、aではなく定冠詞であるtheを用いる必要があります。

EXERCISE

Part 1. Complete the Sentence

1. My grandfather has always bought cars from the same automobile company. They are _____ only cars he drives.
   A. a
   B. an
   C. the
   D. some

2. Did you know that they have competitions for ugly dogs, where they choose the one that is _____ ?
   A. ugliest
   B. uglier
   C. ugly
   D. more ugly

3. The money that was spent on this house by the new corporate owners was not as _____ as the money spent on that house.
   A. more
   B. much
   C. most
   D. many

4. The results of the people who took their time and double-checked their work were more accurate _____ those of other groups.
   A. like
   B. from
   C. by
   D. than

5. There are plenty of hard metals. However, diamond has proved to be the _____ known to man.
   A. harder
   B. hardest
   C. difficult
   D. more difficult

6. The male cardinal chirped pleasantly in the branches of the willow tree but _____ the melodic yellow warbler.
   A. as sweetest as
   B. as sweet as
   C. not as sweeter as
   D. not as sweetly as

7. The responsible teenager was not _____ frivolous as her friend, who spent her whole paycheck on a manicure.
   A. is
   B. as
   C. better
   D. for

Grammar

Listening

Reading

Writing

Speaking

Appendix

8. Grizzly bears are much _____ than Arctic polar bears but just as ferocious.

    A. small

    B. smaller

    C. smallest

    D. most small

Part 2. Error Correction

9. A necklace made with gold, diamonds, and platinum is most precious than one made from sterling silver and semiprecious stones.

    A. with gold

    B. most

    C. one

    D. semiprecious

10. The car collector's 1957 Chevy was cleanest than the brand new Cadillac parked next to it.

    A. car collector's

    B. cleanest

    C. parked

    D. it

11. After the students bit into oranges and lemons, they determined that oranges were not like tart as lemons.

    A. After

    B. bit into

    C. they

    D. like

12. Dogs are pack animals that enjoy socializing and are easily trainable, while cats are more solitary from dogs and are very difficult to train.

    A. that

    B. trainable

    C. from

    D. to train

13. I don't stay out very late; midnight is usually the late I stay out.

    A. I don't

    B. very

    C. is usually

    D. late

14. Not all metals are created equal. For example, iron alloys are a mixture of two or more metals that make them strongest than pure metal.

    A. are created

    B. For example

    C. two or more

    D. strongest

Grammar

Listening

Reading

Writing

Speaking

Appendix

Chapter 8 代名詞

代名詞の選択

　iTEPの文法セクションでは、様々な場面で正しい代名詞を選択する能力が試されます。これは時に難問となることがあります。代名詞は人や場所、物、考えのいずれかを表す名詞の代わりに用いられますが、代名詞の形は名詞の性別など多くの要因によって異なります。代名詞は所有格、単数形または複数形、文中の主語または目的語のいずれかになることもあります。iTEPの問題には、それぞれ正しい代名詞を選択するためのヒントがあります。この章では、iTEPの文法セクションで出題される可能性の高い、代名詞に関する様々な問題の一部をご紹介します。

> このチャプターでは太字になっている項目についてテストします
>
> - 動詞の形
> - **構文**
> - 接続詞
> - **品詞**
> - 冠詞と前置詞
> - 分量の表現
> - **代名詞**

例題1　**Complete the Sentence**

My grandfather bought the house in 1948, but _____ has renovated it many times since then.

    A. he

    B. she

    C. they

    D. him

　正解は**A**です。grandfatherは男性なので、男性を指す代名詞が用いられます。Bは女性を指す代名詞なので不正解です。この文中でgrandfatherは1人だけで、2人以上ではないのでCは不正解です。Dは代名詞の目的格なので不正解です。

例題2　**Complete the Sentence**

My grandparents bought the house in 1948, but _____ have renovated it many times since then.

A. them

B. they are

C. they

D. he

正解は**C**です。grandparents は複数形なので、代名詞も複数形である必要があります。Aは代名詞の目的格なので不正解です。この文では主格が正解です。Bでは動詞が不自然な形になってしまうため不正解です。Dは単数形なので不正解です。

例題3 **Error Correction**

The president spoke about <u>the need</u> for more affordable housing, but <u>they</u> failed <u>to address</u> the lack <u>of</u> jobs and opportunity.

A. the need

B. they

C. to address

D. of

正解は**B**です。presidentは1人なので、複数形の代名詞theyは不正解です。この文では単数形の主格代名詞heかsheが必要になります。

例題4 **Complete the Sentence**

The members of the group did not realize that the story was about _____ because their names had been changed.

A. them

B. they

C. her

D. their

正解は**A**です。前置詞aboutが前にあるため、代名詞の目的格が必要です。Bは主格代名詞なので不正解です。Cのherは単数形ですが、文中のmembersは複数形なので不正解です。Dはtheirが所有格なので不正解です。

Grammar

Listening

Reading

Writing

Speaking

Appendix

関係代名詞

　関係代名詞を使って形容詞節を作ることは、質の高いライティングスキルを身につけるために欠かせない要素です。形容詞節は、文中の人物や場所、物、アイデアを特定し、定義する働きを持ちます。もちろん、関係代名詞の使用と形容詞節は、英語に共通するパターンに従って形成されます。iTEPの文法セクションでは、これらのパターンを認識できるかどうかが試されます。

　まず、受験者はwhoとwhomの違いを知っておく必要があります。関係代名詞としてのwhoは主格の形容詞節に、whomは目的格の形容詞節に使われます。

The principal warned students **who** take that bus that they must report to the bus stop five minutes prior to the scheduled pickup time.

　この例文では、who take that busはstudentsを修飾する形容詞節です。この場合、whoが形容詞節の中でstudentsを表し、students take the busという文があると見なすことができるため、主格の形容詞節と考えられます。

　目的格の形容詞節は、形容詞節の中で関係代名詞が目的語を修飾するときに作られます。この目的語が人の場合は、次の例文のように関係代名詞whomが使われます。

The employees **whom** the company hired before the merger were allowed to keep their positions.

　この例文では、whom the company hired before the mergerがemployeesを修飾する形容詞節です。この場合、whomが節の中でemployeesを表しており、The company hired the employees before the merger.のような文を想定することができるため、目的格の形容詞節と考えられます。この場合、employeesは目的語になります。

　主格の形容詞節では、whoやthatは使えますが、whomは使用できません。目的格の形容詞節では、whomやthatは使えますが、whoは使えません。

Grammar

例題5 **Complete the Sentence**

To make your company successful, you should hire people _____ you can trust.

    A. whom

    B. who

    C. for

    D. which

　正解は**A**です。whomは人を表し、you can trust peopleが適切なフレーズなので、これは目的格の形容詞節ということになり、whomを用います。

例題6 **Error Correction**

The doctors <u>for</u> performed the surgery said <u>that</u> the patient <u>had</u> a good chance of <u>a full recovery</u>.

    A. for

    B. that

    C. had

    D. a full recovery

　正解は**A**です。The doctors who performed....と修正します。

EXERCISE

Part 1. Complete the Sentence

1. _____ issue is with the warehouse supervisor's poor communication skills and attendance policy.
   A. Hers
   B. She
   C. Her
   D. Herself

2. My mother was too impatient to wait for me, so she cleaned the house _____.
   A. themselves
   B. ourselves
   C. myself
   D. herself

3. The teacher approached me after class to ask why I had forgotten to bring _____ books.
   A. me
   B. my
   C. mine
   D. I

4. Evan plays basketball every Thursday, and he left _____ shoes at the last practice.
   A. his
   B. the
   C. he's
   D. her

5. Our cabin is just over the hill; _____ is another ten miles beyond ours.
   A. ours
   B. theirs
   C. we
   D. them

6. _____ have received a passing grade on Mr. Henry's history final exam.
   A. I
   B. Me
   C. He
   D. She

7. You went to the doctor to receive the results of _____ medical tests.
   A. your
   B. you're
   C. there
   D. they're

Grammar

Part 2. Error Correction

8. There has to do it, and do it quite well, to pass the test.
   - A. There
   - B. has
   - C. it
   - D. to pass

9. He doesn't like eating dark chocolate, so I don't think you should have bought for him.
   - A. doesn't
   - B. eating
   - C. don't think
   - D. bought for

10. The president does run the country. However, he does not make all of the rules herself.
    - A. does run
    - B. However
    - C. all of
    - D. herself

11. Themselves did the hard work and reaped the reward, which included a pay raise.
    - A. Themselves
    - B. the
    - C. reaped
    - D. included

12. A country's laws reflect the values, morals, and ethical standards of your people.
    - A. country's
    - B. reflect
    - C. and ethical
    - D. your

13. Frida Kahlo explored many different themes, such as identity, race, and gender in your paintings.
    - A. explored
    - B. such as
    - C. race
    - D. your

14. I worked herself to the bare bone despite not receiving a paycheck.
    - A. herself
    - B. despite
    - C. not
    - D. a paycheck

Listening
Reading
Writing
Speaking
Appendix

Chapter 9 名詞

名詞の形 (-less, -ness, -ism, -tion)

英語の単語は、別の語尾をつけると品詞が変わることがあります。例えば、形容詞kindに-nessを加えてkindnessとすると、名詞形にすることができます。iTEPの文法セクションでは、このような名詞の語尾を正しく用いることができるかどうかを問う問題が出題されることがあります。

> このチャプターでは太字になっている項目についてテストします
>
> - 動詞の形
> - **構文**
> - 接続詞
> - **品詞**
> - 冠詞と前置詞
> - 分量の表現
> - **代名詞**

例題1 Complete the Sentence

Chefs can find _____ of this recipe everywhere, but the basic ingredients of milk, sugar, and flour are common in all of them.

- A. variations
- B. various
- C. vary
- D. variable

　正解は**A**です。空欄には動詞findの目的語が入り、目的語は名詞である必要があります。**B**と**D**は形容詞なので不正解です。**C**は動詞なので不正解です。

例題2 Error Correction

<u>Although</u> we <u>found</u> a few <u>different</u> between the two films, they <u>both</u> contained similar themes.

- A. Although
- B. found
- C. different
- D. both

Grammar

正解は **C** です。動詞 found には目的語が必要で、between の前には名詞がありません。この場合、differences が正しい形です。

there、their、they're について

iTEP の文法セクションでは、文中の似たような音の単語を区別する能力があるかどうかを問う問題が出題されることがあります。there、their、they're という単語はすべて全く同じ発音ですが、それぞれ意味や用法が異なります。以下の3つの例文を見てみましょう。

例題3 **Complete the Sentence**

The scouts searched for berries, seeds, and edible plants, but _____ was nothing to be found in that desert environment.

    A. they're

    B. their

    C. there

    D. they

正解は **C** です。A は、are と was という2つの動詞が重なってしまうので不正解です。B は、所有格代名詞 their の後に名詞が続く必要があるため、不正解です。D は、この複数の主格代名詞の後に単数形の動詞 was が続いてしまうので、不正解です。

例題4 **Complete the Sentence**

The scouts searched for berries, seeds, and edible plants, but _____ leader instructed them to quit because he knew that there were none to be found.

    A. they're

    B. their

    C. there

    D. they

例題4では、正解は **B** です。空欄のすぐ後に leader が続くので、所有格代名詞 their 以外は当てはまりません。

例題5　**Error Correction**

The scouts <u>will search</u> for berries, seeds, and <u>edible plants</u>, but <u>there</u> unlikely <u>to find</u> any because it is a desert environment.

     A. will search

     B. edible plants

     C. there

     D. to find

英語でよくある間違いにthere、their、they'reを混同してしまうことがあります。これら3つは全く同じ発音ですが、文脈に合わせて正しく使い分けなければなりません。この場合、scoutsを意味する代名詞はtheyでなければなりません。この文ではthey'reとする必要があります。よって、**C**が正解です。

名詞節

　名詞句は、英語を母語としない人にとってはまぎらわしい文法概念です。名詞節は、who、where、that、whichなどのように、形容詞節の場合と同じ単語に導かれるため、似ているように見えます。さらに名詞節には、whoやwhatのような疑問詞が用いられるため、疑問文と混同されることも多いのです。特にthatを使った名詞節はまぎらわしいです。名詞節にthatが含まれている場合、それは本当の状況、状態、または出来事を意味しています。こういった点に注意しつつ、以下の例文を見てみましょう。

　名詞節は名詞と同じように、文中で主語、目的語、前置詞の目的語、補語としての役割を持ちます。以下の例文で、名詞節がどのように使われているかに注目してみましょう。

主語としての名詞節

- **Who caused the accident** is not the main concern right now as we must care for the injured.
- **Where William will decide to live after college** is a mystery because he has not told anyone.
- **When you graduate from the university** is not important as long as you finish.
- **That you are the class president** does not mean you have special privileges on campus.

Grammar

目的語としての名詞節

- The teacher asked us to tell her **whom we wanted to speak to our class**.
- Nobody knew **that James had become so ill**.

前置詞の目的語としての名詞節

- The group talked about **who should become the next president of their organization**.
- The scope and vastness of the universe is well beyond **what we can understand**.

補語としての名詞節

- The biggest mistake that the CEO made was **that he did not let his managers make their own decisions**.
- This is **what we saw when we walked into the room**.

例題6   Complete the Sentence

The principal chose _____ the picnic would be held.

    A. might

    B. from

    C. where

    D. who

　正解は**C**の**where**です。Aは、助動詞では2つの節をつなぐことができないので不正解です。この文は主語と動詞を含む2つの節があるので、前置詞では2つの節をつなぐことができません。そのため、Bは不正解です。Dのwhoは人を表しますが、the picnic は人ではないため、不正解です。

例題7   Error Correction

It is up to <u>the people</u> in the community to decide <u>for when</u> their <u>local</u> government should <u>be</u> run.

    A. the people

    B. for when

    C. local

    D. be

　正解は**B**です。この文では前置詞forは必要ありません。また、この文には時間表現がないので、whenをhowに変える必要があります。

EXERCISE

Part 1. Complete the Sentence

1. Kevin received a raise because his _____ was pleased with his job performance.
   A. employed
   B. employing
   C. employer
   D. employee

2. He decided that _____ he needed was a cup of tea.
   A. what
   B. who
   C. think
   D. where

3. She knew she had a _____ to clean her room soon.
   A. responsible
   B. response
   C. responsive
   D. responsibility

4. After five minutes, he finally decided _____ he wanted.
   A. when
   B. what
   C. how
   D. then

5. Danny's _____ helped him get accepted to college.
   A. diligent
   B. diligently
   C. diligence
   D. diligentness

6. _____ Linda ordered for lunch, she would need to eat quickly.
   A. Whoever
   B. How
   C. There
   D. Whatever

7. _____ they were going to dinner that night, Kelly wanted chicken.
   A. However
   B. Whoever
   C. Wherever
   D. Whatever

8. The _____ was coming on Tuesday to paint the old storage shed.
   A. painting
   B. painter
   C. paints
   D. painted

Grammar

Listening

Reading

Writing

Speaking

Appendix

Grammar

Part 2. Error Correction

9. They were ready to go on a trip to how they all grew up.
   - A. They
   - B. to
   - C. how
   - D. up

10. Because of the blizzard, Renee could not see that was in the distance.
    - A. Because
    - B. could
    - C. that
    - D. in

11. When shopping for a refrigerator, Devin found that there were many alternatively.
    - A. When
    - B. for a
    - C. found
    - D. alternatively

12. A person where sees the glass as half empty struggles to find silver linings.
    - A. where
    - B. as
    - C. struggles
    - D. linings

13. Byron liked going to the art museum because it inspired his creative.
    - A. liked
    - B. art
    - C. because
    - D. creative

14. That left the door open let leaves blow into the living room.
    - A. That
    - B. the
    - C. leaves
    - D. into

Chapter 10 条件文

Grammar

Listening

Reading

Writing

Speaking

Appendix

時間と条件文

　第２章の副詞の「論理的なつながりを表す語句」の項で
も、条件文の用法を紹介しました。条件を表す用法や文は、
iTEPの試験ではかなり出題されますので、より深く調べて
おきましょう。特に重要なのは時間的な関係を判断するこ
とと、それを表現する正しい動詞を使うことです。

　また、条件文は因果関係を表す文として見ることもでき
ます。その場合、原因と結果、どちらが先にくるでしょう
か。もちろん論理的には、原因が結果の前に来ます。また、
時間を表現する場合、過去と現在、または現在と未来どち
らが先に来るでしょうか。もちろん、過去は現在よりも先
に、現在は未来よりも先に来ます。英語では動詞で表現さ
れる時制を用いて、条件文の中での原因と結果の時間関係

を表現しています。英語には様々な条件文の種類がありますが、どれも動詞の時制を用いて
因果の時間関係を表現しています。この場合、原因を条件と考えることもできます。

このチャプターでは太
字になっている項目に
ついてテストします

- **動詞の形**
- **構文**
- **接続詞**
- 品詞
- 冠詞と前置詞
- 分量の表現
- 代名詞

条件文の種類	
直説法の条件文	仮定法過去完了
仮定法過去	普遍的真実（事実）を述べる条件文

普遍的真実を述べる条件文

　必ず起こる因果関係を表現する文は、「普遍的真実を述べる条件文」として知られていま
す。この構文は、科学的または普遍的な出来事を説明するためによく用いられ、事実を述べ
る条件文としても知られています。これらの文では、原因と結果を示す節の時制は両方とも
現在です。

Grammar

例文

- When the temperature <u>falls</u> below 32 degrees, water <u>freezes</u>.
- If James <u>comes</u> home late from school, his mother <u>gets</u> angry.

例題1 **Complete the Sentence**

He is usually alert and ready for work if he _____ enough sleep.

    A. get

    B. gets

    C. will get

    D. to get

正解は **B** です。これは普遍的真実の条件文なので、he を主語とする節に現在時制の動詞が用いられます。A は不正解です。he が主語なので、動詞は三人称単数形である必要があります。C は、未来表現がこの条件文での正しい形ではないので不正解です。D は、to 不定詞を主語 he の後に続けることができないので不正解です。

直説法の条件文

直説法の条件文もまた事実を表現しており、この点では、普遍的真実を述べる条件文と似ています。しかし、普遍的真実の条件文が頻繁に、あるいは定期的に起こる事柄の因果関係を表すのに対し、直説法の条件文は一度しか起こらないことを表現する際に用いられます。また、条件文であることを表すために、結果を表す節の動詞に未来表現を用いるという違いもあります。

例文

- If the prices of wheat and other farm commodities continue to fall, the country <u>will borrow</u> more money to pay its expenses.
- If I find a job in the city, I <u>will sell</u> my house and get an apartment downtown.

Grammar

Listening

Reading

Writing

Speaking

Appendix

例題2　**Error Correction**

If Bill gives <u>his</u> wife <u>a</u> present, she <u>was</u> very <u>happy</u>.

  A. his

  B. a

  C. was

  D. happy

正解は**C**です。この直説法条件文では、原因を表す節に現在形の動詞givesが来ています。結果は原因の後に起こるので、結果を表す文の動詞には未来表現を用います。will beが正解です。

仮定法過去

普遍的真実を述べる条件文や直説法の条件文が真実や事実を表すのに対し、仮定法過去の文は条件の内容が実際には起こっていないことなので、事実に反する、または実現不可能なことを示す文と言われます。仮定法過去の文は、非現実的な仮定の下での状況を表しています。仮定法過去は、実際に起こったことではなく、可能性がある事象を表現します。仮定法過去は、最初の節で条件を表す「if+主語」と過去形の動詞が、次の節で「would」と動詞の原形が用いられ、架空の状況を表現しています。

例文

- If Victor <u>treated</u> his classmates more nicely, he <u>would have</u> more friends.
- More patients <u>would survive</u> heart attacks if they <u>got</u> to the hospital faster.

例題3　**Complete the Sentence**

Julie would buy a nicer car if she _____ more money.

  A. make

  B. is making

  C. will make

  D. made

正解は**D**です。この例題では、結果を表す節が最初に来ており、その中でwould buyという述語動詞が使われています。これは、条件が事実に反していることを示しており、原因を表す節では過去形が使われます。過去形の選択肢は**D**だけです。

Grammar

仮定法過去完了

　仮定法過去の文と同様に、仮定法過去完了の文も原因や条件が実際に起こっていないため、事実に反する、または実現不可能なことを示す文であると認識されています。この文では、原因または条件、そして結果の両方が過去のことを表します。条件を表す節には過去完了形の動詞が用いられ、結果を表す節には、wouldと動詞の完了形が用いられます。

例文

- If the bank <u>had not taken</u> steps to lower interest rates, the economy <u>would have declined</u>.
  質問：実際には銀行は金利を下げたのでしょうか？　回答：はい、下げました。

- My parents <u>would have moved</u> to California if my mother <u>had gotten</u> the job with that company.
  質問：実際には母は仕事に就いたのでしょうか？　回答：いいえ、就きませんでした。

例題4 **Error Correction**

If <u>the</u> dam had not been built, <u>this</u> whole area <u>will</u> have been <u>flooded</u>.

    A. the
    B. this
    C. will
    D. flooded

　正解は**C**です。この仮定法過去完了の文では、実際にはダムが建設されていますが、されなかった場合を想定した文となっています。この場合、結果を表す文ではwould+完了形が用いられます。この文中で誤っている単語はwillです。ここではwouldが正解です。

EXERCISE

Part 1. Complete the Sentence

1. Their parents would have punished them _____ they had not done their chores this week.
   - A. would
   - B. so
   - C. if
   - D. as

2. If more people had voted for the law regarding a neighborhood curfew, it would have been _____ .
   - A. pass
   - B. passed
   - C. past
   - D. passing

3. If you have your hair dyed platinum blonde, you will look so much prettier than _____ now.
   - A. I does
   - B. me do
   - C. you does
   - D. you do

4. _____ Kate has enough time off from her job, she will take a trip to Europe over the summer.
   - A. If
   - B. Should
   - C. Maybe
   - D. Despite

5. If Mom does not have her coffee first thing in the morning, she _____ extremely irritable and fussy.
   - A. get
   - B. gets
   - C. getting
   - D. got

6. If Brian _____ to give you some money to buy lunch, you will pay him back tomorrow.
   - A. decide
   - B. decides
   - C. decision
   - D. deciding

7. If everyone in the world had access to medication, _____ would be a lot less disease.
   - A. then
   - B. they
   - C. there
   - D. that

8. _____ had put air in the tires before you took the road trip, you wouldn't have gotten a flat tire.
   - A. If your
   - B. If you
   - C. Even if your
   - D. Even if you

Grammar

Part 2. Error Correction

9. <u>Even if the</u> new highway <u>is a</u> quicker route <u>to travel</u>, <u>people</u> will stop using the back roads.
   A. Even if the
   B. is
   C. to travel
   D. people

10. <u>Unless me</u> Mom goes <u>to the</u> supermarket <u>this afternoon</u>, she will buy <u>some</u> tomatoes for my dinner.
    A. Unless me
    B. to the
    C. this afternoon
    D. some

11. <u>Despite</u> Jane won <u>the</u> lottery, she would go <u>on a</u> trip <u>around</u> the world.
    A. Despite
    B. the
    C. on a
    D. around

12. <u>Should Peter have</u> bought that house <u>in the</u> city, <u>he</u> would have had to <u>remodel</u> the bedroom.
    A. Should Peter have
    B. in the
    C. he
    D. remodel

13. Even if Robin had <u>spent</u> all of her money, <u>I will</u> not be able <u>to buy</u> <u>this painting</u>.
    A. spent
    B. I will
    C. to buy
    D. this painting

14. If you <u>study hard</u> in <u>your</u> Spanish class, you <u>got</u> a good grade <u>at the</u> end of the year.
    A. study hard
    B. your
    C. got
    D. at the

15. <u>Should</u> Mary can <u>find</u> the book <u>that</u> <u>she</u> borrowed from me, she will give <u>it</u> back.
    A. Should
    B. find
    C. that she
    D. it

Grammar

Listening

Reading

Writing

Speaking

Appendix

Chapter 11 並列構造

並列構造の形成

　iTEPの試験では、並列構造を持つ文を正しく構成する能力があるかどうかを試す問題も出題されます。これらのタイプの問題では、名詞や動詞、形容詞、副詞、または節など様々な品詞が並列されますが、どの場合も並列される対象は全て同じ品詞である必要があります。以下の例を比較してみましょう。

> このチャプターでは太字になっている項目についてテストします
>
> ● 動詞の形
> ● **構文**
> ● 接続詞
> ● **品詞**
> ● 冠詞と前置詞
> ● **分量の表現**
> ● 代名詞

A. The most important skills we are looking for in a new manager are **efficiency, precision, and cooperation**.

B. The new manager should be **efficient, precise, and cooperative**.

C. It is important that the new manager work **efficiently, precisely, and cooperatively**.

　上記の例では、文末の一連の単語がすべて同じ品詞であることに注目しましょう。例文Aでは、太字の単語はすべて名詞です。例文Bでは太字の単語はすべて形容詞、例文Cではすべて副詞です。また、動名詞(動詞の -ing形で、名詞の働きをするもの。skiing、cooking、cyclingなど) が並列される対象となる場合もあることを覚えておいてください。以下の例題1を見てみましょう。

| 例題1 | **Complete the Sentence** |

Sometimes when my mom is cooking, she starts _____, dancing, and performing as if she is on Broadway.

    A. singing

    B. to singing

Grammar

C. sing

D. sung

正解は**A**です。この文中では、動名詞dancingとperformingが並列されているので、この並列構造に合致する選択肢はsingingのみです。この文中では、singingが名詞であることに注意しましょう。

例題2 **Error Correction**

Modern grocery <u>stores</u> can be <u>confusing</u> because they <u>offer</u> many choices, <u>sale</u>, and coupons.

A. stores

B. confusing

C. offer

D. sale

正解は**D**です。この文中で並列されているものの中で、sale以外の名詞はすべて複数形です。正しくはsalesです。

並列構造を作る

3つ以上の単語を並列する場合、英語では一般的にandかorのいずれかで各単語をつなぎます。

andを使った場合の例文

Next year she will study English, history, **and** algebra.

orを使った場合の例文

We will decide tomorrow if we will study biology, chemistry, **or** physics.

andを使い、節をつなぐ場合の例文

The teacher said that she was an excellent student because she completed her work on time, solved her lab problems accurately, **and** demonstrated motivation.

また、ほかにもthenを用いて順序を表現したり、neitherとnorを用いて否定を表現することもあります。

Chapter 11 並列構造

Grammar

Listening

Reading

Writing

Speaking

Appendix

thenを使った例文

The principal prefers that teachers greet students, begin an activity, **then** take attendance.

norを使った例文

The mother decided she wanted neither the red ones, the blue ones, **nor** the green ones.

例題3　**Complete the Sentence**

When the disappointing tour guide explained the history of the city, he was neither thorough, passionate, _____ friendly.

    A. and

    B. or

    C. then

    D. nor

正解は**D**です。この文中では並列構造がneitherで始まっているため、空欄に当てはまるのはnorだけです。

例題4　**Error Correction**

The director instructed the actors to smile, wave, nor take a bow.

    A. The

    B. instructed

    C. smile

    D. nor

正解は**D**です。この選択肢は文中にneitherがないので誤りです。この場合はnorではなく、thenかandが最後の並列対象の前に入ります。

Grammar

EXERCISE

Part 1. Complete the Sentence

1. Last time he went to the store he
   got _____ and salami.
   A. milk and cheese
   B. milk and cheese,
   C. milk, cheese,
   D. milk cheese

2. Eric loves to go hiking, _____
   or mountain biking.
   A. fish
   B. fish,
   C. fished
   D. fishing,

3. Have you ever wondered why
   Tolkien and Lewis fans argue,
   when their themes of _____,
   valor, wonder, and philosophy
   rarely conflict?
   A. love
   B. loves
   C. loved
   D. loving

4. He didn't want to go to
   the _____, or the
   optometrist.
   A. doctor plus the dentist
   B. doctor nor the dentist
   C. doctor and the dentist
   D. doctor, the dentist

5. *American Idol* judges should learn
   to listen more closely to vocal
   _____.
   A. tone and pitch and quality.
   B. tone plus pitch, plus quality.
   C. tone or pitch or quality.
   D. tone, pitch, and quality.

6. When my dad got us a cat,
   we thought it would run, _____
   and leap around, but it just sleeps
   all day.
   A. plays
   B. play,
   C. playing
   D. playing,

7. Within each jar were collections of
   ribbon candies, exotic chocolates,
   _____ a host of other treats.
   A. for
   B. since
   C. and
   D. from

Grammar

Listening

Reading

Writing

Speaking

Appendix

Part 2. Error Correction

8. <u>My new</u> puppy likes <u>to play</u> fetch, to take naps, <u>likes</u> to eat his puppy <u>chow</u>.

A. My new

B. to play

C. likes

D. chow

9. When <u>she's</u> bored <u>at home</u>, she likes <u>to play</u> video games, read books, <u>not</u> take a nap.

A. she's

B. at home

C. to play

D. not

10. The police <u>contacted</u> each member <u>of the council</u> with a report <u>on</u> cut lawns, <u>and stray</u> dogs, and overpriced lemonade stands.

A. contacted

B. of the council

C. on

D. and stray

11. He <u>not only</u> learned to play the flute; he <u>too</u> learned <u>to play</u> the piano.

A. He

B. not only

C. too

D. to play

12. Alice <u>would rather</u> sing in front <u>of a</u> crowd than <u>giving</u> a speech in front of a class or perform a play <u>in front of</u> an audience.

A. would rather

B. of a

C. giving

D. in front of

13. <u>Finished</u> the recipe <u>means</u> adding sea salt, apple cider vinegar, <u>and a</u> host <u>of spices</u>.

A. Finished

B. means

C. and a

D. of spices

Grammar

Chapter 12 法助動詞

法助動詞の語形

法助動詞は、ある行動が起こる可能性、能力、義務、許可などを表すために使用される特殊な動詞です。英語ではmodal verbs、またはhelping verbsとも呼ばれます。法助動詞の例は、以下の表を参照してください。

might　許可、推量	may　許可、推量
can　能力、可能	could　過去の可能
must　義務、強要	should　義務、必要
would　過去の意志、仮定	will/won't　意志
shall　意志	

> このチャプターでは太字になっている項目についてテストします
>
> - **動詞の形**
> - **構文**
> - 接続詞
> - 品詞
> - 冠詞と前置詞
> - 分量の表現
> - 代名詞

法助動詞が持つ複数の意味を覚えておきましょう。また、法助動詞の後には動詞の原形が続きます。決してto不定詞や動名詞ではありません。

例題1　Complete the Sentence

The teacher said I could _____ early to go to my locker.

 A. to leave

 B. leaving

 C. leave

 D. leaves

例題1では、**C**が正解です。couldの後に続くことができるのはleaveだけです。to不定詞のto leaveや動名詞のleavingは法助動詞の後に続くことはできません。

Dは不正解です。法助動詞の後に来る動詞は主語の単複に応じて変化することはなく、法助動詞自体も主語が単数か複数かに依存しません。つまりcansやshouldsは誤りです。

　最後に、法助動詞はそれ自体が助動詞なので、否定文や疑問文を作るために追加の助動詞を必要としません。

Should I wait?　>>>　~~*Do I should wait?*~~

They shouldn't wait.　>>>　~~*They don't should wait.*~~

例題2　**Error Correction**

The players must to stay overnight because their last game starts at 8 pm.
- A. The
- B. to stay
- C. their
- D. starts

　正解は**B**です。前述のように、法助動詞の後にto不定詞を置くことはできません。この場合、mustの後には動詞stayの原形が続きます。

Grammar

EXERCISE

Part 1. Complete the Sentence

1. A careful student _____
   cram for an exam the night before
   the test.
   A. do
   B. does
   C. want
   D. won't

2. Any given politician _____
   be fully trusted to tell the truth.
   A. have not
   B. should not
   C. do not
   D. does not

3. My mom _____ allow me to
   drive when I am 15.
   A. was
   B. has
   C. are
   D. might

4. The coach said I should _____
   my game skills at home.
   A. practiced
   B. to practice
   C. practicing
   D. practice

5. In the spirit of Gandalf, "You
   _____ pass!"
   A. ought not
   B. shall not
   C. have not
   D. could not

6. You choose: _____ we eat at
   a five-star restaurant or have fast
   food?
   A. shall
   B. have
   C. want
   D. are

7. All citizens must _____ their
   responsibilities seriously.
   A. take
   B. to take
   C. taking
   D. taken

8. Gravity dictates that what goes up
   _____ come down.
   A. ought
   B. must
   C. did
   D. what

Grammar

Listening

Reading

Writing

Speaking

Appendix

Part 2. Error Correction

9. Serious <u>athletes</u> ought to <u>coming</u> to <u>practice</u> <u>regularly</u>.

   A. athletes

   B. coming

   C. practice

   D. regularly

10. A <u>serious</u> soldier <u>do</u> pay <u>particular</u> attention to <u>keeping</u> his weapon clean.

    A. serious

    B. do

    C. particular

    D. keeping

11. One <u>ought</u> <u>to think</u> twice before <u>to smoke</u> cigarettes because they <u>damage</u> one's lungs.

    A. ought

    B. to think

    C. to smoke

    D. damage

12. You <u>have</u> wear a hat <u>today</u> <u>as it</u> is <u>very</u> sunny.

    A. have

    B. today

    C. as it

    D. very

13. <u>Running</u> away from <u>responsibilities</u> could <u>ending up</u> <u>resulting</u> in serious problems.

    A. Running

    B. responsibilities

    C. ending up

    D. resulting

14. My best friend <u>knew</u> that his <u>choices</u> <u>ought</u> end up <u>affecting</u> his popularity.

    A. knew

    B. choices

    C. ought

    D. affecting

15. Gorillas must <u>enjoying</u> eating bananas <u>since</u> they <u>eat</u> so many of them!

    A. enjoying

    B. eating

    C. since

    D. eat

UNIT 2
LISTENING

Introduction to LISTENING

iTEPのリスニングセクションは、一般的な高校（iTEP SLATE）、大学（iTEP Academic）、ビジネス（iTEP Business）の環境で耳にするような英語をどれだけ理解できるかを判定します。聴解力が問われ、問題文の内容に関する予備知識は必要ありません。全ての問題は、基本的なリスニング能力で選択肢の情報を判別することで解答することができます。iTEPのリスニングセクションは全体で20分かかり、3つのパートから構成されています。

最初にiTEPのリスニングセクションで出題される5つのタイプの問題について、詳しく解説していきます。

問題の5つのタイプ

1. 趣旨

ここで取り上げる問題では、ある人物による講義や、2者間の会話について、その趣旨が何かを正しく判断できるかどうかが問われます。

2. 内容理解

ここで取り上げる問題では、リスニングでの基本的な理解力と記憶力が問われます。会話、議論、または講義の基礎となるポイントをメモすることが求められます。

3. 内容の関連づけ

ここで取り上げる問題では、議論や講義、または会話の中の重要な情報の関連づけができるかどうかが問われます。

4. 推測

ここで取り上げる問題では、会話中で述べられるある特定の状況に基づいて、会話の中の出来事について、文脈を推測することが求められます。

出題構成

このセクションでは次のような項目に関する問題が出題されます

試験時間：**20分間**

レベル：**CEFR A〜C**

パート1
CEFR A1-A2

4つの短い会話と、それに関する4問の多肢択一問題

パート2
CEFR A2-B2

2〜3分間の会話と、4問の多肢択一問題

パート3
CEFR B2-C2

4分間の講義と、それに関する6問の多肢択一問題

Grammar

Listening

Reading

Writing

Speaking

Appendix

5. 目的の特定

　ここで取り上げる問題では、会話の中の出来事の理由を特定することが求められます。さらに、ここでは講義の概要を理解しているかどうかを試されることもあります。

リスニングの心得

　リスニングセクションで高得点を取るためには、最も重要な情報をメモして記憶につなげることが大事です。このユニットでは会話や講義を聞きながら、メモを取る練習をしてみましょう。リスニング中には、〈アクティブリスニング〉と呼ばれるテクニックを使う必要があります。ラジオやポッドキャストを聞くときのように、特に情報を特定したり覚えたりせずに何かを聞くことを〈パッシブリスニング〉といいますが、反対に講義を聞くときは、聞いた情報を理解して記憶しなければなりません。これをアクティブリスニングといい、練習すれば身につけることができる能力です。

　リスニングセクションで高得点を獲得した受験者の多くは、会話や講義の中で重要な情報を記憶するためにメモを取っています。このユニットで会話や講義を聞きながら、メモの練習をしてアクティブリスニングのスキルを磨きましょう。アクティブリスニングとアクティブリーディングは、どちらも鍛錬によって向上させることができる能力であり、この情報収集能力は、何気なく何かを聞くときに使われるパッシブリスニングでは身につかないことを覚えておきましょう。

　メモを取る際は、能動的に聞き、重要度に応じて情報を選別することが大事です。そのためには〈インタビュー〉というテクニックを用いましょう。これは、会話や講義に対して以下の観点からアプローチすることです。

　1. 誰が話しているのか？
　2. 複数の発言者がいる場合、発言者同士の関係は何か？
　3. 言及されている問題は何か？

　アクティブリスニングのその他のコツについては、以降の章で説明します。

設問に対する心得

　会話や講義の後に続く設問に取りかかる際、正しい答えを導き出すのに役立つ一般的なテクニックとして、消去法（POE）があります。消去法とは、不正解だとわかっている答えを取り除き、設問をより単純にすることです。以降の章の例題の後で、消去法を使いこなすコツについて説明します。

Listening

Chapter 1　内容理解

　内容理解の問題では、リスニングの基本的な理解力と記憶力が試されます。このタイプの問題では、会話や議論、講義の基礎となるポイントをメモしておくことが求められます。リスニングのパート1と2(対話)では、会話の中の特定の情報について出題され、リスニングのパート3(講義)では特定の日付や、複数の似たような情報からある重要な情報を識別することが求められます。インタビューを行う際に、会話のテーマや日付、物事の発生順序など、重要な情報に気づけるよう練習しましょう。これは、特にパート1の短い会話の聞き取り時に役立ちます。リスニングの問題音声を聞くには、https://itepexamjapan.com/practiceguideのリンクにアクセスしてください。このセクションでは、それぞれの例題について、音声を聞く必要があります。音声を聞いて、以下の例題を解いてみましょう。

例題1　**Finals** 🔊

What do we know about the man?

　　A. He works and goes to school at the same time.

　　B. He goes to school full-time.

　　C. He does not go to school full-time.

　　D. He works part-time.

　正解は**C**です。会話の中では働くことについては何も触れられていないので、A と D は不正解です。男性は定時制の学校に通っていると言っているので、B は不正解です。

例題2　**Focus on School** 🔊

How is the man paying for school?

　　A. with money he saved

　　B. with savings and loans

　　C. with loans only

　　D. with a scholarship

　正解は**C**です。会話中に貯金や奨学金についての発言はありません。またこの問題では、受験者に会話から隠れた意図を読み取ったり、推測したりする力を求めているわけではありません。そのため、消去法を使えば、A、B、D の選択肢を消去することができます。女性は男性が融資を受け

ていると述べているので、正解はCです。

例題3　Take Out the Trash 🔊

When is the man supposed to take the trash out?

    A. in the evening

    B. when he is reminded

    C. after school

    D. before school

　正解は**D**です。　会話から、この男性が学校に行くのは朝だと推測する人もいるかもしれませんが、この問題は推測を求めるものではありません。時間帯についての言及がないので、AとBはどちらも消去できます。女性は学校に行く前にゴミを出すようにと男性に伝えているので、正解は**D**です。

例題4　Cook Dinner 🔊

The woman did not cook dinner because:

    A. She did not have the ingredients.

    B. The store did not have chicken.

    C. The restaurant was recommended.

    D. She wants to eat chicken at a restaurant.

　正解は**A**です。　ここでも、消去法を用いることで正解にたどり着くことができます。女性は店には行かなかったと述べているので、Bは不正解です。女性がなぜ会話に出てくる店に行きたいのかについては言及されていないので、Cは不正解です。また男性は翌日に食べるものの選択肢にチキンを挙げているので、Dは不正解です。

Listening

Chapter 2 推測

　何が推測できるか、何が示唆されているかを問う問題を解く際には、話者の口調に着目しましょう。また、会話や講義に対してインタビューを行ったり、何が示唆されているかを問う問題でメモを取ったりするときには、話し手が話題や考えに対して好意を示しているのか、また何か他の感情を示しているのかを確認するようにしましょう。

　下記の例題を参照してください。

※ https://itepexamjapan.com/practiceguide を開いて音声を聞くことができます。

例題1　Finals 🔊

What likely happened to the man last semester?

　　A. He did well at school.

　　B. He lost his job.

　　C. He did poorly at school.

　　D. He moved into a new house.

　正解はCです。この答えは消去法（POE）で見つけることができます。まず、家や仕事についての言及がないので、選択肢のBとDを消去することができます。また女性の「男性が同じ結果にならないことを願う」という発言から、男性が前学期に学校で良い成績を残せなかったことがわかります。そのためAは不正解です。また男性が、今年は去年より十分に対策を取るように言われていることからも、彼の去年の学期の成績が悪かったと推測することができます。

例題2　Focus on School 🔊

What is likely true about the man's school performance?

　　A. It is getting better.

　　B. It is exactly what it should be.

　　C. It is below expectations.

　　D. Working has helped his performance.

　正解はCです。この問題は何が真実である「可能性が高いか」を問うているので、聞き手が正解を見つけるには推測を行う必要があると判断できます。彼の学校での成績については特に言及され

ていません。しかし、女性は彼がもっと学校での勉学に集中すべきだと述べているので、彼の学校での成績が向上する可能性が高いと推測できます。彼の学校での成績について肯定的な言及がないので、A、B、Dの答えは不正解です。

例題3　**Take Out the Trash** 🔊

What can we assume has happened prior to the conversation?

 A. The man has forgotten to take out the trash in the past.

 B. The man has always taken out the trash.

 C. The woman has forgotten to take out the trash.

 D. The man has taken out the trash every day.

　正解は**A**です。この会話からはゴミを出す頻度がわからないので、Dは不正解です。女性がゴミを出すという発言はないので、Cは不正解です。女性が「男性に毎回ゴミ出しをちゃんとするように言わなきゃ」と発言しているので、男性はこれまでにゴミ出しを忘れたことがあると推測できます。よって、Aが正解です。

例題4　**Cook Dinner** 🔊

What can be assumed about the woman's schedule?

 A. She is very busy.

 B. She cooks a lot.

 C. It does not change too much.

 D. She has lots of free time.

　正解は**A**です。この設問では、解答者は会話から入手できる情報に基づき、推測を行うように求められます。女性がどれくらいの頻度で料理をしているかはわからないので、Bは不正解です。彼女は突然の予定の変更については言及していないので、Cは不正解です。女性は時間がなく店に行かなかったので、彼女には自由な時間があまりなく、とても忙しいのではないかと推測することができます。

Listening

Chapter 3　趣旨

　趣旨が何かを問う問題では、選択肢を比較する際、以下のような観点からアプローチするといいでしょう。

> 1. 会話／講義を10〜12語でどう要約するか。
> 2. 会話／講義の概要を大まかな言葉で捉えているのはどの選択肢か。
> 3. 会話／講義全体を通して言及されるテーマを反映した選択肢はどれか。

　以下の例題と解説を見てみましょう。

　この会話の音声を聞くには、https://itepexamjapan.com/practiceguide にアクセスしてください。

例題1　Finals 🔊

What is the main idea of this conversation?

  A. comparing exam results

  B. trying to perform better in school

  C. how to reduce stress

  D. trying new things

　正解はBです。この会話は期末試験の前に行われており、まだ結果が出ていないので、Aは不正解です。新しいことに挑戦するという言及はないため、Dは不正解です。男性はストレスについて話していますが、会話の論点はストレスを減らすことではなく、むしろ試験で良い結果を出すことにあります。したがって、Cは不正解であり、Bが会話の趣旨を最もよく反映しています。

例題2　Focus on School 🔊

What is the main idea of this conversation?

  A. It is best not to worry so much about grades.

  B. It is better to work than to study.

  C. It is best not to pay back loans.

  D. It is best to find balance between work and study.

Grammar
Listening
Reading
Writing
Speaking
Appendix

　正解は**D**です。**A**は、会話内に成績についての言及がないので不正解です。会話の中では、融資の返済のために働く必要があることが述べられていますが、発言者は仕事の方がより重要だとも、男性の融資を返済すべきではないとも述べていません。したがって、**B**と**C**は不正解です。会話は主に経済的責任と学校の責任の両方を果たすことについて述べられています。

例題3 **Take Out the Trash** 🔊

What is the main idea of the conversation?

  A. deciding who should take out the trash

  B. fulfilling responsibilities

  C. where to take the trash

  D. how to take out the trash

　正解は**B**です。この会話の趣旨は、男性はゴミを出すことを忘れてはいけないということです。会話の中には「どこで」「どのように」ゴミを出すのかが述べられていないので、**C**と**D**は不正解です。ゴミを出すのは明らかに男性の義務なので、**A**の答えも不正解です。

例題4 **Cook Dinner** 🔊

What is this conversation mostly about?

  A. which restaurant to go to

  B. the best place to eat chicken

  C. making dinner plans

  D. eating at home

　正解は**C**です。**B**は会話で言及されておらず、不正解です。**A**と**D**の情報については会話中で簡単に触れられていますが、どちらも会話の主な情報ではありません。会話全体の主な目的は、夕食について話し合ったり、計画を立てたりすることです。多くの場合、非常に具体的な説明では趣旨を捉えられないことが多いので、趣旨を大まかな言葉で説明した選択肢を見つけることが大事です。

Listening

Chapter 4 目的の特定

　目的は何かを問う問題では、話し手が述べたある事柄について、なぜ話し手はそれを述べたのか、または会話／講義全体の目的は何かが問われます。いずれの場合も、話し手の声のトーンは目的を判断する良い指標となります。このタイプの設問の練習をする際には、つなぎ言葉や、話し手が意見の相違や好意を示す瞬間はいつか、をメモしましょう。

　この会話の音声を聞くには、https://itepexamjapan.com/practiceguideにアクセスしてください。

例題1 **Finals** 🔊

Why does the woman say that she doesn't "want a repeat of last year"?

　　A. because she was very stressed

　　B. because she did poorly at school

　　C. because the man only attended part-time

　　D. because the man did poorly last year

　正解は**D**です。会話の論点は、男性の学校での成績がどうかであり、女性についての情報はほとんどありません。したがって、A と B は不正解です。女性の関心事は、男性がフルタイムで学校に通っているか、定時制で通っているかではないので、C も不正解です。

例題2 **Focus on School** 🔊

Why does the woman mention that the man's loans do not need to be paid back immediately?

　　A. because she knows that he does not need to repay the loans

　　B. because she thinks he should work more

　　C. because the man is worried about his schoolwork

　　D. because the man is worried about repaying the loan

　正解は**D**です。女性は、男性が学業とのバランスを取るために、あまり働かない方がいいと述べていますが、ローンを返済しない方がいいとは述べていません。したがって、A は不正解です。彼女は明確に男性はあまり働かない方がいいと言っているので、B は不正解です。男性はローンを返

Grammar

Listening

Reading

Writing

Speaking

Appendix

済するために働かなければならないと言っているだけで、学業については言及していないので、C
は正しくありません。女性は男性にもっと学校に集中してほしいと思っており、男性がローンの返
済についてあまり心配するべきではないと言っています。

例題3 **Take Out the Trash** 🔊

Why does the woman say she shouldn't have to remind him?

    A. because he always remembers

    B. because she thinks he should remember

    C. because it is not necessary to remind him

    D. because she likes taking out the trash

ほとんどの選択肢はある文脈や状況では正しいかもしれませんが、女性の発言の目的を表してい
るのはBだけです。男性はよくゴミを出すのを忘れるようなので、この状況ではAとCは不正解で
す。女性がゴミを出すことについては言及されていないので、Dは不正解です。女性は、男性がゴ
ミを出し忘れることに不満を感じているので、**B**が正解です。

例題4 **Cook Dinner** 🔊

Why does the man mention eating chicken tomorrow?

    A. because he especially wants chicken for dinner

    B. because he doesn't want to eat chicken tonight

    C. because he is fine with adjusting the dinner plans

    D. because he'd prefer to eat in a restaurant

正解は**C**です。男性は夕食にレストランに行くという代替案を提案していますが、彼は好きな食
べ物について述べてはいません。A、B、Dは、いずれも男性の好みについて言及しているため、消
去することができます。

Listening

Chapter 5　内容の関連づけ

　　内容の関連を問う問題では、より長い会話が出題されます。「どこで、どのように勉強するか」についての会話には、4つの関連する質問があり、会話中の様々なポイントを関連づける必要があります。各設問の後に解説があります。この会話の音声は、Listening 2 の Dialogues（一般的に CEFR B2-C1 レベル）の一例です。

　　この会話の音声を聞くには、https://itepexamjapan.com/practiceguide にアクセスしてください。

例題1　**Where and How to Study** 🔊

Why was the man frustrated?

　　A. The library was closed.

　　B. The café where he studies is too noisy.

　　C. He has difficulty studying while listening to music.

　　D. Studying in the library for long periods is uncomfortable.

　　正解は **D** です。女性は、会話の冒頭で男性が不満を抱えているように見えると述べていますが、その理由が図書館の椅子にあることは、何度かやりとりを重ねて初めて明らかになります。Cは会話の中での発言としては正しいのですが、これが男性の不満の原因ではありません。図書館が閉館したことについての言及はないので、Aは不正解です。カフェで勉強しているのは男性ではなく女性なので、Bは不正解です。また、彼女は騒音に不満を感じているわけではありません。

例題2

Why will the man visit the woman's dorm room tonight?

　　A. She will share some music with him.

　　B. They will complete an assignment together.

　　C. They will study for an exam on classical music.

　　D. He will bring her a book from the library.

　　正解は **A** です。この問題の正解は消去法で見つけることが可能です。会話中で課題や特定の本について言及されていないので、BとDは除外することができます。同様に、試験については言及さ

Grammar

Listening

Reading

Writing

Speaking

Appendix

れていますが、特定の科目や共同のクラスについては言及されていないため、Cは不正解です。女性は男性に音楽をコピーしてあげてもいいと言っています。

例題3

What helps the woman concentrate while studying?

     A. listening to people speak German

     B. listening to popular music

     C. listening to music without words

     D. working in the library where it is quiet

　正解はCです。会話の中で、女性はある種類の音楽を聞くと勉強がはかどることに言及しています。彼女が唯一歌詞のある音楽として挙げているのはドイツ語のオペラ音楽で、彼女はドイツ語を話しません。彼女の集中力を高める音楽は歌詞がないか、彼女が理解できる歌詞が使われていないものなので、Cが正解となります。

例題4

Why do the man and woman talk about music?

     A. It helps the man to study.

     B. It helps the woman to study.

     C. They both study music.

     D. The music in the café is too loud.

　正解はBです。女性は会話の中で音楽が集中力を高めてくれると話しています。一方で男性は音楽を聞きながら勉強するのは難しいと述べています。男性と女性のどちらがどの教科を勉強しているかは明確に述べられていないので、Cは不正解です。カフェの音楽の話は、音楽に関して行われた会話中でほんのわずかしか言及されていないので、Dは不正解です。

Listening

Chapter 6 長めの会話（パート2）

　このセクションでは、iTEPのリスニングのパート2で出題される内容を扱います。この
パートでは、前の5つの章で学んだことが全て凝縮されています。まずは「講義の登録につ
いて」の会話を聞いた後、以下の例題と解説を確認して出題の傾向をつかみましょう。

　この会話の音声を聞くには、https://itepexamjapan.com/practiceguide にアクセス
してください。

例題1　**Registration Issues** 🔊

What class does the professor teach?

    A. nursing

    B. world economics

    C. world literature

    D. accounting

　正解は**C**です。このような詳細を問う問題では、会話を聞きながらメモを取ることが重要です。
会話の冒頭で、学生は教授の世界文学の講義を受けていることを話しています。学生は看護を勉強
していますが、これは教授が教えていることではありません。したがって、Aは不正解です。会話
で述べられているのは奨学金であり、経済学の講義ではないので、Bは正しくありません。最後に、
教授はアドバイスをしていますが、アドバイスをすることについて教えているわけではないので、
Dは不正解です。

例題2

Why does the student talk to the professor?

    A. She needs to graduate.

    B. She is concerned about her grade.

    C. She wants to add his class.

    D. She is worried she is taking too many classes.

　正解は**C**です。この学生は教授の講義への登録について問題を抱えているので、彼女の目的は受
講する講義の追加を依頼することです。彼女は春に卒業したいと思っていますが、これは教授が解
決できることではありません。したがって、Aは正しくありません。学生は自分の成績に問題はな

いと述べているので、Bは不正解です。教授は学生が受講している授業の数について懸念を示していますが、学生はそうは思っていません。したがって、Dは不正解です。

例題3

Why does the student need to add the class?

  A. She wants to graduate in the summer.

  B. She wants to graduate in the spring.

  C. She is majoring in world literature.

  D. She is majoring in nursing.

　正解は**B**です。この問題では、会話の内容の関連づけができるかどうかを問われています。前の章で説明したように、いかにメモを上手に取れるかどうかが正解にたどり着く鍵となります。この学生は夏に看護師としてフルタイムで働きたいと考えているので、夏までに卒業に必要な単位を取得する必要があります。学生は夏までに卒業したいと思っているので、Aは不正解です。Cは、学生の専攻が看護学であるため、不正解です。Dは、文学の講義は看護学やその他の専攻の必須科目として言及されていないため、不正解です。文学と看護学は関連がないため、これは彼女の専攻の必須科目ではない可能性が高いと言えます。

例題4

What is this conversation mostly about?

  A. graduating early

  B. dealing with student debt

  C. getting a job recommendation

  D. asking for advice

　正解は**D**です。会話の中ではCを除くすべての選択肢の内容について述べられていますが、会話の趣旨は、学生がアドバイスを求めているということです。学生はすでに早期卒業の方法や奨学金の解決方法については熟知しており、アドバイスを求めているわけではありません。したがって、AとBは趣旨を捉えておらず、不正解です。趣旨を問う問題では、会話全体の内容を的確に捉えている選択肢を探すことを心がけましょう。

Listening

Chapter 7 講義（パート3）

　このセクションでは、iTEPのリスニングのパート3で出題される内容を扱います。講義の音声の後に例題と解説を確認して出題傾向をつかみましょう。講義の音声はhttps://itepexamjapan.com/practiceguideで聞くことができます。この例題は中上級〜上級レベル（CEFR B2-C2）です。

例題1　Fuel Cells and Hydrogen Power 🔊

According to the professor, which of the following statements is true?

　　A. Natural gas and methane are fossil fuels.

　　B. Hydrogen is a fossil fuel.

　　C. Solar power comes from hydrogen.

　　D. Natural gas and methane are sustainable resources.

　正解は**A**です。B、C、Dは講義の内容からすると正確ではありません。メモをしっかり取ることで、消去法で正解にたどり着くことができます。教授は、水素発電は天然ガスやメタンを用いて簡単に行うことができるが、これらは化石燃料であり、グリーンエネルギーとは言えないと説明しています。

例題2

What is the talk mainly about?

　　A. green energy versus fossil fuels

　　B. how hydrogen fuel is affecting climate change

　　C. hydrogen as a power source for the future

　　D. the role of solar power in green energy

　正解は**C**です。この設問は、講義の趣旨を問うものです。この講義の趣旨はグリーンエネルギーではありますが、教授はグリーンエネルギーのある1つの形、すなわち水素発電にのみ焦点を当てています。その他のグリーンエネルギーである太陽光発電や、気候変動については簡単にしか言及されていませんが、水素発電については長く説明されているので、A、B、Dが不正解であると結論づけることができます。

例題3

What is the professor's purpose in giving the lecture?

    A. to explain the advantages and disadvantages of hydrogen power

    B. to explain recent changes in how hydrogen power is used

    C. to warn about the dangers of hydrogen power

    D. to warn about the dangers of climate change

　正解は**A**です。この講義では水素発電の潜在的な利点と課題が主に説明されているので、選択肢Aが講義の目的を最も的確に表していると言えます。教授は学生を説得しようとしているのではなく、教育しようとしています。そのためBは不正解です。また、教授は学生に危険について警告しているわけではないので、CとDも不正解です。

例題4

What does the professor imply when she says the below?

"Over the coming decades, significant investment may need to be made in order to get over this hurdle and transform the economy from one based on diminishing fossil fuels to one based on hydrogen and clean energy."

    A. Only private companies will be able to produce hydrogen in the future.

    B. It will be easy to start hydrogen production.

    C. Hydrogen production will have major benefits.

    D. Both private and public resources will be needed to start large-scale hydrogen production.

　正解は**C**です。Aは、水素発電を開発するための資源が民間企業にしかないとは述べられていないので、不正解です。この発言ではクリーンな水素の製造を始めるためには、克服すべき課題があることを暗示しているため、Bは不正解です。Dは一見正しく見えますが、この発言では水素発電への投資を誰が行うのかについて特に暗示されていないため、Dは不正解です。教授はこの発言で、水素発電の開発に成功すれば大きなメリットをもたらすと考察していることがわかります。

Listening

According to the professor, what is hydrogen power's primary advantage?

    A. It is not a fossil fuel and burns cleanly.

    B. It can replace natural gas and methane.

    C. It can store energy when it is overproduced.

    D. It can store energy when it is underproduced.

    正解は**A**です。教授は水素発電をある特定のエネルギー源の代わりとして位置づけているわけではないので、Bは不正解です。CとDは、水素ではなく、風力や太陽光による発電についての説明なので、不正解です。信頼性の高い環境に優しいエネルギーの源であることは、教授が説明している水素発電の最大の利点です。

EXERCISE

iTEPのリスニングセクションを一通り学んだどころで、練習問題に挑戦しましょう。
SLATEとAcademicの2パターンがあります。問題音声は、https://itepexamjapan.com/practiceguideのリンクにアクセスしてください。[スクリプトはp. 290]

[スクリプトはp. 290]

SLATE　Part 1

🔊 Schedule

1. Who told the man his schedule?
   A. the woman
   B. he got it himself
   C. the man's boss
   D. the woman's boss

🔊 The Dance

2. From the conversation, what can we assume about the man?
   A. He is confident and bold.
   B. He is intelligent.
   C. He is shy and reserved.
   D. He is sickly and ill.

🔊 The Paper

3. According to the conversation, when did the man finish the paper?
   A. this morning
   B. this afternoon
   C. last week
   D. yesterday

🔊 Would It Be Okay?

4. Where does this conversation likely take place?
   A. at a football field
   B. in a classroom
   C. in the cafeteria
   D. in a house

SLATE　Part 2

🔊 Too Much Homework

5. What class does the woman teach?
   A. history
   B. math
   C. literature
   D. science

6. Why does the student talk to the teacher?
   A. He is struggling to understand the class.
   B. He is concerned about his grade.
   C. He wants to change classes.
   D. He is worried about the amount of homework for the class.

Listening

7. Why will the student call his classmates?
   A. to tell them not to do a homework assignment
   B. to help complete a homework assignment
   C. to ask for a homework assignment
   D. to clarify a homework assignment

8. What is this conversation mainly about?
   A. getting help with class
   B. asking a teacher for options to improve his grade
   C. understanding the length of an assignment
   D. asking for advice

SLATE Part 3

🔊 Pavlov's Dog Experiment

9. According to the professor, which of the following statements is true?
   A. Dogs learn quicker with a bell.
   B. Pavlov's results were not accepted during his lifetime.
   C. Dogs do not learn to produce saliva.
   D. It is more difficult to train a dog that is older.

10. What is the lecture mainly about?
    A. a famous experiment
    B. training your dog
    C. the benefits of saliva in dogs
    D. the role of bells in dog training

11. Why does the professor mention a dog leash?
    A. to explain a good way to train a dog
    B. to show how people can control dogs
    C. to persuade the reader to be a responsible dog owner
    D. to give an example of a conditioned response

12. Which of the following could be implied from this lecture?
    A. Pavlov's findings are no longer relevant.
    B. Pavlov trained dogs to do many different things.
    C. It would be possible to condition dogs to salivate by using a violin instead of a bell.
    D. Pavlov's experiment would be considered unethical by today's standards.

13. What class does the professor teach?
    A. history
    B. biology
    C. psychology
    D. zoology

14. How does the professor describe Pavlov's experiment?

   A. It is complex and difficult to understand.

   B. It is complex but easy to understand.

   C. It is quite simple but difficult to understand.

   D. It is quite simple and easy to understand.

Academic Part 1

🔊 82nd Street

1. Where will the bus driver stop?

   A. 82nd and Main Street

   B. 82nd and Broad Street

   C. Broad Street only

   D. The driver's bus is not in service.

🔊 Dishes

2. When will the man wash the dishes?

   A. tomorrow

   B. later in the day

   C. next week

   D. soon

🔊 The Last Question

3. What is true about the man's homework assignment?

   A. The last answer is incorrect.

   B. He already handed it in.

   C. It's at his home.

   D. It is not yet complete.

🔊 Presentation

4. What does this conversation mostly concern?

   A. working out a scheduling problem

   B. succeeding on the presentation

   C. the best time to do the presentation

   D. getting help from classmates

Academic Part 2

🔊 Applying for Loans

5. Why should a student visit the studentloans.ed.gov website?

   A. to apply for loans only

   B. to apply for grants only

   C. to apply for loans and grants

   D. to check one's bank account

6. From the conversation, what can be assumed about the man's parents?

   A. They do not make a lot of money.

   B. They are paying for all of his expenses.

   C. They are very wealthy.

   D. They have many other children.

Listening

7. Why does the man talk to the woman?
   A. He wants to learn about loans and grants.
   B. He wants to teach her about improving her credit score.
   C. He wants to encourage her to apply only for grants.
   D. He wants to teach her how to apply for loans and grants.

8. Why is the woman reluctant to apply for loans?
   A. She thinks it's too difficult and time consuming.
   B. She already owes a lot of money.
   C. She thinks she will not qualify.
   D. She does not know how.

Academic Part 3

🔊 **Epigenetics**

9. According to the professor, which of the following statements is true?
   A. We have some control over how our genes affect our health.
   B. Genes determine everything about our health.
   C. We can turn some genes on but not off.
   D. We can turn some genes off but not on.

10. What is the lecture mainly about?
    A. how genes affect our health
    B. using genes to predict illnesses
    C. how our behaviors affect our genes
    D. which genes control disease

11. What does the professor imply when he says the below?
    "It can be useful to think of epigenetics in terms of an analogy. Our genes can be thought of as a series of light switches. Imagine the genes that you inherit from your parents as the light switches in a house. Now imagine that each room in the house has one or more light switches. Depending on where you spend your time in the house, some of those light switches will be turned on more often than others."
    A. Our genes will determine if we get sick.
    B. We have no control over our lives and if and when we get sick.
    C. We have complete control over our lives and if and when we get sick.
    D. We have some control over our lives and if and when we get sick.

12. What is the professor's purpose in giving the lecture?

A. to introduce a scientific concept

B. to encourage students to change their diet

C. to describe how genes affect our behavior

D. to describe a dangerous type of gene

13. According to the professor, which of the following has the least impact on genetic expression?

A. pills

B. diet

C. behavior

D. exercise

14. Why does the professor mention identical twins as adults?

A. to explain how genes may increase the likelihood of suffering from a disease

B. to explain how genes never change from birth

C. to describe how genes are affected by lifestyle choices

D. to encourage healthy living

Grammar

Listening

Reading

Writing

Speaking

Appendix

UNIT 3
READING

READING
LISTENING
WRITING
SPEAKING
GRAMMAR

Introduction to READING

iTEP試験のリーディングセクションでは、2つ以上の文章が提示され、各文章の後にその内容についての問題が出題されます。

SLATEでは、パート1で50語の短い文章が2題、パート2で250語の文章が1題、パート3で450語の文章が1題、の計4題が出題されます。

AcademicまたはBusinessのテストを受験する場合は、パート1で250語の文章が1題、パート2で450語の文章が1題、の計2題が出題されます。

リーディングセクションでは、5つの異なるタイプの問題が出題されます。

1. 趣旨
2. 細部の把握
3. 語彙
4. 推論
5. 整序

このユニットの各章の例題と解説は、読者のiTEPのリーディングセクションに対する理解を深め、高得点を取るための戦略を立てる手助けとなるよう作成されています。リーディングセクションの所要時間や解答形式については以下の表をご覧ください。

出題構成

このセクションでは次のような項目に関する問題が出題されます

試験時間：**20分間**

レベル：**CEFR A〜C**

Academic パート1
CEFR A2-B2

250語の中級レベルの文章1題　多肢択一問題 4題

Academic パート2
CEFR B2-C2

450語の上級レベルの文章1題　多肢択一問題 6題

SLATE パート1
CEFR A2-B1

50語の文章 2題
多肢択一問題 2題

SLATE パート2
CEFR A2-B2

250語の中級レベルの文章1題　多肢択一問題 4題

SLATE パート3
CEFR B1-C1

450語の中上級レベルの文章 1題　多肢択一問題 6題

セクション	試験の種類	設問の形式と設問数	時間
リーディング パート1	iTEP Academic/Business 250語の文章1題	iTEP Academic/Business 多肢択一問題4問	20分間
	iTEP SLATE 50語の文章2題	iTEP SLATE 多肢択一問題2問	
パート2	iTEP Academic/Business 450語の文章1題	iTEP Academic/Business 多肢択一問題6問	
	iTEP SLATE 250語の文章1題	iTEP SLATE 多肢択一問題4問	
パート3	iTEP SLATE (only) 450語の文章1題	iTEP SLATE (only) 多肢択一問題6問	

　下記は、リーディングの試験を始めるときに表示される画面です。この試験はAcademic
のパート1の問題の一部です。

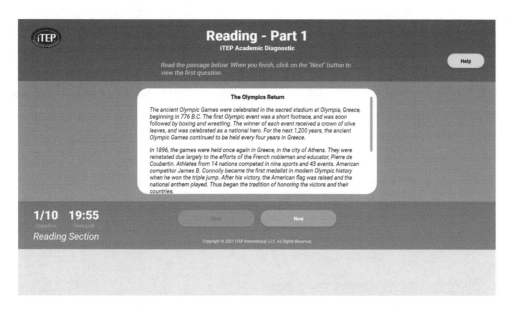

TIP ▶ この文章のタイトル、"The Olympics Return"に注目してください。
タイトルは、その文章が何についてのものかを知る最初の重要な手掛かり
になります。iTEPで良いスコアを出すためには、単に文章を読むだけでは
なく、文章に対して「インタビュー」を行う必要があります。

文章にインタビューを行う

受験者は文章に対して何をインタビューすればいいのでしょうか？　まず、以下の３つの重要な質問をします。
   1. 文章が何について述べたものなのか？
   2. 文章中で、誰が、または何が言及されているか？
   3. 文章中で何か問題や変化が述べられているか？

例題

下記の文章を読み、その下にある質問を使ってインタビューをしながら文章を要約してみましょう。
注：以下の文章はあくまで例であり、実際の試験の文章よりも短くなっています。

Friendly Little Creatures

When most people think of mice, they think of small pests that nibble through the walls or snack on food on countertops. Mice are also often used in research labs, in medical experiments, or as food for carnivorous animals such as snakes. But mice are more than just pests or prey for reptiles. Mice make great pets for small children. Mice are social animals that, when treated well, are affectionate and playful companions. Although many people think mice are dirty or carry diseases, they're actually self-cleaning animals and don't require washing. So, as long as their cages are cleaned weekly, they never need to be bathed. Mice are quite content to be left alone in their cages for hours at a time, such as when children are at school. Since mice are fairly low maintenance, they make good pets for children.

まず、この文章をインタビューしてみましょう。

質問：この文章は何について述べているのか？

回答： ネズミです。ペットとして飼われるネズミと、他の目的で使われるネズミについて書かれています。

質問：文章中で、誰が、または何が言及されているか？

回答： ネズミが主なテーマです。また、ネズミをペットとして、あるいは研究のために使用する人についても述べられています。

質問：文章の中で何か問題や変化は述べられているか？

回答：タイトルのFriendly Little Creaturesから、筆者のネズミに対する考え方を少し知ることができます。ネズミは有害な小動物だが、ペットでもある。ネズミは人懐っこく、きれい好きだということです。

趣旨

　文章に対するインタビューが終わったところで、設問の例をいくつか見てみましょう。まずは、文章の趣旨についての問題です。

Main idea: **Which of the following best supports the main idea of the passage?**
   A. Mice are important for medical research.
   B. Mice are fed to carnivorous animals.
   C. Mice require lots of attention and care.
   D. Mice can be excellent pets for children.

先ほどのインタビューの結果を見直せば、自信を持って**D**を答えとして選ぶことが可能です。

TIP1 **正しい答えよりも間違った答えを見つける方が簡単なので、消去法（POE）を使い、まずは誤った選択肢を除外します。**
趣旨に関する設問では、間違った選択肢には通常、次の2つのうちのいずれかの特徴があります。
1. **文章の一部分だけに焦点を当てすぎている。**選択肢BのMice are fed to carnivorous animals.は正確ではありますが、この文章全体の内容のほんの一部に過ぎません。したがって、これはこの文章の趣旨ではありません。
2. **文章中の情報と矛盾している。**Cは文章中で述べられている内容のうちの1つと異なっています。文章では、ネズミは最小限の世話しか必要としないペットであると明言されています。

細部の把握

次は、細部の把握に的を絞った設問を見てみましょう。

Catching Details: **According to the passage, what is one reason that mice make good pets?**
   A. They are friendly with snakes.
   B. They are useful for medical research.
   C. They can be left alone for many hours.
   D. They need to be kept in cages.

消去法を用いれば、選択肢A、B、Dを消去することができます。すなわち、正解は**C**です。

語彙

次に、語彙に関する設問を見てみましょう。語彙力を問う設問では、特定の単語や語句について問われることがあることを覚えておいてください。このタイプの設問では、対象となる単語が文章中でどのように使われているかが問われているので、あまりなじみのない単語について聞かれても、文章の中でその単語がどのように使われているか、すなわち文脈から正しい答えを見つけ出すことができます。

Vocabulary: **As used in the passage, the word "pests" means:**
   A. unwanted creatures
   B. cuddly pets
   C. invited guests
   D. predatory animals

正解は**A**です。pestsは人の家に入ってきて被害を与えると説明されているので、Aの「有害な生き物」が最適です。

Grammar

Listening

Reading

Writing

Speaking

Appendix

推論

　ここまで、趣旨、細部の把握、語彙に関する設問をざっと見てきました。この３つの設問は、単純でわかりやすいもので、正答を見つけるためには、基本的に趣旨や細かい情報に目を向ける、などそれぞれの設問の指示に従えばよいのです。ですが、この後の２種類の設問、「推論」問題と「整序」問題は分析と、ある程度のスキルが必要になります。

　例えば推論問題では、文章中の情報に基づいて、関連づけや推論を行うことが求められます。そのため、内容理解を問う問題とは異なり、答えとなる選択肢には、文章中に直接記載されず、暗示されている情報が含まれていることがあります。

　　Synthesis: **According to the passage, what does the author think is important when considering pets for children?**

　　　　A. Pets should come from a pet store.

　　　　B. Pets should require little care and cleaning.

　　　　C. Pets should not be reptiles.

　　　　D. Pets should have simple diets.

　正解は**B**です。文章中はすべてのペットについて直接述べられているわけではありませんが、ネズミは手厚い世話を必要としないので、良いペットになりえることが示唆されています。消去法を使うと、筆者はＡを裏付けることを何も述べていないので、これを除外することができます。また、著者は爬虫類に言及していますが、ペットとすることについては何も述べていませんし、示唆もしていません。

整序

　最後に、整序問題が出題されます。この問題は、単純にある文を文章内の正しい場所に挿入するものです。段落内に４つの選択肢が与えられており、挿入する文の情報に基づいて、どの場所が最適かを選択しなければなりません。段落内の一連のポイントの中で、その文が最もあてはまる場所がどこかを考える必要があるため、整序問題と呼ばれています。

Sequencing: At which point—marked by four letters [A, B, C, D]—would the following sentence best fit if added to the passage?

It is true that they're sometimes troublesome and destructive.

When most people think of mice, they think of small pests that nibble through walls or snack on food on countertops. Mice are also often used in research labs, in medical experiments, or as food for carnivorous animals such as snakes. [A] But mice are more than just pests or prey for reptiles. [B] Mice make great pets for small children. [C] Mice are social animals that, when treated well, are affectionate and playful companions. Although many people think mice are dirty or carry diseases, they're actually self-cleaning animals and don't require washing. So, as long as their cages are cleaned weekly, they never need to be bathed. Mice are quite content to be left alone in their cages for hours at a time, such as when children are at school. [D] Since mice are fairly low maintenance, they make good pets for children.

正解は**A**です。挿入される文に含まれる情報は、ネズミには悪い点があることを認めているので、文章の冒頭に提示された考えの続きです。しかし同時に、この文はこの後に逆の考えが続くかもしれないことを示しています。

総括

● ただ文章を読むだけでなく、常にインタビューを行うことを心がけましょう。
● リーディングでは、下記の5つのタイプの問題が出題されます。
　　　趣旨
　　　細部の把握
　　　語彙
　　　推論
　　　整序
● 消去法を用い、誤った選択肢を消去することを忘れずに。

　この後の章では、問題の種類ごとに、正答を見つけるための戦略について学んでいきます。それではさっそくやっていきましょう！

Chapter 1 趣旨

　今度はもう少し深く掘り下げて、より長い文章問題を見てみましょう。趣旨を問う設問では、文章に「インタビュー」を行い、その文章の焦点と目的の両方を素早く判断することが重要です。

　このページ以降に、アクティブリーディングとインタビューを行う能力を高めるための3つの文章を用意しました。最初の文章では、第1のステップとしてインタビューを行う練習をしていきます。インタビューを行う際は、メモを取りつつ、下記の3つの観点から文章にアプローチするように心がけましょう。

　　文章へのインタビュー
　　　　1. この文章は何について述べているか？
　　　　2. 誰が、あるいは何がこの文章中で言及されているか？
　　　　3. その文章中で何か問題や変化が起こっているか？

例文1　**The Great Depression**

　　The Great Depression is one of the most famous historical periods of the 20th Century. This era is recognized mainly in the United States, but the time period affected the entire world. This period, also known as simply the Depression, was a financial crisis that started with the collapse of the stock market on October 29, 1929. Thousands of investors were wiped out on this single day. The effects of this crash continued to hurt the world's financial markets for the next 10 years.

　　The Depression lasted from 1929 until 1939. The worst years were between 1932 and 1934, when unemployment rates were highest. In the United States, unemployment rates reached 25%, meaning one out of four people could not find a job. In an effort to solve this problem, American president Franklin Delano Roosevelt created the Works Progress Administration. This program, known better as the WPA, used government funds to hire Americans to work on construction projects, buildings, and roads. The WPA also funded other projects in other fields, such as creative visual arts and theater.

　　The Depression ended in 1939, partly because of the WPA's programs and

Reading

also due to other factors. Some historians believe that as many countries entered World War II, the world's economy began to accelerate. Economists today still refer to the lessons learned from the Depression. Whenever economies slow down or contract, they are considered to be in a recession. When this occurs, experts frequently debate which actions might be necessary to avoid another Depression.

1. この文章は何について述べているか？

「世界大恐慌」

2. 誰が、あるいは何がこの文章中で言及されているか？

アメリカの株式市場における投資家たちと、ルーズベルト大統領

3. その文章中で何か問題や変化が起こっているか？

仕事を失う人やお金を失う人、将来への教訓を学んだ経済学者たち

例題1　趣旨を問う問題

Which of the following best expresses the main idea of the passage about the Great Depression?

A. It led to the stock market crash in 1929.

B. It is believed to be the major cause of World War II.

C. It could have been avoided by President Roosevelt.

D. It is a period that helps experts understand economics.

趣旨を問う問題で正しい答えを見つけるためには、下記の2つの方法が役立ちます。
　1. メモを取る
　2. POE（消去法）を用いる
この2つを同時に用いて、正答がどれかを考えてみましょう。

選択肢A-1929年の株式市場の大暴落につながった。

これは誤りです。株式市場の大暴落が世界大恐慌を引き起こしたのであって、その逆ではありません。誤った選択肢には物事の順序が逆になっているものもあるので、よく読むようにしましょう。

選択肢B-第二次世界大戦の主な原因になったと考えられている。

これも不正解です。大恐慌は第二次世界大戦の直前に起こりましたが、この文章のどこにも大恐慌が原因であるとは書かれていませんし、示唆もされていません。

選択肢C-ルーズベルト大統領によって回避できたかもしれない。

これも不正解です。メモによると、ルーズベルト大統領はこの文章中で重要な人物ですが、彼は問題の解決に貢献したとされており、原因にはなっていません。

選択肢D-専門家が経済学を理解するのに役立つ時代である。

これが最後の答えだからといって、自動的に正しいとは限りません。よく選択肢を読んでみましょう。これは本質的に、人々はまだ今もこの大恐慌から教訓を学んでいると述べており、文章中で何度か述べられている考え方です。

したがって、**D**が正解です。

例文2　Doctor Who

Doctor Who is a famous British television show about a mysterious alien who travels through time and space in a "police box." Along with other friends of good will, the chief character, Doctor Who, fights numerous enemies and saves civilizations. In England, where the show was created, a police box is like a large public phone booth. It has a phone on its outside, which has a direct line to the police. For the purposes of the television show, this odd disguise makes for some interesting encounters for Doctor Who.

Doctor Who is one of the longest-running programs on TV, despite several breaks in production over the years. Its first season was in 1963, and 44 years later *Doctor Who* was still one of the best-loved shows in the world. This science-fiction, time-travel narrative started as a way to teach children history, but it has evolved into a modern pop-culture phenomenon with a vibrant and involved audience of loyal fans. The show has a devoted following in the United Kingdom, where even the queen follows it closely.

Because the show has been around for so long, it has had many different casts. The casting of the main role is always a source of interest and amusement for *Doctor Who* fans. In the show's history, there have been 12 different actors who have played Doctor Who.

1. この文章は何について述べているか？

イギリスのテレビ番組「ドクター・フー」

2. 誰が、あるいは何がこの文章中で言及されているか？

テレビ番組、番組のキャスト、ファン、イギリスの女王

Reading

3. その文章中で何か問題や変化が起こっているか？

文明を守ること、年々変わるキャスト

例題2 趣旨を問う問題

Which of the four choices best represents the main idea in the paragraph?

    A. *Doctor Who* is generously supported by the queen of England.

    B. *Doctor Who* shows how time travel is scientifically possible.

    C. *Doctor Who* has been a successful television show for many years.

    D. *Doctor Who* is a television show that helps police solve crimes.

まず、それぞれの選択肢を見てみましょう。

選択肢A-「ドクター・フー」はイギリスの女王から惜しみない援助を受けている。

メモによると、女王は番組のファンであると言及されていますが、文章のどこにも女王が何らかの形で番組を援助しているとは書かれていません。Aは不正解です。

選択肢B-「ドクター・フー」はタイムトラベルが科学的に可能であることを示している。

この文章では、「ドクター・フー」が時間旅行をすることが書かれていますが、この番組はSFであり、時間旅行の方法を視聴者に教えているわけではないとも書かれています。Bは不正解です。

選択肢C-「ドクター・フー」は長年にわたって成功したテレビ番組だ。

一見すると、この答えは漠然としていてピンと来ないかもしれません。選択肢が正解かどうかを確認するには、メモと文章の両方をチェックしましょう。「ドクター・フー」はテレビ番組でしょうか？　イエスです。では、何年にもわたって成功しているでしょうか？文章によると、多くのファンを持ち、50年以上前の1963年に開始されたそうです。これはテレビ番組としては長い時間です。Cは正しいかもしれません。

なぜ「かもしれない」なのか？　ある答えが正しいという強い確信があっても、必ずすべての選択肢を確認するようにしましょう。

選択肢D-「ドクター・フー」は、警察が犯罪を解決する助けになっています。

この文章では、ドクター・フーが文明を救い、「交番」で旅をしていると書かれていますが、彼がしていることと実際の警察の仕事との間に関係はありません。選択肢Dは不正解です。

つまり、この問題ではCが正解です。

例文3 **Oscar Wilde**

Oscar Wilde was one of Ireland's most controversial and prolific writers. It is difficult to say whether he is better known for his life as a writer and well-dressed socialite in London high society, or for his witty remarks and one-liners. One of his most famous quotes is something he said in a hotel in Paris at the end of his life: "I am fighting for my life with this wallpaper. Either it goes or I do."

Wilde was born in Dublin, Ireland, and moved to England to attend university in Oxford in 1874. At Oxford, he earned himself high grades for studying the classics. Soon after, he moved to London, where he gained fame and notoriety for his new philosophical positions about art and aesthetics.

Though his life was often filled with much movement in social circles, he is probably best remembered for his written works. He wrote only one novel, *The Picture of Dorian Gray*, but it is considered a great story. His plays, including *The Ideal Husband, Salome,* and *The Importance of Being Earnest*, are still performed all over the world. They are celebrated for their entertaining comedy and social satire. Wilde is remembered today as one of Ireland's greatest literary figures, and there are various tributes to him in Ireland as well as other locations around the world.

1. この文章は何について述べているか?

アイルランドの作家である、オスカー・ワイルド

2. 誰が、あるいは何がこの文章中で言及されているか?

ワイルド、オックスフォード、ロンドン、アイルランド、パリ

3. その文章中で何か問題や変化が起こっているか?

ワイルドは哲学科の学生で、その後作家となった

例題3 **趣旨を問う問題**

Which of the four choices best represents the main idea in the paragraph?

    A. Oscar Wilde was a great Irish writer who wrote many novels.

    B. Oscar Wilde was celebrated in Oxford for his philosophy.

    C. Oscar Wilde is mainly appreciated for his plays and clever quotes.

    D. Oscar Wilde wrote many plays about Paris at the end of his life.

Reading

それでは、正解を考えてみましょう。

選択肢A-オスカー・ワイルドはアイルランドの偉大な作家で、多くの小説を書いた。
文章によると、ワイルドはアイルランドの作家ですが、1つの小説しか書いていません。
この選択肢は半分正しく、半分間違っているので、不正解です。

選択肢B-オスカー・ワイルドは、オックスフォードでは彼自身の哲学で有名だった。
この文章では、ワイルドがオックスフォードで古典を学んで良い成績を挙げたことは書かれていますが、哲学を学んでいたことには触れていません。また、古典への言及は文章の一部分に過ぎず、趣旨ではありません。Bは不正解です。

選択肢C-オスカー・ワイルドは主に彼の戯曲と巧妙な引用で評価されている。
この文章では、ワイルドがウィットに富んだ引用や喜劇のために人々の記憶に残っていると複数の箇所で述べられています。この答えは、全体を通して文章の情報に沿ったものと言えます。Cは正しいかもしれません。

選択肢D-オスカー・ワイルドは、人生の最後にパリについての多くの戯曲を書いた。
注意してください。文章中で、彼が多くの戯曲を書き、人生の終わりにパリにいたと述べられていますが、これらの2つの間には何の接点もないので、Dは不正解です。

よって、選択肢Cが正解です。

総括

さて、趣旨を問う問題についてはどうでしたか？　ここで、このタイプの問題に取り組む際の手順をもう一度おさらいしましょう。

- 文章に対してインタビューを行い、メモを取る。
- 文章から明確な裏付けを得られない選択肢は消去する。
- 半分だけ合っている選択肢は誤り。文章中の細かい情報を誤って伝えている選択肢を選ばないようにする。
- 正しいと思う答えを見つけても、必ず全ての選択肢を確認することを忘れずに。

Chapter 2 細部の把握

　ここまでは、大局的な視点から文章を見て、文章の中のポイントがどのように組み合わされて全体の主張を形成しているかを、インタビューを中心に探していく方法を学んできました。次は細部を問う問題で、具体的なポイントに注目してみましょう。細部を問う問題では、著者の主張を形成する重要なポイントを特定できるかを試されます。あなたは、文章中のある部分について、それが文章全体の主張にとってどのような役割を果たしているかを判断する必要があります。

　下記は、テストで出題される「細部の把握問題」の例題です。

　左側に文章、右側に設問が表示されます。画面に表示されているように、文章の特定の段落や一文に関する設問が提示されることがあり、その場合、該当する段落を示す矢印が表示されています。これらの問題の攻略法は、まず文章で述べられている詳細な情報に注目し、それを使って解答することです。慎重に読めば、必ず答えを見つけることができます。

　以下例題を示します。

Reading

例文1 **The Great Depression**

The Great Depression is one of the most famous historical periods of the 20th Century. This era is recognized mainly in the United States, but the time period affected the entire world. This period, also known as simply the Depression, was a financial crisis that started with the collapse of the stock market on October 29, 1929. Thousands of investors were wiped out on this single day. The effects of this crash continued to hurt the world's financial markets for the next 10 years.

The Depression lasted from 1929 until 1939. The worst years were between 1932 and 1934, when unemployment rates were highest. In the United States, unemployment rates reached 25%, meaning one out of four people could not find a job. In an effort to solve this problem, American president Franklin Delano Roosevelt created the Works Progress Administration. This program, known better as the WPA, used government funds to hire Americans to work on construction projects, buildings, and roads. The WPA also funded other projects in other fields, such as creative visual arts and theater.

The Depression ended in 1939, partly because of the WPA's programs and also due to other factors. Some historians believe that as many countries entered World War II, the world's economy began to accelerate. Economists today still refer to the lessons learned from the Depression. Whenever economies slow down or contract, they are considered to be in a recession. When this occurs, experts frequently debate which actions might be necessary to avoid another Depression.

例題1 **細部の把握問題**

According to paragraph 2, what is one action that President Roosevelt did to respond to the Great Depression?

    A. He contracted the economy.
    B. He consulted top economic experts.
    C. He boosted the stock market.
    D. He created the Works Progress Administration.

ここでは第2段落について問われています。以下の段落の太字の部分が例題1の答えになっています。正解は **D** です。

The Depression lasted from 1929 until 1939. The worst years were between 1932 and 1934, when unemployment rates were highest. In the United States,

120

unemployment rates reached 25%, meaning one out of four people could not find a job. **In an effort to solve this problem, American president Franklin Delano Roosevelt created the Works Progress Administration.** This program, known better as the WPA, used government funds to hire Americans to work on construction projects, buildings, and roads. The WPA also funded other projects in other fields, such as creative visual arts and theater.

では、次の例題です。

例題2　細部の把握問題

According to the passage, in which period of time were the worst years of the Great Depression?
　　A. 1929 to 1939
　　B. 1932 to 1934
　　C. 1929 to World War II
　　D. 1934 to 1939

　この問題では、文章の特定の部分が示されていないので、文章全体を精査する必要があるかもしれません。選択肢を見てわかることは、年で区切ったある期間について正解を聞いているということです。下記の太字部分が正解を示しています。

　　The Depression lasted from 1929 until 1939. **The worst years were between 1932 and 1934**, when unemployment rates were highest. In the United States, unemployment rates reached 25%, meaning one out of four people could not find a job. In an effort to solve this problem, American president Franklin Delano Roosevelt created the Works Progress Administration. This program, known better as the WPA, used government funds to hire Americans to work on construction projects, buildings, and roads. The WPA also funded other projects in other fields, such as creative visual arts and theater.

　正解は**B**の「1932年から1934年」です。

Reading

例文2　**Doctor Who**

Doctor Who is a famous British television show about a mysterious alien who travels through time and space in a "police box." Along with other friends of good will, the chief character, Doctor Who, fights numerous enemies and saves civilizations. In England, where the show was created, a police box is like a large public phone booth. It has a phone on its outside, which has a direct line to the police. For the purposes of the television show, this odd disguise makes for some interesting encounters for Doctor Who.

Doctor Who is one of the longest-running programs on TV, despite several breaks in production over the years. Its first season was in 1963, and 44 years later *Doctor Who* was still one of the best-loved shows in the world. This science-fiction, time-travel narrative started as a way to teach children history, but it has evolved into a modern pop-culture phenomenon with a vibrant and involved audience of loyal fans. The show has a devoted following in the United Kingdom, where even the queen follows it closely.

Because the show has been around for so long, it has had many different casts. The casting of the main role is always a source of interest and amusement for *Doctor Who* fans. In the show's history, there have been 12 different actors who have played Doctor Who.

例題3　細部の把握問題

According to paragraph 2, what was the inspiration for the creation of *Doctor Who*?

    A. to teach children about history

    B. to help scientists understand time travel

    C. to help police investigate crimes

    D. to entertain the queen of England

では、第2段落を見てみましょう。正解を述べた部分を太字で示しています。

Doctor Who is one of the longest-running programs on TV, despite several breaks in production over the years. **This science-fiction, time-travel narrative started as a way to teach children history**, but it has evolved into a modern pop-culture phenomenon with a vibrant and involved audience of loyal fans.

正解は**A**の「歴史について子供に教えること」です。

例文3　**Oscar Wilde**

　　　Oscar Wilde was one of Ireland's most controversial and prolific writers. It is difficult to say whether he is better known for his life as a writer and well-dressed socialite in London high society, or for his witty remarks and one-liners. One of his most famous quotes is something he said in a hotel in Paris at the end of his life: "I am fighting for my life with this wallpaper. Either it goes or I do."

　　　Wilde was born in Dublin, Ireland, and moved to England to attend university in Oxford in 1874. At Oxford, he earned himself high grades for studying the classics. Soon after, he moved to London, where he gained fame and notoriety for his new philosophical positions about art and aesthetics.

　　　Though his life was often filled with much movement in social circles, he is probably best remembered for his written works. He wrote only one novel, *The Picture of Dorian Gray*, but it is considered a great story. His plays, including *The Ideal Husband, Salome,* and *The Importance of Being Earnest*, are still performed all over the world. They are celebrated for their entertaining comedy and social satire. Wilde is remembered today as one of Ireland's greatest literary figures, and there are various tributes to him in Ireland as well as other locations around the world.

例題4　**細部の把握問題**

According to passage 3, what is the name of the only novel Wilde wrote?
　　　A. *The Picture of Dorian Gray*
　　　B. *The Ideal Husband*
　　　C. *Salome*
　　　D. *The Importance of Being Earnest*

　選択肢として挙げられた4つのタイトルのうち、1つだけが小説で、残りは演劇です。以下に、例文3の重要な部分を太字で強調して示します。

　　　Though his life was often filled with much movement in social circles, he is probably best remembered for his written works. **He wrote only one novel, *The Picture of Dorian Gray*, but it is considered a great story**. His plays, including *The Ideal Husband*, *Salome*, and *The Importance of Being Earnest*, are still performed all over the world. They are celebrated for their entertaining comedy and social satire. Wilde is remembered today as one of Ireland's greatest literary figures, and there are various tributes to him in Ireland as well as other locations

Reading

around the world.

正解は**A**の「The Picture of Dorian Gray」です。

例題5　細部の把握問題

According to the passage, where was Oscar Wilde born?
A. Oxford
B. Paris
C. London
D. Dublin

この問題の正解を導き出すには、文章を精査し、POE（消去法）を用いる必要があります。

選択肢A-オックスフォードはワイルドが学んだ場所ですが、生まれた場所ではありません。した
がって、**A**は不正解です。

選択肢B-パリはワイルドが人生の最後にホテルの部屋についてウィットに富んだ発言をした場所
ですが、彼が生まれた場所ではありません。したがって、**B**は不正解です。

選択肢C-ロンドンはワイルドが上流社会と交わった場所ですが、彼が生まれた場所ではありませ
ん。したがって、**C**は不正解です。

選択肢D-ダブリンは、文章によると彼が生まれた場所です。第2段落によると、「ワイルドはアイ
ルランドのダブリンで生まれ、1874年にオックスフォードの大学に通うためにイギリ
スに移った」とあります。

つまり、正解は**D**のダブリンです。

総括

内容理解問題を解く上で、以下のことを覚えておきましょう。

● 正しい答えに関連がありそうな箇所を探し、メモしておく。
● POE（消去法）を使って、文章の裏付けがない選択肢を除外する。
● 設問文に出てくる単語と似たようなキーワードを文章中に探すことで、正解を述べてい
る箇所を特定する。

Chapter 3 語彙

何か新しい言語を学ぶにあたり、その言語の単語と、それが持つさまざまな意味を学ぶことは欠かせないことです。iTEPテストの語彙問題では、特定の語句の意味に関する問題が出題されますが、いずれの場合も文脈の中で語句が提示されます。単語の基本的な意味を学ぶだけではなく、それが文章の中でどのように使われているかを判断することが重要です。

語彙のショッピング

皆さんはショッピングが好きですか？　ショッピングモールや市場に行き、売られている商品を比べ、気に入ったものを買って帰るのはとても楽しいですよね。実は、語彙力問題を解くコツは、ショッピングをするときのコツととてもよく似ているのです。皆さんはショッピングをする際、以下の点に気を付ける必要があります。

実際に買い物をする前に、必ず自分が何を探しているのかを把握しておくこと。

何も考えずに店に入ると、全く役に立たないものを買ってしまい、家に帰ってから「なんでこれを買ったんだろう」と後悔する羽目に陥ります。でも、買い物リストをあらかじめ作っておけば、自分が本当に必要なものや、欲しいものを手に入れられるチャンスが増えます。語彙問題に取り組む際にも同じことが言えます。自分が何を見つけようとしているのかを知る「リスト」を作るまでは、正解を探しに「ショッピング」に行かないようにしましょう。リストは長く複雑にする必要はありませんが、可能な限り明確にするようにしましょう。

さあ、ショッピングに出かけよう！
次のページの例題には、前章と同じ３つの文章が出題されています。今回は、それぞれの文章の中にある語彙の要素に焦点を当てています。アクティブリーディングやインタビューの訓練のため、以下の例題に取り組んでみましょう。

Reading

例文1 **The Great Depression**

The Great Depression is one of the most famous historical periods of the 20th Century. This era is recognized mainly in the United States, but the time period affected the entire world. This period, also known as simply the Depression, was a financial crisis that started with the collapse of the stock market on October 29, 1929. Thousands of investors were wiped out on this single day. The effects of this crash continued to hurt the world's financial markets for the next 10 years.

The Depression lasted from 1929 until 1939. The worst years were between 1932 and 1934, when unemployment rates were highest. In the United States, unemployment rates reached 25%, meaning one out of four people could not find a job. In an effort to solve this problem, American president Franklin Delano Roosevelt created the Works Progress Administration. This program, known better as the WPA, used government funds to hire Americans to work on construction projects, buildings, and roads. The WPA also funded other projects in other fields, such as creative visual arts and theater.

The Depression ended in 1939, partly because of the WPA's programs and also due to other factors. Some historians believe that as many countries entered World War II, the world's economy began to accelerate. Economists today still refer to the lessons learned from the Depression. Whenever economies slow down or contract, they are considered to be in a recession. When this occurs, experts frequently debate which actions might be necessary to avoid another Depression.

例題1 **語彙問題**

As used in the passage, "funded" means:
    A. dropped down
    B. rented out
    C. paid for
    D. made better

　語彙問題を解くコツは、筆者がその単語をどんな意図で使用しているかを示す手がかりを見つけることです。そのためには、その単語が出てくる前の1～2行も併せて確認する必要があります。この例題でも、まず「funded」という単語が出てくる段落全体を見てみましょう。

This program, known better as the WPA, used government resources to hire Americans to work on construction projects, buildings, and roads. The WPA also funded other projects in other fields, such as creative visual arts and theater.

次に、その単語を削除して、別の単語や語句に置き換えるための手がかりを探します。それができたら、選択肢を見てみましょう。

This program, known better as the WPA, used government resources to hire Americans to work on construction projects, buildings, and roads. The WPA also _____ other projects in other fields, such as creative visual arts and theater.

では、その手がかりはどこにあるのか？まず、「WPAは何をしたのか？」というように、what の答えを探してみましょう。例えば直前の文では、WPAについて次のように述べています。

"…used government resources to hire Americans…."

さて、using resources to hire peopleを別の言い方で表現すると、using money to pay people とすることができます。すると using money to pay people に最も合う選択肢はどれで しょうか。

もう一度例題を見てみましょう。

As used in the passage, "funded" means:
    A. dropped down
    B. rented out
    C. paid for
    D. made better

元の文にpaid forを当てはめると、The WPA also **paid for** other projects in other fields, such as creative visual arts and theater. となります。
最も適しているのは**C**です。これで正解を「ショッピング」することができましたね。

では、次の問題です。

Reading

例題2　語彙問題

The Great Depression is one of the most famous historical periods of the 20th Century. This era is recognized mainly in the United States, but the time period affected the entire world. This period, also known as simply the Depression, was a financial crisis that started with the collapse of the stock market on October 29, 1929.

As used in the passage, "crisis" means:
- A. bounty
- B. windfall
- C. crime
- D. disaster

次に、crisisという単語を削除して、whatを考えながら別の語句に置き換えましょう。大恐慌は、1929年10月29日の株式市場の崩壊から始まった金融の「何」でしょう？

文章中に何か手がかりがないか調べてみましょう。

The Great Depression is one of the most famous historical periods of the 20th Century. This era is recognized mainly in the United States, but the time period affected the entire world. This period, also known as simply the Depression, was a financial *"what?"* that *started with the collapse* of the stock market on October 29, 1929.

この例文では、whatについて「崩壊から始まった」と述べられています。これを踏まえ、再度どの答えが一番しっくりくるか、設問文を読んでみましょう。

As used in the passage, "crisis" means:
- A. bounty
- B. windfall
- C. crime
- D. disaster

消去法で正解を探してみましょう。
A. bountyとは、「報酬」や「ボーナス」のことで、collapse（崩壊）とは反対の意味です。よって、Aは不正解です。

B. windfall-これは「幸運」を意味し、多くの場合、金銭面での意味として使用されます。これも崩壊ではありません。Bは不正解です。

C. crime-「犯罪」は違法ですが、崩壊ではありません。

D. disaster-これは崩壊から始まる可能性があるものなので、最も可能性の高い選択肢です。元の文にdisasterを挿入すると、次のようになります。

「大恐慌」は、1929年10月29日の株式市場の崩壊から始まった金融災害である。

よって、正解は**D**です。

例文2　Oscar Wilde

Oscar Wilde was one of Ireland's most controversial and prolific writers. It is difficult to say whether he is better known for his life as a writer and well-dressed socialite in London high society, or for his witty remarks and one-liners. One of his most famous quotes is something he said in a hotel in Paris at the end of his life: "I am fighting for my life with this wallpaper. Either it goes or I do."

Wilde was born in Dublin, Ireland, and moved to England to attend university in Oxford in 1874. At Oxford, he earned himself high grades for studying the classics. Soon after, he moved to London, where he gained fame and notoriety for his new philosophical positions about art and aesthetics.

Though his life was often filled with much movement in social circles, he is probably best remembered for his written works. He wrote only one novel, *The Picture of Dorian Gray*, but it is considered a great story. His plays, including *The Ideal Husband, Salome,* and *The Importance of Being Earnest*, are still performed all over the world. They are celebrated for their entertaining comedy and social satire. Wilde is remembered today as one of Ireland's greatest literary figures, and there are various tributes to him in Ireland as well as other locations around the world.

例題3　語彙問題

As used in the passage, "gained" means:

    A. grouped

    B. accomplished

    C. interested

    D. surrendered

Reading

下記がgainedが含まれる一文です。

Soon after, he moved to London, where he *"what?"* fame and notoriety for his new philosophical positions about art and aesthetics.

最大の手がかりは直前の文にあります。

At Oxford, he earned himself high grades for studying the classics.

もしgainedをearnedに置き換えると、

Soon after, he moved to London, where he *earned* fame and notoriety for his new philosophical positions about art and aesthetics.

つまり、正解はearnedの類義語である**B**のaccomplishedです。

まとめ

語彙力問題を解く際は、次のことを心がけましょう。

● 賢くショッピングをしましょう！
● what?を考えましょう。設問文の中の単語をwhatに置き換えましょう。
● 手がかりを使いましょう。関連する文章の中に手がかりがないか探し、どのような単語を「ショッピング」すべきかを判断します。
● 正答をショッピングしましょう！　POE（消去法）を使って選択肢を精査し、ショッピングリストに一致するものを見つけます。

Chapter 4 推論

これまでの問題では、以下のような能力を評価してきました。

・文章を全体的に見て、趣旨は何かを考える。
・細部の把握を通じて具体的な内容に注目する。
・語彙問題で特定の単語がどのように使われているかを精査する。

　いろいろな意味で、これらのタイプの問題（趣旨、細部の把握、語彙）は、whatの問題でした。これらの問題には、whatを考えることで解答できます。この言葉の意味は何か？　ある年に何が発見されたか？　趣旨は何か？　しかし、これから扱う種類の問題では、Whyを考える必要があります。

　推論問題は、筆者がどのようにして文章中で議論を構築し、主要な論点を説明しているかに焦点を当てています。この種の問題は、筆者がある情報を述べた理由を問うものです。なぜそれが関係しているのか？　なぜそれが言及されているのか？　この種の問題を解くには、自分が取ったメモを参照したり、文章中の筆者の主張を追ったりする必要があります。重要なのは、常に趣旨を意識することです。なぜなら、筆者が文章中に何かを述べる主な理由は、趣旨を説明することだからです。

　また、推論問題では、筆者の主要な論点の間の関係を考え、筆者の主張を効果的に伝えるために各論点がどのような役割を果たすのかを判断することが求められます。また、筆者の議論の主要な要素を分解し、再構築する必要があります。

例文1　The Great Depression

　　The Great Depression is one of the most famous historical periods of the 20th Century. This era is recognized mainly in the United States, but the time period affected the entire world. This period, also known as simply the Depression, was a financial crisis that started with the collapse of the stock market on October 29, 1929. Thousands of investors were wiped out on this single day. The effects of this crash continued to hurt the world's financial markets for the next 10 years.

　　The Depression lasted from 1929 until 1939. The worst years were between 1932 and 1934, when unemployment rates were highest. In the United States, unemployment rates reached 25%, meaning one out of four people could not find a job. In an effort to solve this problem, American president Franklin Delano Roosevelt created the Works Progress Administration. This program, known better as the WPA, used government funds to hire Americans to work on construction projects, buildings, and roads. The WPA also funded other projects in other fields, such as creative visual arts and theater.

The Depression ended in 1939, partly because of the WPA's programs and also due to other factors. Some historians believe that as many countries entered World War II, the world's economy began to accelerate. Economists today still refer to the lessons learned from the Depression. Whenever economies slow down or contract, they are considered to be in a recession. When this occurs, experts frequently debate which actions might be necessary to avoid another Depression.

例題1　推論問題

Why does the author mention "creative visual arts and theater" in the passage?

    A. to tell how the U.S. shifted to a service economy

    B. to explain how actors adjusted to high unemployment

    C. to demonstrate the diversity of the WPA projects

    D. to show that Roosevelt was a great speaker

この推論問題では、どうPOE（消去法）を用いればよいでしょうか。

まず、この文章では、なぜ芸術に言及されているのでしょうか？

より具体的に言うと、経済についての文章で、なぜ独創的な芸術について言及しているのでしょうか？

答えは、趣旨につながるものでなければなりません。

まず、先ほどの例文をインタビューしたときのメモを確認しましょう。

1. この文章は何について述べているか？

    「世界大恐慌」

2. 誰が、あるいは何がこの文章中で言及されているか？

    アメリカの株式市場における投資家たちと、ルーズベルト大統領

3. その文章中で何か問題や変化が起こっているか？

    仕事を失う人やお金を失う人、将来への教訓を学んだ経済学者たち

これらのメモによると、筆者は以下の考えを裏付けるために芸術に言及しています。

・ルーズベルトは大恐慌に立ち向かうために WPA を利用した。
・WPA の目的の一つは、さまざまな分野で雇用を創出することだった。

では、もう一度メモを用いて、正解を探していきましょう。

Why does the author mention "creative visual arts and theater" in the passage?
　　　A. to tell how the U.S. shifted to a service economy
　　　B. to explain how actors adjusted to high unemployment
　　　C. to demonstrate the diversity of the WPA projects
　　　D. to show that Roosevelt was a great speaker

選択肢A- この主張は文章中では述べられていません。よって A は不正解です。
選択肢B- 俳優について言及している点は主題に沿っていますが、文章とは直接関係のない関連づけを行っています。したがって、B は不正解です。
選択肢C- WPA プロジェクトの多様性について述べています。この主張が正しいことがわかる本文中の文章が以下です。C が正解です。

This program, known better as the WPA, used government funds to hire Americans to work on construction projects, buildings, and roads. **The WPA also funded other projects in other fields, such as creative visual arts and theater.**

選択肢D- これは主題とは関連がありません。よって D は不正解です。

例題2　推論問題

Based on the passage, which of the following could be one of the "other factors" the author mentions in the last paragraph?
　　　A. the stock market crash of October 29, 1929
　　　B. investors adjusting their funding strategies worldwide
　　　C. the WPA becoming a permanent program in the U.S.
　　　D. the beginning of World War II and its effect on the world economy

先ほどのメモと、著者が「その他の要因」について述べている最後の段落を確認することで、消去法を使いつつ不正解の選択肢を排除することができます。

Reading

選択肢 **A** - 株式市場の暴落は、大恐慌の原因として述べられており、大恐慌を終わらせるものではありません。したがって、**A**は不正解です。

選択肢 **B** - 投資家の変化が大恐慌の終結につながったとは言及されていませんし、示唆もされていないので、**B**は不正解です。

選択肢 **C** - WPAプロジェクトには言及されていますが、これらのプログラムが永続的に行われたことを示す記述はありません。したがって、**C**は不正解です。

選択肢 **D** - 著者が「他の要因」に言及した直後に、歴史家による以下の説明がなされています。

The Depression ended in 1939, partly because of the WPA's programs and also due to other factors. **Some historians believe that as many countries entered World War II the world's economy began to accelerate.**

この記述は、文章で主張されていることと一致しているので、選択肢 **D** が正解です。

例文2　Doctor Who

Doctor Who is a famous British television show about a mysterious alien who travels through time and space in a "police box." Along with other friends of good will, the chief character, Doctor Who, fights numerous enemies and saves civilizations. In England, where the show was created, a police box is like a large public phone booth. It has a phone on its outside, which has a direct line to the police. For the purposes of the television show, this odd disguise makes for some interesting encounters for Doctor Who.

Doctor Who is one of the longest-running programs on TV, despite several breaks in production over the years. Its first season was in 1963, and 44 years later *Doctor Who* was still one of the best-loved shows in the world. This science-fiction, time-travel narrative started as a way to teach children history, but it has evolved into a modern pop-culture phenomenon with a vibrant and involved audience of loyal fans. The show has a devoted following in the United Kingdom, where even the queen follows it closely.

Because the show has been around for so long, it has had many different casts. The casting of the main role is always a source of interest and amusement for *Doctor Who* fans. In the show's history, there have been 12 different actors who have played Doctor Who.

Grammar

Listening

Reading

Writing

Speaking

Appendix

例題2　推論問題

Why does the author mention the queen of England in the second paragraph?

　　　A. to indicate that Doctor Who is part of the royal family

　　　B. to show that *Doctor Who* is liked by many different people

　　　C. to show how *Doctor Who* teaches students about English monarchy

　　　D. to explain why *Doctor Who* uses a police box for time travel

まず、メモを再確認しましょう。

1. この文章は何について述べているか?

　　イギリスのテレビ番組「ドクター・フー」

2. 誰が、あるいは何がこの文章中で言及されているか?

　　テレビ番組、番組のキャスト、ファン、イギリスの女王

3. その文章中で何か問題や変化が起こっているか?

　　文明を守ること、年々変わるキャスト

選択肢A- 文章中で言及されていない主張なので、不正解です。

選択肢B- 下記のように文章中で言及されています。

The show has a devoted following in the United Kingdom, where *even* the queen follows it closely.

女王で「さえも」「ドクター・フー」を見ていることを示すことで、人気があるだけでなく、イギリスの重要な人物がこの番組を評価しているという点を強調しています。

選択肢C- 部分的には正しいものの、完全に正確ではありません。「ドクター・フー」は学生に歴史を教えるために作られましたが、イギリスの王政については教えていません。したがって、Cは不正解です。

選択肢D- 交番が文章中に出てきますが、交番はイギリス女王とは何の関係もありません。したがって、選択肢Dは不正解です。

選択肢Bだけが文中で言及されているため、正解は**B**です。

Reading

例文2 **Oscar Wilde**

Oscar Wilde was one of Ireland's most controversial and prolific writers. It is difficult to say whether he is better known for his life as a writer and well-dressed socialite in London high society, or for his witty remarks and one-liners. One of his most famous quotes is something he said in a hotel in Paris at the end of his life: "I am fighting for my life with this wallpaper. Either it goes or I do."

Wilde was born in Dublin, Ireland, and moved to England to attend university in Oxford in 1874. At Oxford, he earned himself high grades for studying the classics. Soon after, he moved to London, where he gained fame and notoriety for his new philosophical positions about art and aesthetics.

Though his life was often filled with much movement in social circles, he is probably best remembered for his written works. He wrote only one novel, *The Picture of Dorian Gray*, but it is considered a great story. His plays, including *The Ideal Husband, Salome,* and *The Importance of Being Earnest*, are still performed all over the world. They are celebrated for their entertaining comedy and social satire. Wilde is remembered today as one of Ireland's greatest literary figures, and there are various tributes to him in Ireland as well as other locations around the world.

例題3 **推論問題**

Why does the author include the quotation from Wilde about wallpaper?

A. to give an example of how clever Wilde was

B. to show Wilde was interested in traveling

C. to demonstrate how living in Paris was unhealthy for Wilde

D. to indicate a source of inspiration for Wilde's plays

まずはメモを見て、手がかりがないかどうか確認しましょう。

1. この文章は何について述べているか？

アイルランドの作家である、オスカー・ワイルド

2. 誰が、あるいは何がこの文章中で言及されているか？

ワイルド、オックスフォード、ロンドン、アイルランド、パリ

3. その文章中で何か問題や変化が起こっているか？

ワイルドは哲学科の学生で、その後作家となった

選択肢A- 筆者がワイルドのユーモアのセンスが垣間見える例としてこの引用を行っていると述べられています。直前の文では、ワイルドがウィットに富んだ発言で知られていることが述べられているので、このユーモラスな引用文はその主張を裏付けるものです。Aは正解の可能性が高いと言えるでしょう。

もう一度引用文を見てみましょう。

One of his most famous quotes is something he said in a hotel in Paris at the end of his life: "I am fighting for my life with this wallpaper. Either it goes or I do."

選択肢B- 例文の内容に直接沿ったものではありません。文章中で、ワイルドがいくつかの国の間を行き来していたことに言及されていますが、その点と引用文の間には明確なつながりがありません。よって、Bは不正解です。

選択肢C- 文中でもワイルドが人生の最後をパリで過ごしたことが言及されているので、正しいように思えるかもしれません。しかし、パリにいることが彼にとって実際に不幸であったことを示す情報は、この文中にはありません。したがって、Cは不正解です。

選択肢D- 少しまぎらわしいです。文中ではワイルドの戯曲について触れられてはいますが、この特定のせりふと彼の喜劇との間には明確な関連性はありません。選択肢Dは不正解です。

選択肢B、C、Dが不正解のため、正解はAです。

総括

推論問題を解く際は、以下の点に気を付けてください。

● 理由を探す。なぜ筆者が主要な論点を説明するために、特定の情報を導入したのかを考えましょう。

● 趣旨に関連づける。文章に対してインタビューしたときのメモを使って、常に設問の情報を文章の趣旨に関連づけて考えましょう。

● 点と点をつなぐ。なぜ特定のポイントが文章中の重要な情報であるのかを理解できるように、筆者の文章に一貫して通っている主張が何なのかを見つけましょう。

Reading

Chapter 5 整序

　ただ文章を読むだけではなく、その文章中の適切な場所に1文を加えることができるかどうか、それが整序問題で出題されます。この問題では、文章中のある1つの段落をパズルのようなものと仮定し、そのパズルに欠けているピースを当てはめなければなりません。そのためには、そのピースが収まる最適な場所を特定する必要があります。コツは、情報の順序を見極めることです。すべての段落には情報の順序があり、まず論点を述べ、それを補足し、最後に結論づけることで、次の段落に移ることができます。

　整序問題は、段落内にいくつかの箇所が選択肢として設けられ、そのうちの1つに1文を追加するもので、iTEPリーディングテストの中で最も積極的なアプローチが求められます。段落内の適切な位置に重要な1文を加えるためには、首尾一貫した段落を構築するにはどうすればよいかを理解している必要があります。

　この問題を正解するためには、その文がどの箇所に最もよく当てはまるかを見極めることが重要です。そのためには、手がかりを探しましょう。文の中に代名詞はあるか？　he、she、またはtheyが用いられていないか？　その文は例を挙げたり、結論を導いたりしているか？　もしそうなら、その文が段落の最初に来る可能性は低いでしょう。

　まず、テストの整序問題を見てみましょう。

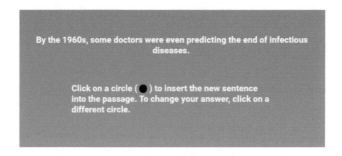

　この例題では、次のような文を挿入するよう指示されます。

By the 1960s, some doctors were even predicting the end of infectious diseases.

段落を見る前に、まずこの文に手がかりがないか探してみましょう。

この文では、その前後に言及されていると思われる事柄について触れているでしょうか？

この文の特徴は、By the 1960sというフレーズです。これはある時代を示しているので良い手がかりになります。もしかしたら、この文は別の時代が言及された文の前か後に入るかもしれません。

試験画面では、それぞれの選択肢に実際に文を挿入して、それが適合するかどうかを確認することができます。

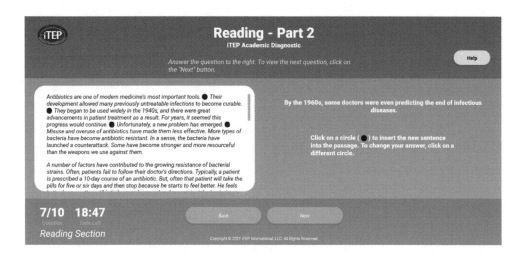

段落の３番目の文では「1940年代」について言及していますが、４番目では時間の経過について述べています。そのため、５番目は「By the 1960s」で始まることになります。もう１つヒントがあります。第４文では病気との闘いにおける「進歩」についても触れられていますが、新たに挿入される文には、the end of infectious diseasesを予測する医師もいたと書かれています。次の第６文ではこう述べています。「残念ながら、新たな問題が発生しました」。 この文は、言及された進歩への希望に対する明確な反応であり、挿入される文がここにうまくマッチしていることをさらに裏付けるものです。

次に、世界大恐慌、オスカー・ワイルド、ドクター・フーの例題について、何問か整序問題を見てみましょう。

例文1　**The Great Depression**

　　The Great Depression is one of the most famous historical periods of the 20th Century. This era is recognized mainly in the United States, but the time period affected the entire world. This period, also known as simply the Depression, was a financial crisis that started with the collapse of the stock market on October 29,

Reading

1929. Thousands of investors were wiped out on this single day. The effects of this crash continued to hurt the world's financial markets for the next 10 years.

The Depression lasted from 1929 until 1939. The worst years were between 1932 and 1934, when unemployment rates were highest. In the United States, unemployment rates reached 25%, meaning one out of four people could not find a job. In an effort to solve this problem, American president Franklin Delano Roosevelt created the Works Progress Administration. This program, known better as the WPA, used government funds to hire Americans to work on construction projects, buildings, and roads. The WPA also funded other projects in other fields, such as creative visual arts and theater.

The Depression ended in 1939, partly because of the WPA's programs and also due to other factors. Some historians believe that as many countries entered World War II, the world's economy began to accelerate. Economists today still refer to the lessons learned from the Depression. Whenever economies slow down or contract, they are considered to be in a recession. When this occurs, experts frequently debate which actions might be necessary to avoid another Depression.

例題1 整序問題

At which point—marked by four letters (A, B, C, D)—would the following sentence best fit if added to the passage?

Others maintain that the banking and fiscal reforms were key to stabilizing and rescuing the economy.

The Depression ended in 1939, partly because of the WPA's programs and also due to other factors. **(A)** Some historians believe that as many countries entered World War II the world's economy began to accelerate. **(B)** Economists today still refer to the lessons learned from the Depression. **(C)** Whenever economies slow down or contract, they are considered to be in a recession. **(D)** When this occurs, experts frequently debate which actions might be necessary to avoid another Depression.

手がかりを見つけるには、まず挿入文をよく読みましょう。

***Others* maintain that the banking and fiscal reforms *were* key to stabilizing and rescuing the economy.**

　最初の手がかりは代名詞othersです。代名詞の前には必ずそれが何かを示す名詞があるので、整序問題を解くのに最適な手がかりとなります。代名詞はすでに導入されている名詞を言い換えたものであり、つまりこの場合、othersはすでにその前に相応の名詞で言及されているはずです。othersが誰であるかを判断するには、前の文のどれかを見ればいいのです。これは正解を見つけるのに大いに役立ちます。

　もう一つの手がかりは動詞の時制です。reforms *were* keyというフレーズから、筆者が過去時制を使用していることがわかります。時間の流れに沿った答えを導くには、出来事が適切な順序となっている必要があります。

　これらの手がかりを総合的に考えると、Bの位置が最も適切そうです。この位置なら、othersは「他のhistorians」を指すことになります。

　　　The Depression ended in 1939, partly because of the WPA's programs and also due to other factors. Some historians believe that as many countries entered World War II the world's economy began to accelerate. ***Others maintain that the banking and fiscal reforms were key to stabilizing and rescuing the economy.*** Economists today still refer to the lessons learned from the Depression. Whenever economies slow down or contract, they are considered to be in a recession. When this occurs, experts frequently debate which actions might be necessary to avoid another Depression.

　正解は**B**です。2つ目の文にothersで受けるべきhistoriansがあります。
　この文を他の場所に挿入すると、順序が合わなくなります。代名詞も合いませんし、時制もおかしくなってしまいます。

　では、次の例題を見てみましょう。

例文2　Doctor Who

　　　Doctor Who is a famous British television show about a mysterious alien who travels through time and space in a "police box." Along with other friends of good will, the chief character, Doctor Who, fights numerous enemies and saves civilizations. In England, where the show was created, a police box is like a large public phone booth. It has a phone on its outside, which has a direct line to the police. For the purposes of the television show, this odd disguise makes for some interesting encounters for Doctor Who.

Reading

Doctor Who is one of the longest-running programs on TV, despite several breaks in production over the years. Its first season was in 1963, and 44 years later Doctor Who was still one of the best-loved shows in the world. This science-fiction, time-travel narrative started as a way to teach children history, but it has evolved into a modern pop-culture phenomenon with a vibrant and involved audience of loyal fans. The show has a devoted following in the United Kingdom, where even the queen follows it closely.

Because the show has been around for so long, it has had many different casts. The casting of the main role is always a source of interest and amusement for Doctor Who fans. In the show's history, there have been 12 different actors who have played Doctor Who.

例題2　整序問題

At which point—marked by four letters (A, B, C, D)—would the following sentence best fit if added to the passage?

Of course, the police box in Doctor Who doesn't connect civilians to the local police.

Doctor Who is a famous British television show about a mysterious alien who travels through time and space in a "police box." **(A)** Along with other friends of good will, the chief character, Doctor Who, fights numerous enemies and saves civilizations. **(B)** In England, where the show was created, a police box is like a large public mailbox. **(C)** It has a phone on its outside, which has a direct line to the police. **(D)** For the purposes of the television show, this odd disguise makes for some interesting encounters for Doctor Who.

まずは挿入文から手がかりを探しましょう。

Of course, the police box in Doctor Who doesn't connect civilians to the local police.

この文は比較的カジュアルな雰囲気を醸しており、たいてい前に述べられていることについて言及するときに使われるof courseというフレーズが含まれています。この文は交番について述べています。この段落では「ドクター・フー」について説明していますが、同時に交番の目的について

も説明しています。したがって正解を見つけるためには、この交番の説明とのつながりを考える必要があります。

TIP POE（消去法）を使いましょう。整序問題は、消去法を使うのにうってつけの問題です。

例えば、Cに文を挿入した場合、文章は次のようになります。

In England, where the show was created, a police box is like a large public mailbox. ***Of course, the police box in*** Doctor Who ***doesn't connect civilians to the local police.*** It has a phone on its outside, which has a direct line to the police.

不自然な文章であることがわかるでしょうか。2つ目の文では、ドクター・フー内の交番は人と警察を結びつけるものではないと書かれていて、3つ目の文ではitが警察に直接関係していると書かれています。これは矛盾しているので、Cは不正解です。

しかし、この場合、間違った選択肢を試すことで、正しい選択肢を見つけることにつながります。Cの箇所は、交番の説明の途中にあります。もしかしたら、of courseの意味を考えると、Dのような、もう少し後に挿入する方がフィットするかもしれません。

Dに挿入すると、以下のようになります。

It has a phone on its outside, which has a direct line to the police. ***Of course, the police box in*** Doctor Who ***doesn't connect civilians to the local police.*** For the purposes of the television show, this odd disguise makes for some interesting encounters for Doctor Who.

この方がずっと自然です。of courseに必要な対比が存在し、文がぴったりと収まっています。したがって、Dが正解です。

例文3　Oscar Wilde

Oscar Wilde was one of Ireland's most controversial and prolific writers. It is difficult to say whether he is better known for his life as a writer and well-dressed socialite in London high society, or for his witty remarks and one-liners. One of his most famous quotes is something he said in a hotel in Paris at the end of his life: "I am fighting for my life with this wallpaper. Either it goes or I do."

Reading

Wilde was born in Dublin, Ireland, and moved to England to attend university in Oxford in 1874. At Oxford, he earned himself high grades for studying the classics. Soon after, he moved to London, where he gained fame and notoriety for his new philosophical positions about art and aesthetics.

Though his life was often filled with much movement in social circles, he is probably best remembered for his written works. He wrote only one novel, *The Picture of Dorian Gray*, but it is considered a great story. His plays, including *The Ideal Husband, Salome,* and *The Importance of Being Earnest*, are still performed all over the world. They are celebrated for their entertaining comedy and social satire. Wilde is remembered today as one of Ireland's greatest literary figures, and there are various tributes to him in Ireland as well as other locations around the world.

例題3　整序問題

At which point—marked by four letters (A, B, C, D)—would the following sentence best fit if added to the passage?

The plays have been translated into over 30 languages and have been enjoyed by audiences from Singapore to Iceland.

Though his life was often filled with much movement in social circles, he is probably best remembered for his written works. **(A)** He wrote only one novel, *The Picture of Dorian Gray*, but it is considered a great story. **(B)** His plays, including *The Ideal Husband*, *Salome*, and *The Importance of Being Earnest*, are still performed all over the world. **(C)** They are celebrated for their entertaining comedy and social satire. **(D)** Wilde is remembered today as one of Ireland's greatest literary figures, and there are various tributes to him in Ireland as well as other locations around the world.

さあ、今回も挿入文から手がかりを探しましょう。

The plays **have been translated into over 30 languages and have been enjoyed by audiences from Singapore to Iceland.**

最初の手がかりはthe playsです。theが付いていることからplaysがすでに前で言及されてい

ることがわかるので、Aは除外されます。

　次の手がかりは、文中の具体的な情報です。これは、前に述べた主張を裏付けるための補足的な情報のように見えます。

　そこで、Cで試してみましょう。

His plays, including *The Ideal Husband*, *Salome*, and *The Importance of Being Earnest*, are still performed all over the world. ***The plays have been translated into over 30 languages and have been enjoyed by audiences from Singapore to Iceland.*** They are celebrated for their entertaining comedy and social satire.

自然な文章になるでしょうか?

　そうですね、この新しい文は、前の文で述べられたall over the worldの主張を補足しています。この文では、言語の数と、シンガポールからアイスランドまでの地理的範囲という2つの詳細が示されています。

　したがって、Cが正解です。

総括

● 整序問題は、パズルのピースを適切な場所に当てはめる問題です。
● 代名詞や時制などの手がかりを探して、段落内の順序を見つけます。
● POE（消去法）を使って、段落内の最適な場所を見つけます。

Reading

Chapter 6 SLATEの文章問題

注：Academic Testのみに臨む場合は、次の章に進んでください。この章は、SLATE Test受験者のみが対象です。

SLATE　パート1

SLATE Testのリーディングには3つのパートがあります。SLATEのリーディングのパート1には、短い文章（50語）とそれに続く2つの設問があります。何かの告知文が出題されることが多く、正しい答えを見つけるためには、点と点をつなぎ、詳細を把握する必要があります。

以下の例題を見てみましょう。

SLATE Reading Passage 1

Next Monday the school's Outdoor Club will visit Golden Reservoir. Students must have a permission slip signed by a parent or guardian by Friday in order to go on the trip. Students will travel by bus after lunch and return to school at 4 pm. Swimsuits are not needed but extra water and sunscreen are recommended.

他の文章問題と同様に、メモを取ることが重要です。

パート1は短いので、メモを多く取る必要はありませんが、この種の文章問題を練習する際には、正確にメモを取ることが重要です。重要なことだけを抽出し、重要でないことは書き出さないように改善していきましょう。自分なりの速記法を身につけ、必要な部分を思い出すためのメモを自分で取れるようにしましょう。

この文章は何について述べているか？

校外学習

誰が、あるいは何がこの文章中で言及されているか？

生徒、アウトドアクラブ、ゴールデン貯水池

その文章中で何か問題や変化が起こっているか?

許可証、昼食、水着

文章問題には、以下の例題のような趣旨を問う問題が含まれています。

例題1　SLATEの趣旨を問う問題

According to the passage, what will happen on Monday?

    A. Students will eat lunch at Golden Reservoir.

    B. Students will have lunch at the Outdoor Club.

    C. Students with permission will take a bus to Golden Reservoir.

    D. Students with permission will go swimming.

想定される正答は何かを考えながら、POE (消去法) とメモを使ってみてください。

選択肢A- 不正解です。この文章では昼食について触れていますが、生徒が貯水池で食事をすると
　　　　は書かれていません。貯水池への移動は、実際には昼食の後に予定されています。

選択肢B- 不正解です。アウトドア・クラブのことには言及されていますが、これは生徒のクラブ
　　　　であり、食事をする場所ではありません。

選択肢C- 生徒がバスで貯水池に行くことを、文章に沿って正確に述べているので、正しいかもし
　　　　れません。

選択肢D- 不正解です。生徒たちが泳ぎに行くと述べていますが、このことは文章中で述べられて
　　　　いません。

したがって、正解は **C** です。

SLATEパート1では、趣旨を問う問題に加えて、推論問題も出題されます。
以下の例題を見てみましょう。

例題2　SLATEの推論問題

What can be inferred from the passage?

    A. The Outdoor Club is for members only.

    B. Students must pay to join the Outdoor Club.

    C. Students will eat dinner at the reservoir.

    D. Students will be outside at the reservoir.

まず、POEとメモを使って正解を検討します。

選択肢A- 不正解です。なぜなら、文章では直接的にも間接的にも、メンバーや会員について何も触れていないからです。

選択肢B- ツアー代金の支払いについて直接的にも間接的にも言及されていないので、不正解です。

選択肢C- 不正解です。ツアーは昼食後に行われますが、生徒たちが貯水池から戻ってくるのは午後4時であり、夕食後ではなくその前です。

選択肢D- 正解かもしれません。厳密に言えば述べられていませんが、学生が外にいることは推測ができます。加えて、貯水池は屋外にある大きな水域です。

これは正解にしては少々あからさまかもしれませんが、推論問題ではこういった選択肢が正解であることもあります。考えすぎないようにしましょう！　**D**が正解です。

総括

SLATEのパート1は、他のSLATEのリーディングの文章と似ていますが、短めです。以下を行うように心がけましょう。

● 文章に対してインタビューを行う
● POEとメモを使って問題を解く

Chapter 7　Academicの文章問題

注：SLATE Testのみに臨む場合は、次の章に進んでください。この章は、Academic Test受験者のみが対象です。

　この章では、Academicのパート2の文章問題について触れていきます。この問題と、これまで扱ってきた文章読解問題との間には、2つの注目すべき違いがあります。まず、このパートはこれまでのものよりも長い文章が出題されます。ここまでのAcademicのパート1では、文章の長さが250語未満でした。

　パート2の文章は、約450語です。設問数はパート1よりも多くなりますが、1つの例外を除いて、ほとんどの場合、今まで扱ったものと同じタイプの問題が出題されます。パート2の趣旨を問う問題は、パート1の趣旨を問う問題とは異なるタイプのものです。パート2の問題は、ある1文が提示され、その文に続く文を6つの選択肢の中から3つ選ぶことで、文章全体の趣旨を説明する文を作るよう求められます。

　以下の例を見てみましょう。

iTEP

Reading - Part 2
iTEP Academic Diagnostic

Help

Answer the question to the right. To view the next question, click on the "Next" button.

Following is a sentence that begins a summary of the main points of the passage:

"Antibiotics have become less effective as bacteria have developed drug-resistance."

Continue the summary by choosing 3 of the 6 sentences below that best represent MAIN points in the passage. Mark your 3 answers by selecting the appropriate checkboxes.

Possible Answers

○ The human body recovers from viral infections because of the effectiveness of the immune system.

○ The best way to prevent further lessening of the effectiveness of antibiotics is through education in their correct use.

○ Both patients and healthcare professionals have erred by using antibiotics for illnesses that do not respond to them.

○ Traces of antibiotics have been found in dairy products.

○ Antibiotics tend to destroy weaker, less virulent bacteria first.

○ As antibiotics have been misused, the strongest, most resistant strains of bacteria have survived.

9/10　**18:21**
Question　Time Left
Back　Next

Reading Section

Copyright © 2021 iTEP International, LLC. All Rights Reserved.

　文章についての要約文が提示され、その文で述べられた考えを完成させる3つの文を特定するように求められます。基本的には趣旨を問う問題なので、3つの文を正しく特定し、全体の趣旨を表現することが求められます。最初は少し難しいと感じるかもしれませんが、一度やってみるとコツがつかめると思います。この章では、この新しいタイプの趣旨に関する

Reading

問題と、Academicパート2で出題される他のタイプの問題の両方を扱っていきます。

まずは例を紹介します。最初にメモを取りながら文章を読み、その後で設問に解答してください。新しいタイプの趣旨に関する問題は、最後に出題されます。

例文1　Blood Falls

If you travel far away to the southernmost continent, Antarctica, you will find a scientific marvel known as Blood Falls. It is a five-story-tall waterfall that flows from Taylor Glacier, and its rusty, red-colored water has puzzled scientists for many years. Scientists used a radar method to learn that bacteria, rust, and salt in the water gave the waterfall its unique coloring. They also used a special machine to capture some of the water before it reached the glacier's surface. Some scientists believe that the sub-glacial water may show how microbes and bacteria survived the Ice Age. Others believe that the same type of unique water may exist on Mars and in other places in our solar system.

The waterfall originates in sub-glacial lakes and rivers filled with brine. A high iron content in the brine gives the water its unique red color when the water bubbles to the surface to begin its journey down the waterfall. Despite the fact that the water is very cold, the high iron content also keeps the water from freezing. The water is much warmer than the surrounding ice. Scientists know that the iron content in the water gets much higher as it nears the glacier's surface. They theorize that this is because water from the melting glacier mixes with the underground water. Scientists also know that the water has an exceedingly high level of salt, which may also help stop the water from freezing. In fact, the combination of salt and iron makes the Taylor Glacier the coldest glacier on earth to have flowing water.

A team of scientists bored into the ice with a special machine so that they could sample some of the water before it reached Earth's surface, and they found that the water is also unique because it contains almost no oxygen. Scientists have studied the water and discovered that at least 17 different microbes live in it. Researchers have not discovered these microbes or bacteria anywhere else on earth. People believe that when the glacier formed 1.5 to 2 million years ago, the environment was completely sealed off. They think that the microbes and bacteria have lived under the ice for all those years. Some researchers also believe that this is an example of how microorganisms survived the Ice Age.

Astrobiologists are also very interested in the discovery of this unique water. They believe that sub-glacial water may exist on other planets, and this water may also contain life. The biologists believe that water on Mars may also be high in iron and salt. Furthermore, they believe that the water may contain bacteria and microbes like the ones the scientists discovered in Antarctica. Some astrobiologists also believe that the moon Europa, which circles Jupiter, may also contain this special water.

文章に対してインタビューを行う
・文章が何について述べているのか？
・文章の中で、誰が、または何が言及されているか？
・文章中で何か問題や変化が述べられているか？

> **TIP**　テクニック：語彙問題では、手がかりを特定し、正解を「ショッピング」する前に「何をショッピングしたいのか？」を確認しましょう。

では、次に実際の設問を見てみましょう。

例題1　語彙問題

As used in the passage, "circles" means:

    A. sharpens

    B. scatters

    C. orbits

    D. holds

例題2　語彙問題

As used in the passage, "survived" means:

    A. prolonged

    B. outlived

    C. neglected

    D. refused

さあ、次は細部を問う問題です。

Reading

According to the passage, what gives Blood Falls its unique coloring?

    A. a mix of bacteria, rust, and salt

    B. a mix of mud, algae, and salt

    C. a mix of oxygen, brine, and rust

    D. a mix of blood, water, and iodine

例題4　細部の把握問題

According to the scientists mentioned in the second paragraph, what probably prevents Blood Falls from freezing?

    A. a mix of 17 different microbes

    B. a combination of iron and salt

    C. heat from the sun

    D. a lack of oxygen

いかがでしょうか。

   ・POE（消去法）は使っていますか？

   ・メモを参照していますか？

   ・設問文で提示された文章中の箇所を実際に確認していますか？

　次は、推論問題、整序問題、そして新しい趣旨を問う問題です。その後、自分の答えが合っているかどうかチェックしましょう（p.155）。

例題5　推論問題

According to the fourth paragraph, why are astrobiologists interested in the discovery of this particular sub-glacial water?

    A. They believe that it is evidence that life could exist on other planets.

    B. They believe it shows that Mars and Jupiter have different glaciers.

    C. They believe it connects Earth's moon to Jupiter's moon.

    D. They believe that it shows how microorganisms survived the Ice Age.

例題6　整序問題

At which point—marked by four letters (A, B, C, D)—would the following sentence best fit if added to the passage?

The falls got its name, Blood Falls, from its striking and strange color.

If you travel far away to the southernmost continent, Antarctica, you will find a scientific marvel known as Blood Falls. **(A)** It is a five-story-tall waterfall that flows from Taylor Glacier, and its rusty, red-colored water has **puzzled** scientists for many years. Scientists used a radar method to learn that bacteria, rust, and salt in the water gave the waterfall its unique coloring. **(B)** They also used a special machine to capture some of the water before it reached the glacier's surface. **(C)** Some scientists believe that the sub-glacial water may show how microbes and bacteria **survived** the Ice Age. **(D)** Others believe that the same type of unique water may exist on Mars and in other places in our solar system.

そして以下が、Academicのパート2でのみ出題される新しいタイプの趣旨問題の例です。前述のように、このタイプの趣旨を問う問題では、文章の趣旨を最もよく表現していると思われる文を6つの選択肢の中から3つ選ぶことになります。また、選ぶ際にヒントとなるキーセンテンスが提示されており、この文がとても重要です。基本的には、この1文で提示された考えに続く3つの文を探すことになります。実際に下記の例題を解いてみましょう。

例題7 趣旨を問う問題

Below is a sentence that begins a summary of the main points of the passage:

The unique colors of Antarctica's Blood Falls are beautiful to see and fascinating to study.

Below are six more sentences. Choose the three that best represent points in the passage and use them to complete the summary.

A. The water gets its red color from high concentrations of iron, salt, and bacteria.
B. Antarctica is the southernmost continent in the world.
C. The sub-glacial water shows how living bacteria could have survived the Ice Age.
D. Water on Mars may also be high in iron and salt.
E. Scientists believe that the same kind of unique water may exist on other planets.
F. The Taylor Glacier is the coldest glacier to have active flowing water.

Reading

この例題のキーセンテンスはThe unique colors of Antarctica's Blood Falls are beautiful to see and fascinating to study.です。

この文は、2つの重要な情報を提示しています。
1. 血の滝は美しい。
2. 血の滝は、研究対象として魅力的だ。

ですから、正解の選択肢は、これらの情報を捉えている必要があります。では、最初の文を精査していきましょう。

A. The water gets its red color from high concentrations of iron, salt, and bacteria.
この文はキーセンテンスの情報に関して述べているでしょうか？ 述べています。滝の構成要素に由来する、美しさの重要な要素を定義しているので、正解と言えるでしょう。これを3つの正解の1つとしてマークしておきましょう。

次の選択肢は、
B. Antarctica is the southernmost continent in the world.
この文はどうでしょうか？ 違います。キーセンテンスの情報を適切に補足しているとは言えません。記述する範囲を少し広げすぎています。文章中の最初でしかこのことに触れられていないので、これは適切な答えではありません。

C. The sub-glacial water shows how living bacteria could have survived the Ice Age.
この文はどうでしょうか？ なぜこの滝が研究対象として非常に魅力的なのか、さらなる根拠を提示しています。これも正解と考えておきましょう。

では、次に行きましょう。
D. Water on Mars may also be high in iron and salt.
この文はキーセンテンスの情報の続きを述べていると言えるでしょうか？ いいえ、具体的すぎてテーマから外れています。火星について語っていますが、火星とキーセンテンス内の情報の間に関連性がありません。したがって、これは正解ではありません。

E. Scientists believe that the same kind of unique water may exist on other planets.
この文はどうでしょうか？ この選択肢は、前の選択肢とは違い、趣旨と他の惑星との関連性を示していますので、これも正解と言えそうです。

では、最後の選択肢です。
F. The Taylor Glacier is the coldest glacier to have active flowing water.

この文はどうでしょうか。この文はあまりにも具体的すぎます。詳細に焦点を当てていますが、趣旨との明確なつながりを示していません。

では、キーセンテンスと、正解の可能性が高い3つの選択肢を再度見てみましょう。
"The unique colors of Antarctica's Blood Falls are beautiful to see and fascinating to study."

    A. The water gets its red color from high concentrations of iron, salt, and bacteria.

    C. The sub-glacial water shows how living bacteria could have survived the Ice Age.

    E. Scientists believe that the same kind of unique water may exist on other planets.

この3つの文が、キーセンテンスで示された趣旨を補足し、説明していることが分かるでしょうか。すなわち、この3つ（**A. C. E.**）が正解となります。

これで、Academicのパート2の趣旨問題の解き方を学ぶことができました。
それでは、他の問題の答えをチェックしましょう。

答え合わせ

まずは、2問の語彙問題を解説していきます。

単語「circles」

例題1で、circlesをwhat?に置き換えると、次のような文になります。

> **Some astrobiologists also believe that the moon Europa, which "*what?*" Jupiter, may also contain this special water.**

what? に入る単語やフレーズは、moon（衛星）が何をするかを説明する必要があります。衛星は惑星の周りを回ります。では、例題の選択肢を見てみましょう。

例題1　語彙問題
As used in the passage, "circles" means:
    A. sharpens
    B. scatters

Reading

      C. orbits

      D. holds

正解は **C** です。goes aroundは「軌道を回る」という意味です。

単語「survived」

survivedをwhat?に置き換えると、次のような文になります。

> **Some scientists believe that the sub-glacial water may show how microbes and bacteria "*what?*" the Ice Age.**

what? を made it throughに置き換えれば、正解のショッピングができるでしょう。

例題2　語彙問題

As used in the passage, "survived" means:

      A. prolonged

      B. outlived

      C. neglected

      D. refused

正解は **B** です。made it throughは「長生きした」という意味です。

例題3　細部の把握問題

According to the passage, what gives Blood Falls its unique coloring?

      A. a mix of bacteria, rust, and salt

      B. a mix of mud, algae, and salt

      C. a mix of oxygen, brine, and rust

      D. a mix of blood, water, and iodine

最初の段落をよく読むと、答えを見つけることができます。

> …known as Blood Falls. It is a five-story-tall waterfall that flows from Taylor Glacier, and its rusty, red-colored water has puzzled scientists for many years. **Scientists used a radar method to learn that bacteria, rust, and salt in the water gave the waterfall its unique coloring**. They also used a special…

156

正解は**A**のa mix of bacteria, rust and salt.です。

例題4　**細部の把握問題**

According to the scientists mentioned in the second paragraph, what prevents Blood Falls from freezing?

  A. a mix of 17 different microbes

  B. a combination of iron and salt

  C. heat from the sun

  D. a lack of oxygen

設問文では、次のような文章を含む第2段落に答えを見つけるように指示しています。

  Scientists also know that the water has an exceedingly high level of salt, which may also help stop the water from freezing. In fact, the combination of salt and iron makes the Taylor Glacier the coldest glacier on earth to have flowing water.

正解は**B**のa combination of iron and saltです。

例題5　**推論問題**

According to the fourth paragraph, why are astrobiologists interested in the discovery of this particular sub-glacial water?

  A. They believe that it is evidence that life could exist on other planets.

  B. They believe it shows that Mars and Jupiter have different glaciers.

  C. They believe it connects Earth's moon to Jupiter's moon.

  D. They believe that it shows how microorganisms survived the Ice Age.

　推論問題は、推論や内容の関連づけを求められることがあるという点で、細部の把握問題とは少し異なることを覚えておいてください。では、第4段落を見て答えを見つけましょう。

  Astrobiologists are also very interested in the discovery of this unique water. They believe that sub-glacial water may exist on other planets, and this water may also contain life.

正解は**A**のThey believe that it is evidence that life could exist on other planets.です。

Reading

At which point—marked by four letters (A, B, C, D)—would the following sentence best fit if added to the passage?

The falls got its name, Blood Falls, from its striking and strange color.

If you travel far away to the southernmost continent, Antarctica, you will find a scientific marvel known as Blood Falls. **(A)** It is a five-story-tall waterfall that flows from Taylor Glacier, and its rusty, red-colored water has puzzled scientists for many years. Scientists used a radar method to learn that bacteria, rust, and salt in the water gave the waterfall its unique coloring. **(B)** They also used a special machine to capture some of the water before it reached the glacier's surface. **(C)** Some scientists believe that the sub-glacial water may show how microbes and bacteria survived the Ice Age. **(D)** Others believe that the same type of unique water may exist on Mars and in other places in our solar system.

POE（消去法）を使うと、選択肢Bは排除することができます。なぜならここに文を挿入すると、直後にある代名詞の theyが指す言葉が取り除かれてしまうからです。CとDも、この時点ですでに論点は滝の独特の色とその名前の話から離れてしまっているので、正しくありません。残ったのはAで、これはBlood Fallsについて述べられていることとつながりがあります。

正解は**A**です。ここに文を挿入すると下記のようになります。

If you travel far away to the southernmost continent, Antarctica, you will find a scientific marvel known as Blood Falls. **The falls got its name, Blood Falls, from its striking and strange color.** It is a five-story-tall waterfall that flows from Taylor Glacier, and its rusty, red-colored water has puzzled scientists for many years.

総括

● Academicのパート2では、メモを取ることとPOEが重要です。
● 趣旨を問う問題では、常に趣旨が何かを意識しましょう。

Chapter 8 SLATEの練習問題

注：Academic Testのみに臨む場合は、次の章に進んでください。この章は、SLATE Test受験者のみが対象です。

[正解はp. 289]

SLATE パート 1 の練習問題：School Library

The school library will close for the summer after final exams are completed. All overdue books must be turned in before 3 p.m. on Friday, and any overdue fees should be paid by then as well. If a book has been lost, you may have to pay for the cost of the book.

1. What is the main purpose of this paragraph?
    A. to explain the schedule for final exams
    B. to encourage students to use the library
    C. to ask students to return their library books
    D. to raise money for the library

2. As used in the passage, "completed" means:
    A. contested
    B. approved
    C. fought
    D. finished

SLATE パート 2 の練習問題：Hoover Dam

Ancient settlers built houses to protect themselves from the weather, and they often built them near rivers, which could be used as water supplies for growing crops. But rivers are temperamental, and their levels can rise and fall, causing havoc for those who depend on them. Rivers may rise due to spring ice-melt or great rainstorms, which may cause flooding to any nearby development. One way

Reading

that people have controlled river flow has been by building dams.

Dams block rivers to form lakes, creating a reliable supply of water, even in dry times. One of the largest dams in the world is the Hoover Dam in the United States. The Hoover Dam blocks the Colorado River to create Lake Mead, the largest man-made lake in the United States. The dam itself is over 700-feet high and made from more than six-million tons of concrete. The dam is constructed to use gravity to keep the concrete in place and is shaped like an arch to use the water pressure to keep the water safe inside the canyon walls. It also has spillways to allow floodwater to run off before it reaches the top of the dam.

The dam does more than simply save water, though. It doubles as a power plant by using 17 turbines to generate electricity for surrounding cities. Water falls through the dam from intake towers at the top to turn the turbines before exiting to the Colorado River at the bottom. Generating this "hydro-power" provides a cleaner, renewable source of energy, and dams around the world have copied this model for over a century.

英文にインタビューを行う

What is the passage about? _____

_____

_____

Who or what is mentioned in the passage? _____

_____

_____

Are there problems or changes mentioned in the passage? _____

_____

_____

例題1 　語彙問題

1. As used in the passage, "temperamental" means:
    A. equal
    B. tentative

C. unpredictable

D. theoretical

例題2　語彙問題

2. As used in the passage, "doubles" means:

　　A. copies itself

　　B. returns itself

　　C. sends two messages

　　D. serves a second purpose

例題3　細部の把握問題

3. According to the first paragraph, what was one possible disadvantage of building cities near rivers?

　　A. Ancient settlers flooded the newly created lakes with their dams.

　　B. The cities could be flooded when river levels rose.

　　C. The banks of rivers could not sustain proper crop yield.

　　D. Ancient settlers were unable to generate sufficient hydropower.

例題4　細部の把握問題

4. According to the second paragraph, which of the following is an accurate description of Lake Mead?

　　A. It is over 700-feet high and used 6-million tons of concrete.

　　B. It is the largest natural lake in the United States.

　　C. It is one of the oldest lakes in the United States.

　　D. It was created by the construction of the Hoover Dam.

例題5　推論問題

5. According to the passage, what causes the greatest risk for cities built near rivers?

　　A. the rise and fall of the water levels

　　B. the cost of maintaining dam construction

　　C. the danger of falling rocks and concrete

　　D. the poor yields of crops grown near riverbanks

Reading

例題6 　趣旨を問う問題

6. Which of the following best expresses the main idea of the passage?

    A. The Colorado River created the Hoover Dam.

    B. The Hoover Dam is impressive and useful.

    C. Lake Mead is the largest man-made lake in the world.

    D. The Colorado River is a great source of power.

例題7 　整序問題

7. At which point—marked by four letters (A, B, C, D)—would the following sentence best fit if added to the passage?

Using valves and levees, they can be opened or closed depending on how much water is available or needed.

    Dams block rivers to form lakes, creating a reliable supply of water, even in dry times. **(A)** One of the largest dams in the world is the Hoover Dam in the United States. **(B)** The Hoover Dam blocks the Colorado River to create Lake Mead, the largest man-made lake in the United States. **(C)** The dam itself is over 700-feet high and made from more than six- million tons of concrete. **(D)** The dam is constructed to use gravity to keep the concrete in place and is shaped like an arch to use the water pressure to keep the water secure inside the canyon walls. It also has spillways to allow floodwater to run off before it reaches the top of the dam.

Chapter 9　Academicの練習問題

注：SLATE Testのみに臨む場合は、次のユニットに進んでください。この章は、Academic Test受験者のみが対象です。

［正解はp. 289］

Academic パート 1 の練習問題：Bald Eagles

Eagles are impressive birds that soar through the sky and have been admired by people throughout history. One particular eagle, the bald eagle, is found primarily in North America, but its name is a little misleading. The birds are not actually bald, but they do have white heads and white tails that starkly contrast with their brown bodies.

Eagles primarily eat fish, so they are often found near large bodies of water. The bald eagle uses its sharp talons to swoop down and catch fish directly out of the water. Bald eagles are well-known for building extraordinarily big nests in trees that can be 4 meters deep and 3 meters wide. In fact, their nests are the largest bird nests in North America and the largest tree nests of any animal discovered so far. Female bald eagles are generally about 25 percent larger than their male counterparts.

The bald eagle is also the national bird for the United States. It appears on official government seals for the United States, holding 13 arrows, which represent the 13 original states, and an olive branch in its talons, representing peace. Until recently, the bald eagle was registered as an endangered species. Fortunately, the bald eagle populations have managed to recover, and this type of eagle is currently a beloved bird species to many people across North America. There are some bald eagles that are held in captivity across the United States, but these birds are either injured or unable to be released into the wild.

英文にインタビューを行う

What is the passage about? _____

_____

_____

Reading

Who or what is mentioned in the passage? _____

_____

_____

Are there problems or changes mentioned in the passage? _____

_____

_____

TIP ▶ テクニック：最初の3問は語彙問題なので、手がかりを探して、「ショッピング」の前にwhat?を確認するようにしましょう。

例題1 語彙問題

1. As used in the passage, "contrast" means:

    A. unify

    B. cancel

    C. complement

    D. differ

例題2 語彙問題

2. As used in the passage, "swoop down" means:

    A. flow smoothly

    B. bite harshly

    C. descend quickly

    D. rise slowly

例題3 語彙問題

3. As used in the passage, "endangered" means:

    A. popular

    B. threatened

    C. incredible

    D. deadly

例題4　細部の把握問題

4. According to the passage, why are bald eagles called "bald"?

    A. Their feathers change colors during winter.

    B. They have brown heads and white bodies.

    C. They have white heads and brown bodies.

    D. They lose their feathers during mating season.

例題5　細部の把握問題

5. According to the second paragraph, what is remarkable about the bald eagle?

    A. It primarily hunts and eats fish.

    B. It builds very large nests.

    C. It has an unusual name.

    D. It is regulated by the government.

例題6　趣旨を問う問題

6. Which of the following statements best expresses the main idea of the passage?

    A. Bald eagles are good builders but not good hunters.

    B. Bald eagles are the national bird for many countries.

    C. Bald eagles are impressive and greatly admired.

    D. Bald eagles are quite different from other eagles.

例題7　推論問題

7. In the third paragraph, why does the author mention 13 arrows?

    A. to show how they have been respected in the United States

    B. to represent how bald eagles hunt for their prey

    C. to show how hunters used arrows to hunt bald eagles

    D. to explain how the birds became endangered in the United States

例題8　整序問題

8. At which point—marked by four letters (A, B, C, D)—would the following sentence best fit if added to the passage?

Habitat destruction and illegal hunting were factors that led to a decline in their population.

Reading

The bald eagle is also the national bird for the United States of America. **(A)** It appears on official government seals for the United States holding 13 arrows, which represent the thirteen original states, and an olive branch in its talons, representing peace. **(B)** Until recently, the bald eagle was registered as an endangered species. **(C)** Fortunately, the bald eagle populations have managed to recover and this type of eagle is currently a beloved bird species to many people across North America. **(D)** There are some bald eagles that are held in captivity across the United States, but these birds are either injured or unable to be released into the wild.

Academic パート 2 の練習問題 : Christmas Trees

When people think of the holiday Christmas, they think of the Christmas tree. But how did the tradition of the Christmas tree begin? Surprisingly, the first Christmas tree did not include lights, decorations, or even have a clear connection to Christianity. It's difficult to pinpoint where it originated because the Christmas tree sprung up in numerous places around the same time. The customs associated with the Christmas tree have undergone many changes over the centuries.

The practice of taking a plant and hanging it for decoration during the winter months most likely began among worshipers of pagan gods. Branches of evergreen firs were used as decorations around the house to remind the occupants that spring was nearing. This custom was eventually picked up by members of the Christian church, who used the evergreen as a symbol of the everlasting love of God. Over time the practice changed, and later resurfaced in Latvia around the early 16th century. There, the trees were called "Paradise Trees," and were used in plays put on in front of the church on Christmas Eve, as a way to tell the stories of the Bible to people who could not read. The Paradise Tree was intended to represent the Garden of Eden. Gradually, the custom evolved and people began to choose trees for more personal reasons. Usually cherry or hawthorn plants were taken inside in the hopes that they would be blooming by the time Christmas came around, while portions were also hung outside for decoration.

Later in the 16th century, religious reformer Martin Luther began adding lights to the tree. According to some historians, one winter night, as Luther was walking home, he was struck by the beauty of the stars shining through the trees. Eager to

Grammar

Listening

Reading

Writing

Speaking

Appendix

explain the sight, he fastened candles to a tree in demonstration. The idea quickly caught on, eventually turning into the practice of putting Christmas lights on trees.

Despite quickly gaining popularity in Europe, the practice didn't reach North America until the late 19th century. With the Puritans largely trying to do away with anything that resembled "pagan practices," decorations for Christmas didn't catch on until a large group of German immigrants brought the practice with them from their homeland. Indeed, the "Yule tree" was an ancient and pre-Christian custom in northern Europe. Finally, during the Great Depression, a group of construction workers put out a tiny spruce tree in the Rockefeller Center as a way to bring cheer to each other during the holiday. Two years later, they put it up again, but added colored lights to it. As the years went on, the Rockefeller Center Christmas Tree became more extravagant. Today it is an international icon and tourist attraction, a 100-foot tree adorned with more than 2,500 lights.

英文にインタビューを行う

What is the passage about? _____

_____

_____

Who or what is mentioned in the passage? _____

_____

_____

Are there problems or changes mentioned in the passage? _____

_____

_____

> **TIP** テクニック：最初の2問は語彙問題なので、手がかりを探して、「ショッピング」の前にwhat?を確認するようにしましょう。

Reading

例題1 語彙問題

1. As used in the passage, "originated" means:

    A. spread

    B. grew

    C. began

    D. organized

例題2 語彙問題

2. As used in the passage, "adorned" means:

    A. simulated

    B. darkened

    C. dressed

    D. admired

例題3 細部の把握問題

3. According to the second paragraph, what was the purpose of the Paradise Tree?

    A. to be a symbol of everlasting love

    B. to be a reminder that spring was approaching

    C. to represent the Garden of Eden

    D. to teach people how to read

例題4 細部の把握問題

4. According to the passage, what was Martin Luther's reaction to seeing stars shining through the trees?

    A. He wrote plays to teach people stories from the Bible.

    B. He began to hang hawthorn trees for decoration.

    C. He designed lights to hang on the Yule Tree.

    D. He put candles on a tree in winter.

例題5 推論問題

5. Why does the author mention the Puritans in the fourth paragraph?

    A. to explain why the Christmas tree was popular in Europe but not in the United States

    B. to show how they made the tree in Rockefeller Center a tourist attraction

C. to support the idea that they left the United States of America after the 19th century

D. to suggest that they brought the first Christmas trees to the United States

例題6　整序問題

6. At which point—marked by four letters (A, B, C, D)—would the following sentence best fit if added to the passage?

Because the play was presented in winter, the tree itself would be quite bare, barren of any fruit, and suitable for this role.

　　The practice of taking a plant and hanging it for decoration during the winter months most likely began among worshipers of pagan gods. **(A)** Branches of evergreen firs were used as decorations around the house to remind the occupants that spring was nearing. **(B)** This custom was eventually picked up by members of the Christian church, who used the evergreen as a symbol of the everlasting love of God. Over time the practice changed, and later resurfaced in Latvia around the early 16th century. **(C)** There, the trees were called "Paradise Trees," and were used in plays put on in front of the church on Christmas Eve, as a way to tell the stories of the Bible to people who could not read. The Paradise Tree was intended to represent the Garden of Eden. **(D)** Gradually, the custom evolved and people began to choose trees for more personal reasons. Usually cherry or hawthorn plants were taken inside in the hopes that they would be blooming by the time Christmas came around, while portions were also hung outside for decoration.

例題7　趣旨を問う問題

7. The following sentence begins a summary of the main points of the passage:

The Christmas Tree actually has many connections to non-religious influences.

Below are six sentences. Choose the three that best represent MAIN points in the passage, and use them to complete the summary. Your choices do not need to be placed in any special order.

Possible answers:

    A. The Puritans tried to avoid associating with German immigrants.

    B. Martin Luther was inspired by the beauty of the stars shining through the trees.

    C. The Paradise Tree was intended to represent the Garden of Eden.

    D. Early members of the Christian Church in Latvia saw the evergreen tree as a representation that God's love lasts forever.

    E. The tree at Rockefeller Center is a major tourist attraction.

    F. The "Yule Tree" was an ancient pre-Christian custom in Northern Europe.

UNIT 4
WRITING

Introduction to WRITING

iTEP試験のライティングセクションは、これまでの章で説明した基本的な英語能力の多くが求められる難易度の高いセクションです。このセクションでは、あなたの英語力をさらに活用していくことが求められます。この試験ではあるトピックが提示され、それに対する自分の意見と、その理由を英語で説明することになります。ライティングスキルを向上させるには、時間と練習が必要です。実際にたくさんの文章を書いて先生に添削してもらい、どこを改善すべきかを常にフィードバックしてもらうことが大事です。

ライティングセクションで高得点を獲得するためには、さまざまな言語スキル（文法力、語彙力、綴りの知識、句読法の知識、読解力）、さらには非言語スキル（思考力、タイピング能力）が試されます。このセクションでは、ライティングセクションの対策について説明します。

出題構成

試験時間：**25 分間**

レベル：**CEFR A〜C**

パート 1
CEFR A1-B1

50~100語の文もしくは手紙
制限時間5分

パート 2
CEFR B1-C1

175~250語の小論文
制限時間20分

ライティングセクションの問題構成

まず、ライティングセクションの問題構成を見てみましょう。
パート1では、シンプルな状況やトピックに対して、短い文章や手紙（50 〜 100語）を書くことが求められます。

▶ 答えはキーボードで入力します。
▶ 制限時間は5分です。
▶ 「Next」をクリックすると、完了したことになります。一度「Next」をクリックすると、問題に戻ることはできません。

パート2では、与えられたトピックについて自分の意見を175 〜 250語で述べることが求められます。高得点のためには、自分の意見を裏付ける理由や例を示す必要があります。

キーボードで文章を入力し、20分間で課題を完成させます。書き終えたら「Next」をクリックして、課題を完了させてください。一度「Next」をクリックすると、解答の変更はできません。戻ることはできないので注意しましょう。

iTEP ライティング・パート1

パート1について

　パート1では、一般的な日常生活のトピックについて50〜100語で解答します。もちろん解答者の英語の習熟度にもよりますが、比較的簡単な問題です。パート1では、以下のようなトピックをもとに、特定の何か（人、場所、物）について説明することが求められます。

▶ 知っている人物について

▶ 好きなものについて

▶ 何かのやり方について

上記のトピックは、通常ある手紙やメモに記載されるものとして出題されます。

パート1では、どのような問題が出題されるのか？

　パート1は通常、パート2で出されるような、提示されたトピックに対する判断や意見の形成を要求するものではありません。しかし、文法力、語彙力、表現力を最大限に発揮し、答えを素早く考え、組み立て、文章にする必要があります。

例題と解説

　パート1に解答する際は、必ず問題文全体を読み、そこで求められている情報を盛り込む必要があります。次の例題を見てみましょう。

　"Write about a good friend and what you have learned from him or her."

　この例題では、以下のように問題の最初の部分のみを踏まえて解答するのでは不十分です。

My best friend is John. He is tall and very handsome with long, blond hair. I like being with him because girls like him, so I meet a lot of nice girls.

　後半部分のwhat you have learned from him or herについても具体的に述べる必要があります。したがって、以下のような解答がベターです。

My best friend is John. He is tall and very handsome with long, blond hair. I like being with him because girls like him, so I meet a lot of nice girls. He always asks them questions about their lives instead of talking about himself. So he has taught me how to make friends and to show people that I care about them.

2つ目の解答を見ると、解答者が親友から学んだことについて、明確に答えていることがわかります。問題文が要求していることに完璧に答えている、良い回答と言えるでしょう。親友についての説明をするだけでなく、彼から学んだことについて詳細に説明しています。この文章では、So he has taught me how to....というフレーズで、2つの解答要素を分かりやすくつなげています。また、何を学んだかを聞かれているので、taughtという動詞を使っていることもポイントです。

パート1

パート1の練習は、いつでも、どこでも行うことができます。パート1では、好きなもの（嫌いなもの）とその理由を答える問題がよく出題されるので、以下のような質問を参考に練習を行いましょう。

- ▶ 学校で一番好きな科目は何ですか？　それはなぜですか？
- ▶ 自由時間に行うのが好きな活動は何ですか？　それはなぜですか？
- ▶ 好きな人は誰ですか？　それはなぜですか？
- ▶ 今度は逆に、一番嫌いなものは何ですか？　それはなぜですか？

実践練習1-アイデアを出す練習

What is your favorite activity when you have free time? Why? Give two or three reasons why.

Reason 1 _____

_____

_____

Reason 2 _____

_____

Reason 3 _____

_____

_____

| What is your least favorite subject at school? Why?

Reason 1 _____

_____

Reason 2 _____

_____

_____

Reason 3 _____

_____

_____

では、実際に解答の下書きを作ってみましょう。以下の空欄を好きなように使って、あなたの好きなことについて書いてみてください。2、3個の理由を挙げるようにしましょう。

_____

_____

_____

_____

_____

_____

最後に、50 ～ 100語になるように実際に解答を作ってみましょう。自分で5分間計りながら、パソコンで解答を作ってみてください。

パート2

　パート2では、提示された課題に対して、20分間で175〜250語の文章で解答をします。通常、自分の意見や、あるトピックについての意見に対する自分の考えを示すことを求められます。パート2では、問題文についてより深く考えることが求められます。多くは、事実や意見を提示した上で、その事柄についてのあなたの意見を求めるものです。

　パート2では、以下のような問題がよく出題されます。
- ▶ 問題文について賛成か反対かを述べる。
- ▶ 問題文に提示されている2つまたは3つの答えから1つを選び、それを選んだ理由を述べる。
- ▶ 議論が分かれるようなテーマについて、自分の考えを述べ、その理由を説明する。
- ▶ 2つの視点を比較し、自分の考えを述べ、その理由を説明する。
- ▶ ある行動や方法について、メリットとデメリットを説明する。
- ▶ 特定の問題や課題に、自分ならどう対処するかを説明する。

> **TIP** 実際に文章を書く前に、提示された課題に対してどうアプローチすべきか、数分かけて計画を立てましょう。明確な主張と、その主張を裏付ける論拠を持った文章を作成した人が、高得点を獲得できます。また、同時に高い文法力と語彙力を示すことが求められます。

自分の意見を考え、展開させる練習

　意見が分かれやすいトピックや、興味のあるトピックについて考えるときは、以下の観点からアプローチするように心がけましょう。
- ▶ そのトピックについてどう思うか？
- ▶ なぜそのように思うのか？
- ▶ そのように感じる理由は何か？
- ▶ その話題について、あなたはどんな事実、詳細、経験、知識、感情、信念を持っているか？

　上記を行うことで、自分の意見を理解し、展開させることができるようになります。iTEPでは、20分間という短い時間で自分の意見を述べ、明確で簡潔な文章を書かなければなり

ません。考える力を養い、さまざまなテーマについて自分の意見を持つことに時間を費やすことで、試験に臨む際に自由にアイデアを出すことができるでしょう。さらに重要なことは、トピックについて考え、例や詳細な情報に裏付けられた明確な意見を表明する方法を学ぶことです。これは、iTEPで高得点を取るために、そして全体的に熟達した文章を書くためには非常な重要なことです。

実践問題1

1. What is a controversial topic? Write it here:

_____

これには、例えば以下のようなトピックを提示することができます。

> Many people think that women should work at home and not have professional jobs, while others feel that women should work in all areas of society. What do you think? Give reasons and examples to support your opinion.

2. What is your opinion about the topic?

_____
_____
_____
_____
_____
_____
_____

　メモを取り、トピックに関する一般的な考えを書き留めておくとよいでしょう。さらに、自分の意見を裏付けるのに使える詳細情報や例を提示する必要があります。メモ自体は整ったものでなくてもかまいません。また、図や写真、数字やカテゴリー分けを使った精度の高

いメモを取るのもいいでしょう。しかし、重要なのは、そのメモがあなたの思考を補助し、整理された文章を組み立てることにつながるかどうかです。また、メモは簡潔に取るようにしましょう。必ずしも自分が書こうとしている文章全体、もしくは単語全てをメモする必要はありません。

TIP　　メモの取り方を確立しましょう。

　よく使う単語を簡略化した形を知っておきましょう。単語やフレーズ全体を書き出すのではなく、例えばandの代わりに「+」、for exampleの代わりに「eg」を用いることができます。また、「=」「<」「>」などの記号も有用です。他にも、technologyはtechと簡略化できます。

　また、自分の解答を表現するためのアイデアや詳細情報を頭の中ですぐに整理できるように、問題文に含まれる単語の簡略形を自分で作るのもいいかもしれません。例えば、前述の例ではwomenをwとすることができます。パート2に備えて、自分の意見について簡単にまとめたり、簡単なメモを書いたりする練習をしておくとよいでしょう。

アイデアの出し方とメモの取り方の例

> Topic: Women should work outside the home.

メモの例1

　Why?
　More interesting
　Better for society
　Need money
　Need fulfillment in life + self-actualization
　Makes a woman a better mother

　もしくは、以下のようにメモを取ってもいいでしょう。

メモの例2

　I. Women should stay at home
　　A. need to take care of children

        a. children need mother
        b. birth
        c. raise + teach
    B. not as strong as men
        a. taking care/children
        b. weaker   NOT = hard jobs
        c. emotionally sensitive
                can't do stress
    II. everyone serves their purpose/society

　目標はメモの練習を重ね、すぐに自分の考えを整理して簡単に表現できるようになること
です。また、練習を重ねることで、詳細情報や例に裏付けられた、明解で一貫性のある小論
文を書けるようになります。

実践問題2

　では、実際にやってみましょう。別の問題を選び、そのトピックについて時間をかけて考
え、メモを取ります。そして自分が何を書くかを吟味し、実際に書いてみましょう。ライテ
ィングの上達には、ひたすら練習あるのみです。
　書いた後はすぐに見返してもいいですし、ユニット4をすべて勉強したあとで修正しても
かまいません。

　さて、ここまでiTEPのライティングセクションの2つのパートを紹介してきました。練
習を重ねることで、上手に書くための戦略を身につけることができます。以下に、ライティ
ングセクションのスコアを上げるための4つのポイントを紹介します。

ライティングセクションで解答するときのポイント

Key #1：タイピングの練習をしよう

1. これに関しては、考えてもみなかった人もいるかもしれません。ですが、iTEPのラ
   イティングセクションでは、解答をキーボードで入力する必要があります。したがっ
   て、可能であれば、試験会場に行き、キーボードのレイアウトが自分になじみのある
   ものであるかどうかを確認しましょう。慣れていない場合は、キーボードの配列を覚

え、それに似たものでタイピングの練習をしましょう。

▶ 一般的によく用いる句読点がキーボードどこに配置されているのかを確認しておきましょう。

▶ キーボードを打ち慣れていない人は、キーボードを打つ練習をして、タイピングのスピードを上げましょう。

▶ キーボードの力学的なキー（スペースバー、シフトキー、エンターキーなど、よく使うキー）の位置を覚えておきましょう。

2. 解答を全部大文字で書いてしまう、あるいは逆に文頭などで大文字にしないなど、よくあるタイプミスをしないようにしましょう。文章を書いているとき、書いた文章を読み返したり、もう一度書いたりすることで、それが合理的であるかどうかを逐一確認するようにしましょう。

3. できる限り自分のアイデアを英語で入力する練習を行い、思考と同じ速さでタイピングできるようにしましょう。

4. 毎日タイピングの練習を行い、書く練習をするときやこのユニットの練習をするときには、同時にタイピングの練習も行うようにしましょう。

Key #2：考える練習をしよう

1. ライティングで高得点を取るためには、自分の主張を裏付ける理由や例を含めて、アイデアを生み出せるかが大きなポイントとなります。受験者の中には、自分の意見を述べたり、なぜそう思うのかを表現するのが苦手な人もいるので、自分の考えを述べたり、その考えを裏付ける理由や例を示す練習をするとよいでしょう。

2. ここまで、あるトピックについてメモを書き出す練習をしてきましたが、これは良い練習になるので、ぜひ継続していってください。さらに、自分が物事に対してどのように感じているかを考えてみましょう。以下は、物事に対するアプローチの一例です。

▶ 伝統的なものを好むか、それとも変化を好むか？

▶ 社会が人を助けるために存在するのか、それとも人が社会を助けるために存在しているのか、どちらだと思うか？

▶ 芸術は重要だと思うか？

▶ 教育についてどう思うか？

▶ 政府についてどう思うか？

▶ お金は諸悪の根源だと思うか、それとも社会の役に立つものだと思うか？

▶ 新しいテクノロジーの影響は、プラスとマイナス面のどちらが大きいと思うか？

3. 毎日、新しいトピックについて考える時間を取り、自分の信念や特定の意見に対して、理由を探ってみましょう。なぜそう思うのか、具体的な例を挙げて考えてみましょう。

4. あるトピックについて肯定・否定いずれかの立場を取り、なぜその立場なのかを考える練習を行いましょう。自分がそれほど強いこだわりを持っていないトピックで、あるいは自分の意見とは反対の立場でやってみてください。それほど強い意見を持たないトピックについても、例を挙げ、明確な理由を持って主張を行うことができるでしょうか？　これは、パート2で素早く、まとまりのある解答を書くための良い練習になります。

Key #3：適切な長さ、時間、スタイルの解答を作成する練習

1. 英語でキーボードを打つ練習や、意見を述べる練習が必要なように、テストの時間内に解答を完了させるように練習することも非常に重要です。タイマーを使い、計画的に文章を書き、自分の書いた文章に間違いがないかを、最後に1分間かけて見直す練習をしましょう。各セクションで与えられた時間内に文章を書く練習をしてください（パート1は5分、パート2は20分）。数分間考え、その考えをもとに文章を書き、最後に自分の書いたものを見直す、という流れを20分間の中で行うことを覚えていきましょう。タイミングに慣れ、その時間内にタイプして自分の考えを伝えることに慣れてくると、ライティング能力が上がり、iTEPのスコアも上がります。

2. 単語数を数える：実際の試験では、作文の長さを把握するための「ワードカウンター」が用意されています。自宅で文章を書く練習を行う際は、自宅のパソコンのワードカウント機能を使って、自分がどれだけの長さの文章を作成しているかを把握しておきましょう。

3. 文章の長さ：250語で解答を書く練習をしましょう。パート2の解答は、175〜250語で解答を作成することが求められます。文法的に正しく、内容が非常に良くても、文

章が短すぎると、スコアは低くなってしまいます。

4. ライティングスキル：このユニットで紹介したライティングの一般的なスキルを伸ばすためには、実践練習あるのみです。特に論文の文章展開力、つなぎ言葉を使う力、文章の首尾一貫性やまとまりを保つ力、具体性の高い文章を正しく構築する力などを伸ばす必要があります。さらに、本書の随所に記載されている英語のスキルを使い、合理的な文章を書く練習をする必要があります。これには、フォーマルまたはカジュアルな単語の使い方、動詞の形、動詞の時制、名詞句などの文法の特徴、同じ単語を繰り返し使用してしまうことによる単調さの回避、その他のヒントやスキルなどが含まれます。

Key #4：自分の意見を表現する練習

書く練習だけでなく、書かずに考える練習をして、自分の意見を表現する力を身につけましょう。

ある意見に基づいた質問への答えは何か、を考える時間を毎日作ることが大事です。自分の国や世界で話題になっていることを考え、それについて意見を聞かれたらどう答えるかを考えてみてください。ニュースを読んだり、インターネットを利用したり、人と話したりするときに、自分の意見は何か、意見を聞かれたら何と答えるかを考えてみましょう。

Chapter 1　ライティングセクションの採点

ライティングセクションはどう評価されるか？

　パート1とパート2の両方を総合的に、また同時に採点します。訓練を受けたiTEPの採点者によって、パート1とパート2の両方が採点されます。2つの文章を精査した後、0～6までのスコアが付けられます（採点者は0、0.5、1と上がっていき、5、5.5、6のように、0.5刻みでスコアリングします）。

　採点は「総合的」に行われます。つまり、採点者は作文をあらゆる側面から精査し、受験者の能力を最もよく表すスコアを割り当てるのです。採点者はさまざまな要素を考慮しますが、受験者が覚えておくべきなのは、文章内の文法や単語が正しく使われているかどうかだけを見られているわけではないということです。受験者は、英語での正確な自己表現能力があることを示し、読み手が文章の構成と表現されたアイデアの両方を理解することができるように、一般的なライティングのテクニックを熟知し、使用する必要があります。

採点要素

[採点基準]

上級（スコア6）

▶ 正確な文法と、さまざまな構文（異なる時制や文の種類）を用いることができる。

▶ 使用されているすべての、あるいはほとんどすべての語彙が正しく使用されており、単語やその語形の選択が多岐にわたっている。

▶ 読み手が文章をわかりやすく理解できるように、また文章の構成をはっきりさせるために、談話標識やつなぎ言葉を巧みに使うことができる。

▶ アイデアを論理的に表現できる。

中上級（スコア5）

▶ 文法や語彙がほぼ正しく、意味に影響しない程度の小さな誤りしかない。

▶ さまざまな構文や表現を使うことができる。

▶ いくつかの小さな誤りを除いて、単語やフレーズが正しく使われ、綴りも正しい。

▶ 文章が明確で理解しやすく、談話標識やつなぎ言葉言葉を用いている。

Writing

上中級（スコア4）

▶ 意図したメッセージを伝えられるだけの文法力・語彙力が備わっているが、間違いや語形の誤りが多い。

▶ 単語の綴りにおおむね間違いがない 。

▶ 単純な文が用いられている。

▶ 談話標識やつなぎ言葉は用いられているとしても、文章の全体的な意味はかなり容易に理解できる。

中級（スコア3）

▶ 基本的な英語の構文は使用されているが、文法や語形の間違いがない文章を組み立てる能力がかなり低い。

▶ 語彙や言い回しのバリエーションが少なく、誤字脱字もあるが、自分が意図した内容を表現できている。

▶ 読み手が構成を理解するための手がかりとなるような表現がなく、論理的な表現の欠落がある。

▶ 明確な答えとその裏付けはあるが、主張の厚みに欠ける。

下中級（スコア2）

▶ 基本的な簡単な文章や単語の形、綴りにも誤りが多い。

▶ 考えが明確に表現されておらず、理解しづらい。

▶ 文章が読みづらく、主張を理解するためにある程度努力が必要。

▶ 短い文章が多い（例：Writing Part 2で175語以下しかない）。

初級（スコア1）

▶ 文法や単語の使い方がほとんどにおいて正しくない 。

▶ 文章がかなり短い。

▶ 文章のほとんどの部分が意味不明である。

初心者（スコア0）

▶ 文章が書かれていないか、数語のみ。

▶ 意味不明である。

※ なお、このスコアは明らかにあらかじめ暗記してきたと思われる内容や、テーマから外れた内容が書かれている場合にも適用されます。

さまざまなレベルのライティングの例

　以下は、テスト受験者の解答例です。それぞれの例について、採点基準を見て、あなたならどんな点数をつけるか、またその理由を記載してください。それぞれのライティング例について、あなたは何に気付きましたか？　何が他の文章より優れているのでしょうか？　まず、これらの例に目を通し、代表採点者がそれぞれの点数とその理由についてどういったことを述べているのか見てみましょう。

　次の各ライティング例では、質問に対する答えを書き、自分の書いたものを振り返ってみましょう。可能であれば、解答について、パートナーや友人、講師と話し合ってください。

例題1

Topic 1: Your friend from Australia sent you a gift for your birthday. Write a note thanking him or her for the gift and explaining why you like it so much.

解答：
　　　hello
　　　how are you.
　　　i'm fine.
　　　you for your gift.

(Words: 10/100)

Topic 2: Some schools require students to wear uniforms. Other schools permit students to choose which clothes they wear. Which policy do you think is better, and why?

解答：
　　　i am goes to ladies high school.
　　　i wear uniform.
　　　uniform is show all student is common.
　　　uniform is hide economy situation and social position of all student.
　　　so same situation go to school.
　　　therefore i agree schools require students to wear uniform.

(Words: 43/250)

Writing

What are the strengths of this answer?

_____

_____

_____

_____

_____

What are the weaknesses of this answer?

_____

_____

_____

_____

_____

What would you improve?

_____

_____

_____

_____

_____

What score would you give?

_____

_____

では、代表採点者がつけた点数とコメントを見てみましょう。

Grammar　Listening　Reading　Writing　Speaking　Appendix

[代表採点者がつけたスコア：1]

コメント：

この解答者は、ピリオド以外の句読点や、大文字を使っておらず、非常に基本的なライティング能力しか持ち合わせていないと言わざるを得ません。ボキャブラリーは質問文に含まれているものに限られ、質問の最も基本的な側面に答える以上の、詳細な情報は全く含まれていません。最初の質問への解答は、解答者が手紙の書き始め方を習ったときに暗記したものであると思われます。2つ目の質問への解答では、おそらく質問に解答する時間を少し長めに確保できたために、少しだけ詳しく内容が説明されています。この文章では主語と動詞の一致が欠けており、解答者は非常に基本的な文のみで質問に解答しています。

例題2

Topic 1: Your teacher has organized an email-friend project. You will write a weekly email to a student living in Australia. Write to your email-friend describing one of your best friends or one member of your family.

　　　Dear My friends live is Colombian, he is tall, he is thing, white face, he has got black, curly hair, he has got big eyes, thin lips, he is very friendly an handsome. another my Mother is very good, she like play basquetball and play very fine, she is intelligent and love

(Words: 52/100)

Topic 2: Nowadays, some people are choosing to teach their children in the home, instead of sending them to traditional schools with other children. This type of education is called homeschooling. Do you think homeschooling is a good choice for a child's education. Why or why not?

　　　Good evening,

　　　I think that is good sending at school because they can talk, play, to given you opinion with other boys, the education not only is learn mathematics, spanish, music, english, too is sociable with other person, learn to listen a teacher, to yours friends, listen other opinions, but is dificult because the parents think different, because there more danger, much violence, maybe they believe that they will good in the home, everyone think different , all the day in new paper read notice sad and children are victims of atacks, in conclutions my opinion is that should learn to be friendly, to responsable, good,

(Words: 105/250)

 Writing

What are the strengths of this answer?

_____

_____

_____

_____

What are the weaknesses of this answer?

_____

_____

_____

_____

What would you improve?

_____

_____

_____

_____

What score would you give?

_____

_____

では、代表採点者がつけたスコアとその理由を見てみましょう。

[代表採点者がつけたスコア：2]

コメント：

最初の質問への解答は、冒頭から文に若干の乱れがあり、良くない状態で始まっています。言葉をうまく使えておらず、それは2つ目の質問への解答にも同じことが言えます。適切に大文字を使っておらず、多くの綴りミスがあり、さらにカンマだけで区切られた1つの長い文があるため、読むのに労力が要ります。スコア2を超えるためには、ピリオドを適切に使用して文を区切る必要があります。基本的な構文を使っていますが、ほとんどが文法的な誤りを含んでいます。

例題3

Topic 1: Your family has planned a one-week trip during the school term. Write to the teacher to inform the school of your absence and to find out how to keep up with your studies while you are away.

Hi, teacher. I will have a trip with my family. This travel need one week. I will go and I promise you I will bring my homework. I will study when I enjoy my trip in the free time.

(Words: 39/100)

Topic 2: Recently, your friend was given a large amount of money. She is considering using the money either to start her own small business or to invest in some established businesses. What do you advise your friend to do with the money? Should she start her own company or put the money into businesses that are already operating?

Hi, my dear friend. First I cheer for you. Now you have enough money to do something that you want. You told me you wanted to be a businesswomen accroding this money. It is a perfect idea. I know you had some problems with your idea. To start a small buiness yourself or to invest in some established buinesses. It is really difficult for you I know. So I have some advises for you. First of all. I think you should to do some small business activities like join another business company and study with your leader. Because it is your first join in bussiness place. You does not have any patner before. Anyone has choice to hurt you if they see you are on person. Second, you can start your own company when you think you are finish your study about business knowledge. To be a small company is a good

choice for you. Third, do not use you any money in one business activity. You need keep enough money to help yourself.

(Words: 174/250)

What are the strengths of this answer?

_____

_____

_____

_____

_____

What are the weaknesses of this answer?

_____

_____

_____

_____

_____

What would you improve?

_____

_____

_____

_____

_____

What score would you give?

_____

_____

では、代表採点者がつけたスコアとその理由を見てみましょう。

[代表採点者がつけたスコア：3]

コメント：

最初の解答はかなり短いものですが、基本的なやり方で、質問されたことに答えることができています。2つ目の答えはより上手に書かれており、いくつかのつなぎ言葉（first や second）を使えていますが、その後に続く文は必ずしも完全なものとは言えません。主語と動詞の一致に難があるだけでなく、いくつかの綴りのミスもあります。少し複雑な構文を使用できており、比較的整理はされているものの、ややぎこちない印象です。どちらの解答も、もう少し長く、より内容の深いものにすべきです。言葉をある程度流暢に使いこなせる兆しは見えています。

例題4

Topic 1: You are going to attend a university in the US and will live on campus in the dorm with another roommate. Write a letter to this university describing a type of roommate you would like to have.

I am really glad that i have been accepted to this great university . hopfully this is the place were i would achive my dreams . so in order to do that i would really appreciate that if you could find mae a roomemate that is respectful and caring for other . so that we both achive our goals

(Words: 56/100)

Topic 2: Some people believe that rich countries should help poor countries. Other people believe that each country is responsible for its own success. What are your thoughts on this topic?

In todays world there are many countries and nations . so in order for every one to live in peace and harmoney we must help each other. every country has responseplties and prioraties. off course every country has to take care off its own people.however, in order for us as humans to live in a peacefull world we must conterbiute to help other countries that has probloms. there are many ways to help other countries like sending supply and voulontiring

Food shorteage is a big issue in smoe poor countries. many people suffer from poverty and unfourtunatley many die because of lack of food. so sending supply and food for these people will help them in many ways. many of us are

fourtunate to have food and water in our reach . and the activities that might look to us as mundane are much hard and difficult in those poor cities . many people have to walk long distances just get water to drink .

   voulontiring is also a way to help those who are in need . many people suffer from deseases that are easy to treat but the lack of medical supply and staff prevent them from healing so many pass away becuase of simple diseases that are easliy to treat . so a lot of doctors travel to these countrries to help people and

(Words: 222/250)

What are the strengths of this answer?

_____

_____

_____

_____

_____

What are the weaknesses of this answer?

_____

_____

_____

_____

_____

What would you improve?

_____

_____

_____

_____

_____

What score would you give?

_____

_____

では、代表採点者がつけたスコアとその理由を見てみましょう。

[代表採点者がつけたスコア：4]

コメント：

不注意によるミスが多い一方で、言葉遣いは流暢で、洗練された語句（例：*mundane*、*easy to treat*）を使っています。ケアレスミスにはあらゆる種類のものがあり（大文字、カンマ、アポストロフィー、綴り、ピリオドの配置など）、どの文にも１つか２つはあります。自然な言い回しを使用しており、全体的にテーマに沿っている内容です。たまに時制が誤っていますが、ほとんどは正確です。文法や話の展開は論理的で、２つ目の解答では良い例を提示できています。文がもっと長くなるように語句を組み合わせるべきですが、クオリティーは十分です。話が上手に展開されています。また、文意を損なうような誤りはありませんが、もう少し正確に書くべきです。

例題5

> Topic 1: Over the weekend, you had to help a friend who was very ill. Thus, you could not complete a homework assignment on time. Write to the teacher explaining why you were not able to do it and ask whether you can still submit it late.

Dear teacher,

　　I'm writting this to apology because I could not complete my assignment on time. My best friend was very ill and in bed and I had to help her because she lives alone here in the city and her parents live far from here. I would like to know if I can still submit the assignment, since it is my biggest interest to demonstrate you that I want to learn and present the homework despite of the situation.

　　Thanks for your help and comprehension. I look forward to hearing for your

(Words: 93/100)

> Topic 2: Nowadays, some people are choosing to teach their children in the home, instead of sending them to traditional schools with other

Writing

children. This type of education is called homeschooling. Do you think homeschooling is a good choice for a child's education. Why or why not?

Nowadays homeschooling is becoming very common in many places. Some parents think that teaching children at home is better than allowing them go to a school. However they forget the importance of social interactions, bonds and relationships build at the school.

In many cities around the world many parents are opting to teach their children at home. In this type of education parents stay with their kids at home and help them with subjects such as history, science, mathematics and language. This system can be good at certain points because education is given at a personalized level and parents know the specific needs and type of learning of their children. However the social part is been left behind.

Schools allow children to build social relationships and bonds. Firstly, it is important to share with many people because it helps on building values and life skills that will help children interact in the future and be prepared for the real life situations that will be in a real context or at a labor field. Secondly there are currently many tools which facilitate learning that are not available at any home. Schools are created, prepared and organized for this purpose, so they are the appropiate place for teaching.

To conclude it is necessary to think about the benefits of being at a school because the most important thing is to do the best for children in order to prepare them to face a real future along with many people.

(Words: 247/250)

What are the strengths of this answer?

_____

_____

_____

_____

_____

What are the weaknesses of this answer?

_____

_____

_____

_____

_____

What would you improve?

_____

_____

_____

_____

_____

What score would you give?

_____

_____

では、代表採点者がつけたスコアとその理由を見てみましょう。

［代表採点者がつけたスコア：5］

コメント：

どちらの解答にも、高い語彙力だけでなく、文章の流暢さ、非常に美しい言葉遣い、教養面・文体面での適格性が表れています。用法や文法に多少の誤りが見られ、いくぶん不自然な箇所がありますが、全体的には非常によくできています。ごくわずかに、ぎこちない言い回しがあり、もう少しカンマを使用してもいいかもしれません。ですが、文章はよく練られており、時間をかけて自分の視点をしっかり説明できています。綴りのミスはほとんどなく、全体的に複雑な社会問題を含むトピックを扱った、よくできた文章です。つなぎ言葉が適切に使われています。

Grammar
Listening
Reading
Writing
Speaking
Appendix

例題6

Topic 1: You are going to take a trip and want to invite your best friend to go with you. Write to your friend both explaining your plans for the trip and inviting him or her to go along.

Dear Millard,

I am going to Florianópolis for Xmas and wanted to know if you would like to come along with me. I would love for you to meet my family. I think they would enjoy getting to know you as well. The city is beautiful. The beaches are great, and I as you love surfing, I know that you will enjoy doing this there. Ah...there are sand dunes you can surf too! Yeah, isn't that unusual? Well, let me know as soon as possible so I can let my mom know,

Debora

(Words: 95/100)

Topic 2: The past 150 years or so have seen an unprecedented number of technological innovations. Which one technological advance from this period do you think has had the most far-reaching effect on humanity, and why?

Internet: the biggest impact on the human race

Of all technological innovations in the last 150 years, the internet has been the one that has had the largest impact in my view. First, it has really transformed the world into a Global village where we can instantly communcate with anyone, anywhere in the world in seconds, in writing or in speaking with the help of Skype. This not only increases the speed of communication, but lowers the cost. Secondly, it has made access to knowledge more democratic. We do not need to buy books in order to acquire information. Using tools like Google provide us with information on anything we want. Third, it has become an efficient way to commercialize products, and do our banking without leaving home. What could be better for the working man and woman?

However, despite these two great aspects, it has also had negative impacts. It has brought pornography closer to us, and also broaden the gap between those who are digitally literate from those who are not. Last, but not least, unfortunately the evil side of mankind has also found a way to interfere, corrupt, hack and insert viruses into the internet. So like all technology, good also comes along with evil.

(Words: 207/250)

では、代表採点者がつけたスコアとその理由を見てみましょう。

［代表採点者がつけたスコア：6］

コメント：

この解答者は、非常に流暢で、自然な英文を作成しています。興味深い内容で、文法的な問題はなく、誤字脱字も1つか2つしかありません。ネイティブスピーカーが書くような文章で、語彙や単語の使い方も高いレベルで洗練されています。楽しく読める文章で、つなぎ言葉を効果的に使用し、文章にまとまりを与えています。構文が非常にバラエティーに富んでおり、それが文章の面白さにつながっています。素晴らしい！（おそらくネイティブスピーカーでも全員がこれほどうまく書けないでしょう！）

Chapter 2 実践と成功のための戦略

ライティング・パート1：実践と成功のための戦略

先に述べたように、ライティングの2つのパートは総合的に評価されます。つまり、採点者は2つのパートで良い文章を書くために必要なすべての要素について考慮し、最終的に1つのスコアを出すことになります。

文法や語彙、その他の言語能力ももちろん重要ですが、自分の考えを巧みに文章に組み込み、質問に対する完結した論理的な答えを作ることも重要です。

このレッスンでは、最終的なスコアに影響する文法やその他の言語能力のことは一旦忘れてください。文を組み合わせて一つのエッセイにするスキルだけに焦点を当てます。

まず、パート1から始めていきましょう。iTEPの試験では、5分間で課題文に答える形で簡単な文章を書きます。

多くの場合、課題文は何かを説明するように求めたり、何かのリストから好きな項目を選ぶように求めたりします。また、ある事柄について手紙を書くように指示されることもあります。いくつか例を挙げてみましょう。

▶ あなたの親友と、その人の一番の特徴を述べてください。

▶ あなたの一番好きなもの（祝日、学校の科目、食べ物の種類など）とその理由を書いてください。

▶ 学校宛の手紙に、その学校に入学したい理由を書いてみましょう。

▶ 取引先の会社に手紙を書いて、自分の会社の製品について説明してください。

例題

下記は、ライティング能力の異なる2人の解答者が、それぞれ特定のトピックについて書いた文章です。2つの解答例を比較し、どちらが上手に書けているかを判断して採点してください。なお、これらのエッセイは文法的には全く問題ないので、あくまで文の内容と構成のみを判断してください。

> Topic A: Write a letter to your friend describing your favorite foods from the city you live in.

解答例1 **Writing Sample A**

Dear John:

Hi, how are you? I hope you are doing well. I've been good here. But I'm eating many good foods. I never knew Mexican food in Japan. Now in USA, it's common. I like it because it is spicy. It uses lots of cheese and lots of tomato sauce. It is kind of like a pizza but with more spice. Well, I have to go to school so I will stop writing now. I hope that you will write to me again soon and tell me about the food there.

Your friend, Yumi

(95 words)

解答例2 **Writing Sample B**

Dear John:

Hi, I hope you are well in your new city. Here in my city, I'm eating many new foods. I never knew Mexican food when I lived in Japan. But now in the USA ,it's a very common food to eat. It's popular and the cost is very reasonable always. I like it also because it's spicy. With lots of cheese and tomato sauce, it is kind of like pizza but with more spice. Well, I plan to explore the new foods here a lot, and I suggest you do the same there.

(93 words)

どちらがより優れているか？　その理由は何か？

　Sample Bの方がいいエッセイと言えるでしょう。まず、Sample Aには、I hope you are doing wellやI've been good hereなど、質問への答えになっていないフレーズがいくつか含まれています。一方、Sample Bの解答者は、同じ制限時間でありながら、自分の考えをダイレクトに表現しています。Here in my city, I'm eating many new foods. という具合です。Aの文章ではYour friend, Yumi.のような関係のない文やフレーズを使っており、貴重な制限時間を無駄にしています。

　もう一つのポイントは、Bの解答者は、食べ物全般についてより詳細に説明し、次のような複合的な文をより多用していることです。With lots of cheese and tomato sauce, it is kind of like pizza but with more spice.しかし、どちらの例も質問に直接答えていません。どちらの例も、自分の好きなメキシコ料理を具体的に挙げて、その料理について説明することで、改善できるでしょう。この種の質問に答えるには、詳細な説明が重要です。

Topic B: What is your favorite day of the week, and why?

Writing

解答例3　Writing Sample A

I'm a student so for me the weekends are my best days, and especially Saturday. On Sunday, I'm already thinking about the week ahead, so it's less enjoyable. But on Saturdays I am in control. I can even decide if I want to study then or wait until Sunday night to study. But usually I need to relax, to do something to refresh my mind. So Saturday is my day of choice for taking care of myself.

(Words: 77/250)

解答例4　Writing Sample B

I'm a student in Jones University studying for my degree in economics. I will tell you why Saturday is my favorite day. On Sunday, I'm already thinking about the week ahead. It's less enjoyable. I worry about what I have to prepare for Monday. But on Saturday I am in control. I can even decide if I want to study. If I don't study Saturday, I study Sunday. Usually I need to relax. I need to do something to refresh my mind. Saturday is my day of choice for taking care of myself. It's the best day of the week.

(Words: 101/250)

どちらがより優れているか？　その理由は何か？

　たいていの人はAをよりよい文章として選ぶでしょう。ただし、ほぼ100語で書かれたBよりも少し短い点に注意してください。解答者の中には、語数を重視するあまり、長い方が高得点を得られると考えている人がいます。しかし、必ずしもそうではありません。短くてもよく書けていれば、長くても多様性や複雑さに欠けるエッセイよりも高得点が得られます。

　AとBの述べている内容はよく似ていますが、Aの解答者は、より多様な構文を使用しており、単純な文を複合的で複雑な文に組み合わせています。例えば、各例の似たような文を比較してみると、Aでは、soという単語を使って文と文をつないでいることがわかります。

Sample A: "On Sunday, I'm already thinking about the week **ahead, so it's** less enjoyable."
Sample B: "On Sunday, I'm already thinking about the week **ahead. It's** less enjoyable."

　Bでは、どこの学校に通っているのか、何を勉強しているのかなど、余分な情報を入れて語数を増やしています。また、I will tell you why... というフレーズは必要ありません。解

答者は、自分の考えを述べる前に、In this essay, I'm going to write about.... のような
フレーズを書くことに時間を費やすべきなのです。

結論

　パート1では、5分間という限られた時間の中で、素早く書くことが大切です。優れた解
答者は、課題に素早く対応し、問題のすべての側面に答えることができます。問題をよく読
み、何を書くかをすぐに判断して書き始めましょう。5分以内に書き終え、できれば文法や
スペルに間違いがないようチェックしてください。総合的に見て、Sample Aの方が優れ
た解答と言えるでしょう。

ライティング・パート2：実践と成功のための戦略

　パート2では、より複雑な問題が出題されます。解答者はよく考えて書く内容を判断し、
より長い時間（20分以内）をかけて解答することが求められます。

　以下に2つの解答例を紹介します。問題文を読んでから、各例を読んでみましょう。両方
とも文法には問題ないので、文の内容と構成に注目してください。

> **TIP**　これらの例では、分析のために、エッセイがパート2で認められている
> 175〜250語よりも短めです。よいエッセイは一般的に175〜250語
> で書かれるべきだとされています。しかし、短いエッセイであっても、一
> 貫性がありよくまとまっていて、明確な論旨を伝えていれば、高得点を獲
> 得することができます。

Topic A: Name one of the most important issues in the world today and
explain why it's important.

解答例1

　　　Energy use is important. We know oil and coal are important sources of
energy. Oil and coal are limited in supplies and one day in the future they will
be scarce. When they become scarce the costs will go up and this will hurt poor
countries and poor people.

　　　If no other energy source is found, the lack of oil and coal might even lead to

wars. Rich countries with more power can have war with poorer countries to control their use of oil or coal or even to steal the oil and coal in those poor countries.

Now, other energy sources are beginning to be used. One promising source is solar power. The sun shines all over the world so any country that can develop or buy the right equipment can get solar power.

解答例2

One of the most important issues facing the world today is energy use. Both oil and coal, the two most common energy sources today, are limited and will become scarce in the future. Scarcity will cause prices to go up, hurting poor countries and poor people. If no alternative energy source is obtained, this might even lead to wars, as richer countries could invade oil or coal-rich areas to take their resources.

Now, other energy sources are being developed, with the most promising being solar power. The sun itself provides a free source, but large amounts of money will be required to harness that power. A key issue in the world's future might well be how solar power is produced and distributed around the globe.

どちらが優れているか？　その理由は何か？　［正解はp. 289］

The stronger essay is: _____

_____

_____

_____

Why? Explain please: _____

_____

_____

_____

_____

Topic B: If you had extra money to spend on one charitable cause, what would it be and how would you support that cause?

解答例3

There are many worthy causes that deserve support, but one that is dear to me is refugee support. Today, there are many wars and disputes that have forced millions of people to leave their homes and become refugees. They have done nothing wrong, other than to have the bad luck to live in a war-torn area.

It bothers me a great deal that some people in richer, more stable countries feel that this is not their problem and are even closing their borders to refugees. If I had the financial resources, I would commit whatever amount possible to assist organizations like the Red Cross to give more assistance to refugees now and in the future.

解答例4

War and disputes have forced millions of people to leave their homes and become refugees. The refugees did not do anything wrong, other than to live in the wrong places. Many people in rich countries don't feel that this is their problem. Some of them even want to close their borders and not accept refugees.

Another issue I care about is clean water. It's amazing and sad that in some areas of the world, people don't even have access to clean water.

I also care about women's rights and I think all women should be respected. Women should be regarded the same way as men, but in some countries they have fewer rights. If I had the money I'd spend some to support women's causes.

どちらがより優れているか？　その理由は何か？　［正解はp. 289］

The stronger essay is: ＿＿＿＿＿＿＿＿＿＿＿＿＿＿＿＿＿＿＿＿＿

＿＿＿＿＿＿＿＿＿＿＿＿＿＿＿＿＿＿＿＿＿＿＿＿＿＿＿＿＿＿＿

＿＿＿＿＿＿＿＿＿＿＿＿＿＿＿＿＿＿＿＿＿＿＿＿＿＿＿＿＿＿＿

＿＿＿＿＿＿＿＿＿＿＿＿＿＿＿＿＿＿＿＿＿＿＿＿＿＿＿＿＿＿＿

＿＿＿＿＿＿＿＿＿＿＿＿＿＿＿＿＿＿＿＿＿＿＿＿＿＿＿＿＿＿＿

Grammar　Listening　Reading　Writing　Speaking　Appendix

Writing

Why? Explain please:_____

_____

_____

_____

Chapter 3 思考力を養う

さまざまなトピックについて自分の意見を述べる力を養いましょう。また、書く内容を素早く頭の中で組み立て、自分の議論や意見を補足するための詳細情報、例、理由を考え出すことも必要です。このセクションは、そういった力を向上させ、あなたの解答をレベルアップさせるのに役立ちます。この章では、iTEPの試験でよく出題されるような5つの課題が用意されています。

課題文を読んで、解答の内容を考えてみましょう。前述のように、トピックについて素早く考え、根拠を持って自分の答えを導き出すことは、ライティング・セクションで求められる重要なスキルです。

それぞれの質問について数分間考えた後、続くコメントを読み、エッセイを読むときに採点者が何を見ているかを理解しましょう。

> Prompt 1: People enroll in higher education with various goals and objectives in mind. In your opinion, why do most adults continue their education at a university or college?

Notes _____

_____

_____

_____

_____

_____

What's your opinion? _____

_____

_____

_____

Writing

_____

_____

What are your reasons and examples?

_____

_____

_____

_____

_____

コメント:

この問題では、解答者は自分自身のことについて述べればよく、話を一般化する必要はありません。*I am going to college because I want to be an engineer.* などと書くこともできますが、これは適切とは言えないでしょう。「多くの人が大学に行く目的は、自分のキャリアの目標を達成し、特定の分野で仕事を見つけるための教育を受けることである」というような主張であれば、エンジニアになるという自分の個人的な目標を例に挙げることができます。

Prompt 2: Who do teenagers learn the most from—parents or teachers? Use specific reasons to support your opinion.

Notes _____

_____

_____

_____

_____

What's your opinion? _____

_____

_____

_____

_____

_____

What are your reasons and examples?

_____

_____

_____

_____

コメント：

この種のエッセイ（あるいは、どんなエッセイにも言えますが）に正解はありません。解答者の意見そのものはさほど重要ではなく、その意見の表現の仕方の方が重要です。ですから、実際には10代の若者は教師から最も学びを得るという考えを持っているにもかかわらず、10代は親から最も多くを学ぶという違う主張をしたとしても、それを裏付ける理由を素早く考え出すことができれば全く問題はありません。

> Prompt 3: Do you believe people learn more by doing or reading? Compare and contrast the knowledge learned from books with hands-on experience. Which learning experience is most valuable in your opinion?

Notes _____

_____

_____

_____

_____

_____

_____

Grammar　Listening　Reading　Writing　Speaking　Appendix

Writing

What's your opinion? _____

_____

_____

_____

_____

What are your reasons and examples?

_____

_____

_____

_____

コメント：

多くの解答者がこの質問に対して、ある１つの事柄を学ことに焦点を絞りすぎてしまうことになりそうです。例えば、ある言語 (iTEP は英語のテストなので、通常は英語) を学ぶには、本で勉強するのがいいのか、それともその言語が話されている場所に住むのがいいのかについて論を展開する解答者が多いのです。これでも良いエッセイになり得ますが、具体的になりすぎず、聞かれた一般的な質問に答えることが重要です。一つの例として、「本から言語を学ぶ方法」と「経験から学ぶ方法」を対比してもかまいませんが、特定の事柄の学習だけでなく、学習全般について質問されていることを意識して解答する必要があるのです。

> Prompt 4: A company plans to build a large amusement park (similar to Disneyland) next to your community. Do you support or oppose the theme park? Explain the advantages and disadvantages this will have on the people living in your community.

Notes _____

_____

_____

What's your opinion? _____

_____

_____

_____

_____

What are your reasons and examples?

_____

_____

_____

_____

コメント:

多くの解答者が、ある事柄のメリットとデメリットの両方についての説明を求められているにもかかわらず、その片側だけにしか焦点を当てないことになりそうです。一方には多くの理由があり、もう一方にはほとんど理由がない、ということでもかまいません。せめて *There are very few disadvantages to...* のように述べ、尋ねられた両方の立場について何らかの記述をする方がいいでしょう。

> Prompt 5: Do you agree or disagree with the following statement? Children living in urban environments grow up with more opportunities than children living in rural environments. Use specific examples to prove why either a city or country environment is better for children.

Writing

Notes _____

_____

_____

_____

_____

_____

What's your opinion? _____

_____

_____

_____

_____

What are your reasons and examples?

_____

_____

_____

_____

_____

コメント：

必ず、子供とその成長過程に焦点を当ててください。ナイトクラブ、大学、仕事の機会といった要素よりも、小学校の教育、医療、公害といった要素を記載することが大事です。

> **TIP** 次のチャプターで実際に文章を書く練習をした後は、上記の問題に対する答えを書く練習をしましょう。その時に備えて、各問題についてメモを取っておいてください。自分の考えを表現し、それを英語で書く練習をする絶好のチャンスです。

Chapter 4　良い文章の特徴

態を理解する

　iTEPのライティング・セクションのおおよその感覚をつかんだところで、今度は良い文章が持つ特徴に注目してみましょう。良い文章を決定づける要素には、趣旨が表現できていること、適切な段落分け、趣旨を補足する情報があること、首尾一貫性、文章全体がまとまっていることなどがあります。これらの要素についてはこの章と次の章で説明しますが、重要なのはどの要素も、前向きに課題に取り組むことで習得できるものであるということです。メモを取り、学んだテクニックをどう実践するかを考え、日々のライティングに応用していくことが大事です。さらにこれまで述べてきましたが、「(英語で)タイプする練習」、「考える練習」、「時間を計って文章を書く練習」、「自分の意見を述べる練習」も同じく高得点を取る秘訣なので、怠らずに鍛錬を行うようにしましょう。

　この後の各章で扱うトピックや解答例は、主にパート2に焦点を当てていますが、パート1に関連する題材も扱います。ライティング・セクションは総合点で評価されるので、良い文章を書くことはどちらのパートにも大事です。

　この章では、thesis statement に焦点を当てます。これは、自分の主張を1つの文で表現することです。特に250語の小論文は、この1文で始めることになるので、非常に大事な要素です。この1文を組み立てる能力を身につければ、ライティングのスコアを、ひいてはiTEPテストのスコアを向上させることができます。

Thesis Statement──自分の主張を表現する文

　では、thesis statementとはいったい何でしょうか？　これは、提示された質問に対する直接的な解答を述べる文です。エッセイの中で最も重要な文であり、エッセイの中に書かれている他のすべての文は、この文を補足している必要があります。thesisとはあなたの主張のことですから、この文が以降のエッセイの内容を左右することになります。パート2で最も重要な1文といっても過言ではありません。

　優れた解答の多くが、明確なthesis(主張)を持っています。第1文以降の文は、その主張について説明や補足を行う役割を担わせる必要があります。特にパート2では、質の高いthesis statementを提示することで、高得点を得られる解答者を作るための幸先のいいス

タートを切ることができます。この章では、課題に応じた短い小論文でthesis statement を書くことに焦点を当てます。本来、出題される課題によって、作成される文章の内容も大きく変わってくるものです。例えば、長い研究論文を書く場合、主張文は長めで複雑なものになり、場合によっては、まったく命題に答えるものではなくなってしまうかもしれません。これから文章を書く力を身につけていく過程で、さまざまな要求に応じた、さまざまな文章を書かなければならない場面に直面するでしょう。しかし、この章では、あくまでもiTEP で高得点を獲得し、自分の英語力を存分に示すための対策にのみ焦点を当てていきます。

良いthesis statementの条件とは？

1. 良いthesis statementは、課題に関する意見や、課題文で質問されたことに対する答えを伝えるものです。
2. thesis statementは、自分がエッセイの中で書こうとしていることの詳細を伝えるためのものではありません。簡潔に自分の意見や要点のみを伝えましょう。
3. 良いthesis statementでは、課題文で提示された言葉の言い換えが行われています。つまり、課題文を読まなくてもエッセイを理解してもらえるように、課題文の要点を再提示するのです。
4. thesis statementは完全で、文法的な誤りがない文でなければなりません。
5. thesis statementでは、トピックと、エッセイ全体を貫く論旨を伝えましょう。つまり、トピックとともに、たいてい課題文に含まれるwhyまたはhowの情報を要約して提示するのです。

> Topic 1: Does the entertainment industry influence people's behavior? Use reasons and specific examples to support your answer.

模範解答例

Entertainment influences the way people communicate with family and friends.

　エンターテインメント業界は人々に影響を与えている、という意見が明確に述べられており、その影響が人々にどのような影響を与えているかという質問に対する答えも提示されています。

　この文では、トピック（エンターテインメントが人々に与える影響）と、論旨（エンターテインメントが人々の家族や友人とのコミュニケーション方法にどのような影響を与えるか）の両方が含まれていることに注目しましょう。

　　　　　　　　　トピック　　　　　　　　　　　　　　　　　論旨
Entertainment influences the way people communicate with family and friends.

書き手の言いたいことが論旨で明確に示されています。

悪い解答例その1

Entertainment influences people in lots of ways.

　解答者は、「エンターテインメントは人々に影響を与える」という意見は述べているものの、lots of waysという表現では、メディアが具体的にどのように人々に影響を与えるかについての情報を提供したことにならず、論旨が伝わらない文になってしまっています。

悪い解答例その2

In this essay, I will write about many reasons why television and movies influence people.

　この文には解答者の意見がなく、ただ自分の意図を表明しただけです。論旨も示されていません。

> Topic 2: In your opinion, how do most people achieve success? Does success usually come from organized planning, unintentional luck, or taking risks? Support your opinion using specific examples and reasons.

模範解答例その1

I believe that people must take chances to be successful in life.

　このthesis statementは、質問に対して明確な解答と意見を提示しています。ここでは、トピックが「人々はチャンスに賭けてみなければならない」であるのに対し、論旨として「人生で成功するためには」リスクが必要であると明確に述べられています。また、mustを使うことで、書き手の意見の強さが強調され、考えをより提示しやすくしています。

模範解答例その2

To be a success, a person must make careful plans when it comes to work and relationships.

Writing

これも明確な解答、立場を表現しており、また言葉の言い換えも効果的に行われています。

悪い解答例その1

Many successful people take chances.

質問に答えておらず、前提について賛成も反対も表明していません。

悪い解答例その2

Careful planning is the reason many people are successful, but some people take risks.

これでは単に話題を変えただけで、質問に答えていないし、明確な意見も提示していません。

[実践練習] **Thesis Statement**

thesis statementについて学んだところで、さっそくこれを書く練習をしてみましょう。まずは以下のトピックを読み、次にthesis statementsの例を見て、その文が良いか悪いかを判断してください。また、その判断についてほかの人と話し合ってみてください。

> Topic: Do you support or oppose the following statement? Clothes impact people and their behaviors.

thesis statements　[正解はp. 290]

1. I believe that the clothes a person wears affect the way they behave.
   (strong/weak)
2. I believe that people behave differently when they wear different clothes.
   (strong/weak)
3. People dress differently based on their mood. (strong/weak)
4. Fashion has a huge effect on people's moods and how they react to others.
   (strong/weak)
5. Few people realize how much fashion affects our everyday lives.
   (strong/weak)
6. This essay will look at how clothes impact people and their behavior.
   (strong/weak)
7. The clothes a person wears tell us a lot about that person. (strong/weak)
8. I do not believe that wearing different clothes affects people's behavior

Grammar

Listening

Reading

Writing

Speaking

Appendix

because my friend's personality stays the same no matter what he wears.

（strong/weak）

9. I do not believe that wearing different clothes affects people's behavior.

（strong/weak）

10. My personality changes when I wear different clothes.　　（strong/weak）

11. I can't say whether clothes affect people's behavior.　　（strong/weak）

12. Clothes impact everything from human emotions to the way they treat others.

（strong/weak）

thesis statementを書く練習

練習課題

　この章にある2つのトピックからそれぞれについて、thesis statementと短いエッセイを書いてみましょう。始める前に、必ず下記の注意点に目を通してください。また、これまでに身につけたスキルも駆使して書いてみましょう。

1. 取り組む課題文を1つ選ぶ。
2. タイマーを20分にセットする。
3. 可能であれば、パソコンを使ってタイプする。
4. トピックに関する自分の意見をメモすることから始める。
5. トピックと自分の意見や主張を含めたthesis statement を作成する。
6. トピックについての短いエッセイを書く（250語以内）。
7. 自分の主張を伝え、それを裏付ける明確な説明をすることに集中する。
8. 十分な補足説明をする。
9. 20分の間に2〜3分取り、自分の書いたものを読み返し、間違いがないか確認する。
10. この課題について振り返り、右ページに自分の考えを書き、それについて他の人と話し合う。

_____

_____

_____

_____

_____

_____

_____

_____

振り返り

　下記の質問に答える形で考えを書きましょう。

1. How did you feel about the ideas and details that you were able to write?

_____

_____

_____

_____

_____

_____

2. How did you feel about your thesis statement?

_____

_____

_____

_____

_____

_____

3. What challenges did you have completing this task?

_____

_____

_____

_____

_____

_____

_____

4. What will you work on next to improve not only your writing of a thesis statement, but also your ability to provide details and examples while writing within a time limit?

_____

_____

_____

_____

_____

_____

_____

Grammar

Listening

Reading

Writing

Speaking

Appendix

Chapter 5 文章を効果的に展開する

要点を押さえる

　これまでの章では、テストの形式と採点方法について説明してきました。さらに、テストの解答例、論文の書き方、成功のためのコツなどを紹介してきました。ここからはいよいよiTEPのライティング・セクションを、特に文章の展開の仕方に焦点を当てて、より詳しく見ていきましょう。これは、「質」と「量」の問題です。

　iTEPの採点者は、分かりやすい構成と詳細情報を備えた文章の書き手を高く評価します。一般的に、そのような文章の方が洗練されていると見なされます。というのも、採点者が書き手に求めているのは、各段落の趣旨から外れることなく、具体例を示し、表現力のある言葉を使い、正しい文法を維持し、さらに自分の主張を裏付ける説明を提示することだからです。

例その1

　以下は、同じトピックについての3つの解答例で、それぞれ展開の仕方が異なります。解答者がそれぞれどのように自分の文章を展開させたかを見てみましょう。

> Topic: What demands do large populations place on society and the environment? What can be done to improve the current situation?

解答例1
レベル：低

　　　　First, fewer people can help the environment. People use many things from the environment such as water, trees, and air. If there were fewer people in Japan, less water would be taken from rivers. Fewer trees would be taken from the forest. Fewer cars would mean cleaner air. Therefore, the environment would be cleaner.

解説：この文章で、筆者は細部にほとんど注意を払わずに一般的な情報を述べています。説明は明快ですが、筆者が主張を表現するために用いている手法は陳腐です。

TIP	常に自分の主張を意識してください。自分の主張を裏付ける詳細な説明と、不可欠ではない情報への言及とのバランスを取ることが、高得点を獲得するための鍵です。

解答例2

レベル：中

First, large populations make large demands on the environment. People need fresh drinking water. Waste such as sewage and garbage needs to be disposed of. Also, new houses and roads need to be built for growing populations. If the population decreases, much of these places could be cleaned up. Instead of cutting down trees to build more roads, these places could be left untouched for nature to flourish.

解説：この例では、筆者は段落の最後に、「木を切って道路を増やしたりせずに、土地を温存して自然の繁栄に任せることができるだろう」という明確な記述を加えています。

解答例3

レベル：高

First, large populations make large demands on the environment. People need fresh drinking water. This puts pressure on Japanese rivers. Waste such as sewage and garbage needs to be disposed of. This puts pressure on landfills and the ocean where the waste is sent. Also, new houses and roads need to be built for growing populations. This puts pressure on the land and forests. If the population decreases, many of these places could be cleaned up. There would be much more open space for people to enjoy. Instead of cutting down trees to build more roads, these places could be left untouched for nature to flourish. In short, the fewer the people, the fewer the demands on the environment.

解説：この最後の例では、筆者は明確な主張を述べ、裏付けとなる証拠を示し、そして多くの詳細情報を提示して要点を分かりやすくしています。明確な説明と結論があり、洗練された構文と適切な言葉選びによって、非常に優れた解答になっています。詳細情報の記述例は以下のとおりです。

▶This puts pressure on Japanese rivers.
▶This puts pressure on landfills and the ocean where the waste is sent.
▶This puts pressure on the land and forests.

Writing

例その2

> Topic: How do declining birthrates affect opportunties for women?

解答例1

レベル：低

    Second, if a family is small, it will spend more for a daughter's education. Women will have more chances to go to a four-year university. In this way, girls will have more opportunities.

解説：この文章は短すぎます。ほとんど詳細が説明されておらず、単純で直線的な文だけで構成されてしまっています。

解答例2

レベル：中

    Second, declining birthrates open up many more opportunities for women. In the past, large families did not have much money to spend on their children's education. Therefore, families usually spent more money on their son's education than their daughter's education. Also, as the number of young people falls, universities need to admit more women to keep the same number of students. A declining birthrate will continue to open up opportunities for women.

解説：この文では、In the past, large families did not have much money to spend on their children's education. のような具体性の高い情報に言及されています。

解答例3

レベル：高

    Second, declining birthrates open up many more opportunities for women. In the past, large families did not have much money to spend on their children's education. Families usually spent more money on their son's education than on their daughter's education. Sons were sent to four-year universities, while the daughters were sent to two-year colleges. The thinking at this time was that men had to provide for families and therefore should be given the better education. Due to enrollment numbers, universities needed to admit more women to keep the same number of students. This has allowed many more women to achieve their educational goals. A declining birthrate will continue to open up opportunities for women.

解説：この文は、下記のようなさらに具体性の高い説明がなされています。

> Sons were sent to four-year universities while the daughters were sent to two-year colleges. The thinking at this time was that men had to provide for families and therefore should be given the better education.
>
> This has allowed many more women to achieve their educational goals.

実践練習

　下記の３つの文章について、解答者がどのように文章を展開し、そしてそれがiTEPのスコアにどうつながっているかを考察してみましょう。

> Topic: What demands do large populations place on society and the environment? What can be done to improve the current situation?

解答例１
レベル：低

　　　Third, Japan does not grow enough food for itself. If there were fewer people, Japan would not have to import so much food from other countries. Farmers could also use more land to grow food.

Why is the detail level low in Version 1?

_____

_____

_____

_____

解答例２
レベル：中

　　　Third, Japan does not grow enough food for itself. If there were fewer people, Japan would not have to import so much food from other countries. Farmers could also use more land to grow food.

How has the writer increased the detail level in Version 2?

_____

Writing

_____

_____

解答例3

レベル：高

      Third, in the past 100 years Japan has found it more and more difficult to feed itself. It is very dependent on food imports from China, the Philippines, America, and many other countries. Currently, Japan produces only 42% of its own food. If there were fewer people in the country, this percentage could be raised. Not only would there be fewer people to feed, but also more land could be used for farming. Japan might not be able to become completely self-sufficient, but at least it could lower its dependence on foreign food imports and support its own domestic food market.

In Version 3, what did the writer do to improve the development?

1. _____

_____

_____

2. _____

_____

_____

_____

_____

3. _____

_____

_____

_____

_____

考察した結果を、周りの人と話し合ってみてください。

Chapter 6　まとまりと一貫性

　cohesionという語は、ラテン語のcohærereに由来し、「まとまる」という意味です。これを紹介した理由は、まとまりのある段落を作るために役立つ概念だからです。ある段落中の各文は、それぞれ一つの主張について述べるものです。つまり個々の主張は、それぞれ別の一で表現されます。主張と文が「一体となって」1つのまとまった段落を構成するのです。文、論旨、詳細な情報がすべて明確に組み合わさっていれば、文章は首尾一貫したものになり、読む人に理解してもらいやすくなります。例え文法が完璧でも、いかにテーマが優れていても、文章にまとまりや一貫性がなければ、iTEPのライティング・セクションで良いスコアを得ることはできません。この章では、あなたの文章にまとまりと一貫性を持たせるための方法をいくつか紹介します。

どうやってまとまりのある文章を書くか？
　テクニックはたくさんありますが、特に以下の4つの要素が重要です。

1. キーワードやその同義語を繰り返し使う
2. 代名詞を使う
3. 限定詞を使う
4. つなぎ言葉を使う

1. キーワードやその同義語を繰り返し使う

　文章を読んでいる人に対して、自分の主張を明確にしておくことが重要です。そのためには、その主張が何であるかを読者に都度思い出させる必要があります。そこで、キーワードを繰り返し用いたり、その同義語を用いることが重要です。この2つのテクニックを併用することが大事で、同じ語句ばかりを繰り返し使うと文章が単調になってしまいます。以下は、よくまとまっている文章の例です。トピックから見てみましょう。

> Topic: People often choose a particular type of work, such as owning a business, working as an employee, or being a consultant. Which type of job is best for you?

Writing

まずは、同じキーワードが繰り返されている文章です。

In most cases, companies offer benefits to their **employees**. These benefits include health insurance, dental insurance, and coverage for eye care. These services are quite expensive if you have to pay for them from your own pocket. For example, my **self-employed** friend did not have health insurance. When he got sick he had to pay so many hospital bills that he almost lost his business. If he had **been an employee**, he would have had health insurance. In addition, companies offer their **employees** retirement benefits. By participating in these retirement programs, **employees** can prepare for their later years over time. People who are not **employees** at a firm have to save for retirement on their own.

次は、そのキーワードを適宜別の同義語に置き換えている文章です。

In most cases, companies offer benefits to their **employees**. These benefits include health insurance, dental insurance, and coverage for eye care. These services are quite expensive if you have to pay for them from your own pocket. For example, my **self-employed** friend did not have health insurance. When he got sick he had to pay so many hospital bills that he almost lost his business. If he had **had a position at a company**, he would have had health insurance. In addition, companies offer their **workers** retirement benefits. By participating in these retirement programs, **employees** can prepare for their later years over time. People who are not **working for a firm** have to save for retirement on their own.

2. 代名詞を使う

　文章が単調にならないようにするには、代名詞を上手に使うことが大切です。これは思ったよりも難しいことです。同じ名前を繰り返さないとか、言及している人、場所、物を繰り返し書いてはいけないという意味ではありません。以下は、代名詞を上手に使った文章です。まずはトピックを確認しましょう。

> Topic: Where is the best place for an international traveler to visit in your country if s/he could only stay for one day? Give recommendations to the visitor and explain why that place was chosen.

例文1

　　　First, a foreigner could learn a lot about Japanese culture by visiting Mt. Fuji. When I climbed Mt. Fuji, I was surprised at how many older people were climbing the mountain. I talked to one of **them** while I was going up the mountain, a man in his seventies! **He** told me that **he and his wife** had dreamed of getting to the top of Mt. Fuji for many years. **He** also told me that **they** both loved nature, and climbing the mountain was a great way of experiencing the outdoors. This man and **his** wife taught me how important nature is to Japanese people. Foreigners could understand the same thing about nature by visiting Mt. Fuji, so I think it is a great place for **them** to visit.

次は代名詞の使い方に難がある文章です。

例文2

　　　First, a foreigner could learn a lot about Japanese culture by visiting Mt. Fuji. When I climbed **it**, I was surprised at how many older people were climbing **it**. I talked to one of **the old people** while I was going up the mountain, a man in his seventies! **The man** told me that **they** had dreamed of getting to the top of **it** for many years. **The old man** also told me that **he and his wife** both loved nature, and climbing **it** was a great way of experiencing **it**. This man and his wife taught me how important nature is to Japanese people. **They** could understand the same thing about nature by visiting **it**, so I think **Mt. Fuji** is a great place for them to visit.

いつ代名詞を使い、いつキーワードを繰り返せばいいのか？

　代名詞を使用する際に最も重要なことは、読み手が、その代名詞が何を指しているのかに疑問を抱かないようにすることです。原則として、キーワードと代名詞を交互に使うか、別の人物、場所、物に新たに言及するまでは代名詞を使うようにしましょう。例文1を参考に、代名詞の使い方を考えてみましょう。ここでは、以下のキーワードが代名詞に置き換えられています。

the old man	the old man's wife	Mt. Fuji
nature	Japanese people	foreigners

　例文2では、特定の代名詞が指している名詞、特にMt. Fuji、nature、Japanese people、foreignersの代わりに使用されている代名詞が何を指すのか読み手が混乱する可能性があります。

3. 限定詞を使う

　文章にまとまりを持たせるには、限定詞を上手に使用することも有効です。限定詞は、文章中で言及されている特定の人、場所、または物の代わりに使用するという点で、代名詞と似ています。しかし、代名詞とは異なり、限定詞はキーワードやその同義語と一緒に使わなければなりません。

限定詞には何があるか?
　限定詞は4つしかなく、おそらく皆さんがすでに知っている単語です。自分の文章の中でどのくらいの頻度でこれらの単語を使っているかを思い返してみてください。4つの限定詞は以下のとおりです。

　　1. this
　　2. that
　　3. these
　　4. those

　次は、限定詞を効果的に使用している文章です。まずはトピックを読んでみましょう。

> Topic: Most people work both to survive and to pay for their basic needs. There are other people who work for various reasons besides money. Explain other reasons why people choose to work.

　　　Secondly, some people work because they love what they do. For example, being a teacher is not easy, and it takes a special person to do the job well. In fact, teachers in France are not paid as well as other professionals such as engineers, lawyers, or accountants. **These professionals** sometimes make three to four times as much as teachers do. However, people who teach do so because they love the job. It takes a special personality to be an effective educator. A person must be patient, organized, and compassionate. If a person has **these traits**, he or she will be a successful instructor and will enjoy teaching no matter how much the pay is.

　次も、限定詞を上手に使用した文章の例です。

> Topic: In your opinion, does technology cause students to learn information faster or does it cause more distractions?

Firstly, in the past, students did not have access to a piece of technology that is very common today: the calculator. **This advanced tool** allows students to solve mathematical problems quickly if it is used properly. In fact, many new calculators have commonly used formulas programmed into the device. The calculator lets the user insert the information into **these formulas** and then quickly displays the solution or answer. **This capability** saves students a lot of time, and allows them to spend more time learning mathematical principles and less time doing tedious calculations.

4. つなぎ言葉を使う

iTEPの関係者の誰もが、パート2で高得点を挙げるにはつなぎ言葉が重要であると口を揃えます。なので、ぜひ時間をかけてでもこれらの使い方はマスターしておきましょう。ここでは、英語の文章で用いられるつなぎ言葉について、理解を深めるための練習問題を用意しています。

なぜつなぎ言葉が重要なのか?

つなぎ言葉が重要なのは、上で紹介した他のテクニックが重要であるのと同じ理由からです。文章の中で読者を誘導し、複数のアイデアを結び付け、文章の意味や方向性を明確にします。採点者が文章の趣旨を少しでも見失ってしまうと、減点されてしまうことを覚えておきましょう。つなぎ言葉の使用は、読み手をあなたの伝えたいことから目を離させないようにするための最善策なのです。

How do writers join ideas? Good essays are easy for readers to understand. This is achieved via many writing avenues. **First and foremost**, the grammar and vocabulary of an essay should be clear and the ideas that the writer wishes to convey should be relevant, organized, and easy to understand. **In addition**, a good essay must have "signals" that help the reader follow the writer's train of thought. These signals are often transition words or/and phrases that join two or more ideas together to support a single point.

上の文章を読み、太字のフレーズFirst and foremostとIn additionに注目しましょう。これらは典型的なつなぎ言葉の例です。Good essays are easy...から始まる文は、良いエッセイが読みやすいことを説明する多くの理由があることを伝えています。そして、その

Writing

うちの２つの理由が、つなぎ言葉の使用によって明確に示されています。

以下は、つなぎ言葉を使用目的別に整理したものです。

複数の説明を行うとき	論調の変化や対比を示すとき	例や、より詳細な説明を行うとき	原因や結果を表すとき	結論を表すとき
First, ... Second, ...	However, ...	For example, ...	... since ...	In conclusion, ...
In addition, ...	In contrast, ...	An example of ...	... because ...	Therefore, ...
The first reason for this is that ...	On the other hand, ...	... is	As a result, ...	
Another reason is that ...		... Specifically,	This results in ...	
		... For instance, ...		

実践練習

他にもたくさんのつなぎ言葉があり、その使い方も無数にあります。下記の例文を読みながら、優れた書き手がつなぎ言葉を駆使して文章を展開する手法に注目してください。

例文1

I believe that math is a very important subject for students to master. First of all, basic math is needed for success in many other subjects such as physics and chemistry. Also, even in many unrelated fields, research requires the use of statistics, which is based on math skills. In addition, learning math helps to keep the brain sharp and is like exercise for the student learning the math formulas and processes.

例文2

I think that cooking at home is better than eating at restaurants for many reasons. One important difference is that by cooking at home, you can save a lot of money. For example, a steak bought at a grocery store might cost five or six times more money if you buy the exact same meat cooked at a fancy restaurant. In addition to the savings, it's fun to enjoy the creation and experimentation while cooking. Overall, cooking a great meal at home really beats going out to a restaurant.

Grammar Listening Reading Writing Speaking Appendix

例文3

　　With the Internet and modern technology, many people think that they can easily work from home, but there are several reasons why it's better to work in a traditional office setting.

　　While it's true that it's convenient to work from home, it's also more difficult to set and keep a specific work schedule. Furthermore, by not separating clearly "home" from "office," a worker might actually work longer days since it's so easy to check emails after traditional work hours, or to finish a project due by working late into the night. Another consideration is that the employer might not be comfortable in every case, not knowing whether workers are really putting in a full day's work. In summary, the convenience of having employees stay at home to work actually carries danger for both the workers and their bosses.

つなぎ言葉の応用

　　つなぎ言葉を2つ3つ覚えて文章の中で使ったとしても、それで十分とは言えません。つたない文章の特徴の一つは、単調であることです。受験者の中には、最も一般的なつなぎ言葉を5つか6つ知っていれば十分だと考えている人がいますが、それだけではいい文章を書くことはできません。英語のライティングを上達させるために覚えておくべきキーワードは「変化」です。段落が1つだけなら、5〜6個のつなぎ言葉を知っていれば事足りますが、パート2では3つほどの段落を含んだ文章を書かなければなりません。そのため、つなぎ言葉に対する深い理解と、その使い方を熟知している必要があります。それが文章に変化を与え、変化が質の高い文章の構成を生み出し、さらにパート2で高得点を取得することにつながります。

単調さと変化

　　文章に変化を持たせる際、エッセイ全体のバランスを考慮しなければなりません。以下に、パート2の解答例を2つ示します。1つ目の文章では、つなぎ言葉にほとんど変化がなく、2つ目の文章ではさまざまなつなぎ言葉が使われています。

> Topic: People have differing views about whether higher education should be available for everyone. In your opinion, should colleges and universities only accept good students?

　　Making higher education available to as many students as possible is a goal of most societies. A university or college degree opens the door to future prosperity. **However**, it is difficult to decide if higher education is right for everyone. I believe that limiting access to colleges and universities is good for everyone.

First, many believe that opening colleges and universities to all students will increase the competitiveness of a country in the global economy. **Indeed**, a well-educated work force is very valuable, as companies need the best workers to beat their rivals. **However**, the value of a college degree in my country, Germany, is not the same as it was when my parents were students. **For example**, my father received a bachelor's degree in engineering and was able to find a good job. **However**, these days, companies usually require new employees to have a master's degree. Therefore, allowing all students into university could make an undergraduate degree less valuable.

Second, sending all students to college or university would require a lot of money. **Therefore**, the government would probably have to allocate more money for education. Many believe that this new money would make universities more stable and improve the quality of the instruction that they provide. **However**, accepting more students requires lowering academic standards. When higher education is exclusive, it means that only the best students can go. **Therefore**, classes that were once taught in high school such as algebra and basic geometry would have to be taught in college.

In conclusion, most countries want to provide as many opportunities to their citizens as possible. **However**, sending all students to college or university is not the best answer because it would have negative consequences. The value of undergraduate degrees would suffer and the quality of higher education would decline. **Therefore**, college and university should only be available to those who qualify to attend.

(however x5, therefore x3)

では、つなぎ言葉がうまく使いこなされた文章例を見てみましょう。

Topic: Many people say not to judge others based on the way they look. Do you agree or disagree with this advice?

In everyday life, it is necessary for us to assess the people with whom we have contact. **Unfortunately**, we do not have time to get to know every person we meet.

Outward appearance is one of many criteria we must use to make good judgments about people. I believe that we must sometimes use only the things we can see to make these judgments.

First, my country, Argentina, is very beautiful. **On the other hand**, there are many dangerous places in Argentina, and we must use our eyes and our brains to make good decisions in order to keep ourselves safe. **Indeed**, we learn how to make these judgments from our parents. **For example**, if a neighborhood looks ruined or deserted, we know we should stay away. **Similarly**, if a person we meet on the street looks careless or aggressive, it is better to avoid contact with that person. **Therefore**, the visual clues we get from people can keep us out of dangerous situations.

Secondly, we must use people's outward appearance in our professional lives as well. **For instance**, I once worked for a woman who was a sales manager for a make-up company in Buenos Aires. One of the most important jobs she had was hiring new salespeople. **However**, she did not always have enough time to meet with people for a long time. **Consequently**, she had to rely very much on her appraisal of their outward characteristics to make her decision. **Of course**, it may not seem fair, but in this situation, it was necessary.

To conclude, the way people present themselves in public says a lot about their self-respect and their respect for others. While I know we cannot all look like a Hollywood star, we can at least keep ourselves looking clean and fit. We do not always have the time to learn about someone's personality. In these cases, we must use the way a person looks to form an opinion of him or her.

(326 words)

以下は、上の文章例で使われたつなぎ言葉の一覧です。それぞれが１回だけ使われています。

Unfortunately	First	On the other hand	Indeed
For example	Similarly	Therefore	Secondly
For instance	However	Consequently	Of course
To conclude			

つなぎ言葉と文構造

つなぎ言葉には多くの種類があり、できるだけ多くの種類を文章中で使うことが望まれま

す。ですが、受験者がつなぎ言葉を使い始めて間もない段階では、文の構造や句読点の使い方を間違えやすいものです。カンマを適切に使用することが、文意を正しく伝える上で重要です。文法、句読点と意味は密接に関連しているからです。また、つなぎ言葉を適切に分類することも、それらを正しく使うためには不可欠です。

　文構造の間違いを防ぐために、英語の文を個別の公式に当てはめてください。つなぎ言葉は分類に応じて公式が異なります。簡単な公式を覚えておけば、文構造を間違えることはないでしょう。ここでは、各公式とそのルールを紹介していきます。

    S - 　大文字で始まる主語

    s - 　小文字で始まる主語

    v - 　動詞

    Ex- 大文字で始まる接続語

    ex - 小文字で始まる接続語

    cc - 等位接続詞

    Sc - 大文字で始まる従属接続詞

    sc - 小文字で始まる従属接続詞

　単純な文は、主語部分と動詞部分の２つに分けられます。以下の文は、単純な公式に従っています。

公式その1：S v

- I drive.
- She drives her car.
- My friend takes the bus to work.
- The government of Italy has created programs to encourage women to have children.
- Children who grow up in the country do not have access to many educational activities.

　単純な構造の文だからといって、必ずしも短いわけではありません。主語と述語（動詞）の各部分全体を捉えることが重要です。

　では、次は別の構造の文です。この公式は、あらゆる接続語に当てはまります。

公式その2：Ex, s v.

- Therefore, parents should educate their own children.
- In addition, the government of Italy has created programs to encourage women to have children.
- Indeed, children who grow up in the city have access to the best libraries.
- Consequently, prices for consumer goods continue to rise.

公式その3：S v, cc s v.

- The air in the city got much worse, so people had to start wearing masks in order to protect their lungs.
- Friends who are different can teach a person about new things, and they can give advice on matters that might be unfamiliar.
- My brother never plans his weekend activities in advance, but he always seems to have a good time.

公式その4：Ex, s v, cc s v.

- For example, my brother never plans his weekend activities in advance, but he always seems to have a good time.
- In addition, friends who have different traits can teach a person new things, and they can give advice on matters that might be unfamiliar.
- However, the air in the city got much worse, so people had to start wearing masks in order to protect their lungs.

公式その5：S v sc s v.

- People from my city need to wear masks because the air has gotten so dirty.
- Children from the country now have access to technology even though they are not near a populated area.
- Children will learn to be responsible if they are required to do household chores.

公式その6：Sc s v, s v.

- While sports programs are important, the primary focus of a university should be academics.
- When I lived in America, I did not have much contact with my neighbors.
- Because people in my country like to save their money, the economy has not been growing as fast as it should.

Writing

では、各公式を知ったところで、受験者がしがちな間違いを見てみましょう。

要素が欠けている文
- For example, students who are not motivated to study.
- The supervisors that inspire their employees.
- For instance, people from poor countries.

　これらの文はどうすれば正しいものにできるでしょうか。共通する問題点は、動詞がないことです。一見動詞があるように見えますが、For example, students who are not motivated to study. では、are not motivated の主語は、関係代名詞の who です。文の主語であるはずの students の述語動詞として機能しているわけではありません。これは非常によくある間違いです。

　つまり、正しい文にするには動詞を加えればいいのです。下の修正文を見てみましょう。
　※動詞は斜体字になっています。
- For example, students who are not motivated to study *require* help.

もしくは
- For example, **there** *are* students who are not motivated to study.

もしくは
- For example, **some** students *are* not motivated to study.

- The supervisors that inspire their employees *are* much more valuable to the company.

- For instance, people from poor countries **often** *have* **no access** to the Internet.

無終止文
　上で動詞が欠けている例を見ましたが、無終止文は逆に動詞が多すぎることが問題です。これは、書き手が文を不適切につなげようとしたときによく起こります。
　以下に無終止文の例をいくつか紹介します。

1. 無終止文の問題点の一つは、等位接続詞(cc)を使わずに文をつなげようとしてしまうことです。修正するには、適切な場所に接続詞を追加しなければなりません。
　以下は、誤った文とその訂正例です。訂正文で、等位接続詞の直前にカンマが使われていることに注目しましょう。

誤文：For example, my friend likes to study in cafes and coffee shops she likes to be surrounded by people. (~~S v s v.~~)

訂正文：For example, my friend likes to study in cafes and coffee shops**, and** she likes to be surrounded by people. (S v, cc s v.)

誤文：For example, my friend knows a lot about American football he has never traveled to America. (~~S v s v.~~)

訂正文：For example, my friend knows a lot about American football**, but** he has never traveled to America. (S v, cc s v.)

2. もう一つは、単純に無終止文を2つの文に分割することです。

誤文：For example, my friend likes to study in cafés and coffee shops she likes to be surrounded by people. (~~S v s v.~~)

訂正文：For example, my friend likes to study in cafés and coffee shops. She likes to be surrounded by people. (S v. S v.)

誤文：For example, my friend knows a lot about American football he has never traveled to America. (~~S v s v.~~)

訂正文：For example, my friend knows a lot about American football. However, he has never traveled to America. (S v. Ex, s v.)

3. 最後は、2つの文を従属接続詞でつなげて修正するパターンです。

誤文：For example, my friend likes to study in cafés and coffee shops she likes to be surrounded by people. (~~S v s v.~~)

訂正文：For example, my friend likes to study in cafés and coffee shops because she likes to be surrounded by people. (S v sc s v.)

誤文：For example, my friend knows a lot about American football he has never traveled to America. (~~S v s v.~~)

訂正文：For example, my friend knows a lot about American football although he has never traveled to America. (S v sc s v.)

Writing

カンマ

1. カンマと従属接続詞

　従属接続詞（sc）を使う際、どこにカンマを使うかはよく迷うところです。以下の公式を覚えておきましょう。

S v sc s v.
もしくは
Sc s v, s v.

以下の例文には誤りがあります。どこが誤りかわかるでしょうか？
- It is very difficult to accept invitations, if one has a full schedule every day of the week.
- For example, my friend learned discipline, because he had to go to his soccer practice every morning.
- Some children become excellent musicians, even though they have no musical training in school.

　上記の文には、実はカンマは必要ありません。では、次の各文を見て、それぞれの間違いを探してみてください。従属接続詞の公式を思い出してください。
- If one has a full schedule every day of the week it is very difficult to accept invitations.
- Because he had to go to his soccer practice every morning my friend learned discipline.
- Even though some children had no musical training in school they became excellent musicians.

　上記の文のいずれにもカンマが必要なのに、入っていません。以下が正しい文です。
- If one has a full schedule every day of the week, it is very difficult to accept invitations.
- Because he had to go to his soccer practice every morning, my friend learned discipline.
- Even though some children had no musical training in school, they became excellent musicians.

2. カンマと等位接続詞

最も一般的に使用される等位接続詞は、and、but、so、yet、そしてorです。等位接続詞と従属接続詞では、使用される文の構造が全く異なるため、その違いを知ることが重要です。等位接続詞は5つしかないので、その違いを覚えるのはそれほど難しくありません。以下の文では等位接続詞が使われていますが、誤りがあります。

S v, cc s v.

- Some storeowners do not know that their products are dangerous so it is important to inform them of dangerous products.
- My father bought a boat to take our family fishing but he sold it soon afterwards.

これらの文を修正するには、単純に、等位接続詞の前にカンマを追加するだけです。以下の修正例を見てください。

- Some storeowners do not know that their products are dangerous, **so** it is important to inform them of dangerous products.
- My father bought a boat to take our family fishing, **but** he sold it soon afterwards.

文を等位接続詞で始められるか？

この疑問については、英語を母語とする人々の間でも賛否両論があります。実際のところ、文頭に等位接続詞を使ってはいけないという正式なルールはありません。

ですが、パート2のエッセイの目標は、アカデミックな論調の文章を書くことです。採点者によっては、文頭に接続詞を使うことを非標準的と見なすかもしれません。また、通例、接続副詞など接続語を使用する方がよりアカデミックな論調を生み出せるため、文頭では等位接続詞を使用せず、代わりに接続副詞などを用いるとよいでしょう。

以下の例文を見て、どうすれば文頭に等位接続詞を使わずに書くことができるかを確認しましょう。まずは文頭に等位接続詞を使用している例です。

- Extended television viewing can damage a child's eyes. And, a child who sits in front of the TV for many hours is not getting enough exercise.
- In the past, many jobs did not require that people know how to read and write. So, reading and writing were not as important as they are today.
- Studying alone can provide a person with the peace and quiet needed to concentrate on one thing. But, studying with other people can help a student stay motivated. And, other people can give you ideas that you might not have had if you had studied alone.

では、次に修正後の文章です。

- Extended television viewing can damage a child's eyes. **In addition,** a child who sits in front of the TV for many hours is not getting enough exercise.
- In the past, many jobs did not require that people know how to read and write. **Therefore,** reading and writing were not as important as they are today.
- Studying alone can provide a person with the peace and quiet needed to concentrate on one thing. **However,** studying with other people can help a student stay motivated. **Moreover,** other people can give you ideas that you might not have had if you had studied alone.

3. カンマと接続語

カンマは、接続語が文頭にある場合はその直後に、文中にある場合は直前と直後両方に使います。パート2で高得点を取るためには、接続語を正しく用いることがとても重要です。以下の例では、誤りとそれをどう修正したかを見てみましょう。

誤文:

However women who stay at home after giving birth fall behind in their careers. Therefore studying in a library is better than studying at home.

訂正文:

However, women who stay at home after giving birth fall behind in their careers. Therefore, studying in a library is better than studying at home.

4. 語句が列挙される中で使用するカンマ

カンマは、3つ以上の項目が列挙される場合、その中で各項目を区別するために使用されます。列挙される単語やフレーズは、それぞれ同じ品詞や語形でなければなりません。下記は、誤っている例文とその修正後の文です。

誤文:

George is known for his strength, kindness, and he is generous.

訂正文:

George is known for his strength, kindness, and generosity.

誤文:

The principal investigated the crime, identified the offending students, and she notified the students' parents about the incident.

訂正文：

The principal investigated the crime, identified the offending students, and notified the students' parents about the incident.

誤文：

I like my best friend because she is trustworthy, helpful, courteous, and she is kind.

訂正文：

I like my best friend because she is trustworthy, helpful, courteous, and kind.

5. 名詞を修飾する２つの形容詞の間のカンマ

- It was a long, tiring hike up the mountain, but we were in shape and made it to the top in two hours.
- I could not wait for the warm, sunny days of summer to come.

6. 同格と形容詞節のカンマ

　最も便利なライティングのテクニックの一つに、同格があります。同格の語句は、ある名詞に情報を追加するという点で、形容詞節と似ています。しかし、同格の語句は節ではないので関係代名詞や動詞を含みません。つまり、who is や which is のない形容詞節と同じだと考えることができます。多くの場合、同格の語句は固有名詞と一緒に使われます。なぜなら、形容詞節と同様に、すでに言及された名詞に関する追加情報を提供するものだからです。下記の例で、同格を使ったいくつかの文を見てみましょう。まず、独立した形容詞節を含む文を紹介します。続いて、同格を使った文を見てみましょう。どちらの場合も、前後のカンマに注意してください。

形容詞節を使った例文

- Bill Gates, who is the founder and president of Microsoft, devotes more of his time to his charitable organizations than to his business.
- The bus tour includes a five-day trip through Hokkaido, which is the northernmost island of Japan.
- *Mugicha*, which is a cold tea made of barley, can be found in most refrigerators in Japan.

同格を使った例文

- Bill Gates, the founder and president of Microsoft, devotes more of his time to his charitable organization than to his business.

- The bus tour includes a five-day trip through Hokkaido, the northernmost island of Japan.
- *Mugicha*, a cold tea made of barley, can be found in most refrigerators in Japan.

誤文：

Reggie my neighbor's dog, barks all day and sometimes wakes us up at night.

訂正文：

Reggie, my neighbor's dog, barks all day and sometimes wakes us up at night.

> **TIP** ▶ できる限り形容詞節ではなく同格を使用するのが望ましいと見なされます。

7. カンマと地名

都市名と国名・州名の間にはカンマを使用します。地名を表す最後の語句となる国名や州名の後に、2つ目のカンマを置きます。

- For example, when I lived in Chicago, Illinois, for three years, I got used to cold weather.
- Barcelona, Spain, hosted the Olympic Games in the summer of 1992.

Chapter 7　フォーマルな文体

　完璧な構造の文を書き連ねたとしても、それだけではパート２でトップスコアを取れる保証はありません。機械的なミス以外にも減点対象となる項目があります。文筆家やライティングの指導者は通常、それらの項目を「文体」というカテゴリーに分類します。文体は主観性が高く、簡単に確立できるとは限りません。採点者がどのように文体を評価するかを理解しておくことが大事です。以下に、採点者が求める文体の要素を、自分の文章に組み込む方法をいくつか紹介します。

同義語によるキーワードの繰り返し

　常に趣旨を明確にしながらエッセイを展開するために、ときにはキーワードやキーフレーズを繰り返す必要があります。前章でも、キーワードやキーフレーズを繰り返すことで、一貫性のある文章を構築できることに触れました。しかし、エッセイ全体で同じ単語を使い続けると、文体が単調で退屈なものになってしまい、減点されることがあります。これを避ける一つの方法は、同義語を用いたり、キーワードと似たような意味を持つフレーズを作り出したりすることです。まず、パート２でよく出題されるテーマを見てみましょう。

Education	Family	Business	Media	Public Policy
Lifestyle	Children	Environment	Work	Money

　以下の文章は、ビジネスと仕事に関するエッセイです。この段落では、どんな単語が頻繁に繰り返されているかを見てみましょう。

　　　First, good supervisors should be interested in the professional development of their workers. That is, they should seek opportunities for their workers to gain new skills and new experiences. A good supervisor knows that workers who are more skilled and have a wide experience are better for the company and make the firm more productive. For example, my friend had a supervisor who never let him try anything new at the company or take on any new tasks. After some time, my friend realized that he would not advance in the company under this supervisor. When he asked the supervisor to give him more responsibility, he told my friend to just do the job he had been given. Finally, because of this supervisor's closed-minded attitude, my friend quit this job and went to work for a competing company.

Writing

supervisorという語の繰り返しが多すぎることが分かります。次に、supervisorを同義語に置き換えた同じ文章を見てみましょう。

First, good *supervisors* should be interested in the professional development of their workers. That is, they should seek opportunities for their workers to gain new skills and new experiences. A good *manager* knows that workers who are more skilled and have a wide experience are better for the company and make the firm more productive. For example, my friend had a *boss* who never let him try anything new at the company or take on any new tasks. When he asked the *supervisor* to give him more responsibility, he told my friend to just do the job he had been given. After some time, my friend realized that he would not advance in the company under *this person's management*. Finally, because of this *manager's* closed-minded attitude, my friend quit this job and went to work for a competing company.

句動詞を同義語に置き換える

iTEPのライティングで高得点を挙げるためには、アカデミックな文体で書くことが重要です。アカデミックな論調を強める方法の一つが、句動詞を使いすぎないことです。ほとんどの句動詞を1単語で言い換えることが可能で、句動詞よりもその単語を使ったほうが、書き手が言葉に習熟しているという印象を読み手に与えるのです。以下の例を見てください。よく使われる句動詞と、それを1語で言い換えるとどうなるかを示してあります。また、両者を確認できる例文も添えました。ここに挙げる句動詞は、iTEPのライティングで最頻出するものに限っています。

分離可能な句動詞

bring up—mention, raise

- Her father's illness was a serious issue, but it was never **brought up** at the dinner table.
- Her father's illness was a serious issue, but it was never **mentioned/raised** at the dinner table.

bring up—raise

- His parents **brought up** five children in difficult circumstances.
- His parents **raised** five children in difficult circumstances.

call off—cancel

- The organizers **called** the picnic **off** due to heavy rain.
- The organizers **canceled** the picnic due to heavy rain.

242

fill out—complete

- I had to **fill** so many applications **out** for the scholarship. It was a lot of work.
- I had to **complete** so many applications for the scholarship. It was a lot of work.

find out—discover

- When she **found out** that she would be working with the famous designer, she was very excited.
- When she **discovered** that she would be working with the famous designer, she was very excited.

give back—return

- For example, my friend borrows books from me all the time but never **gives** them **back.**
- For example, my friend borrows books from me all the time but never **returns** them.

hand in—submit

- My professors at Warsaw University never allowed us to **hand** assignments **in** late.
- My professors at Warsaw University never allowed us to **submit** assignments late.

hold up—delay

- His tardiness **held up** the meeting for 30 minutes.
- His tardiness **delayed** the meeting for 30 minutes.

leave out—omit

- She told me the whole story but **left out** the little details.
- She told me the whole story but **omitted** the little details.

look up—find

- When I was student, I often **looked** words **up** in a dictionary.
- When I was student, I often **found** words in a dictionary.

make up—create

- I thought the best thing to do was to **make up** a new name for the business.
- I thought the best thing to do was to **create** a new name for the business.

pick out—choose
- She stays in the store for hours and never **picks** anything **out**.
- She stays in the store for hours and never **chooses** anything.

put off—postpone
- The deadline for the proposal was only a week away, so he did not want to **put** the meeting **off** again.
- The deadline for the proposal was only a week away, so he did not want to **postpone** the meeting again.

put out—release
- The band usually **puts out** an album once every two years.
- The band usually **releases** an album once every two years.

set up—arrange
- The CEO wanted the matter resolved, so she **set up** a conference between the two disputing vice-presidents.
- The CEO wanted the matter resolved, so she **arranged** a conference between the two disputing vice-presidents.

talk over—discuss
- At the dinner table, my family usually **talked over** what was happening in our lives.
- At the dinner table, my family usually **discussed** what was happening in our lives.

throw away—discard
- For example, in my city, too many people **throw** their trash **away** in the street.
- For example, in my city, too many people **discard** their trash in the street.

turn down—decline
- For example, his boss offered him a position in another office, but he **turned** the offer **down**.
- For example, his boss offered him a position in another office, but he **declined** the offer.

分離不可能な句動詞

get over—recover from

- It took him six months to **get over** his illness completely.
- It took him six months to **recover from** his illness completely.

go over—review

- They start every meeting by **going over** what they had discussed the previous week.
- They start every meeting by **reviewing** what they had discussed the previous week.

look into—investigate

- The boss asked me to **look into** the cause of the problem.
- The boss asked me to **investigate** the cause of the problem.

come across—find

- After I heard about the new drug on television, I **came across** many ads for it in magazines.
- After I heard about the new drug on television, I **found** many ads for it in magazines.

take after—resemble

- Her friends say she **takes after** her mother, but she thinks she takes after her father.
- Her friends say she **resembles** her mother, but she thinks she is more like her father.

wait on—serve

- The person who **waited on** us was thoughtful, so we gave her a big tip.
- The person who **served** us was thoughtful, so we gave her a big tip.

3語の他動詞句

drop out of—quit

- One problem is that many young men **drop out of** school before they graduate.
- One problem is that many young men **quit** school before they graduate.

Writing

get rid of—discard

- When people move into a smaller apartment, they often have to **get rid of** many possessions.
- When people move into a smaller apartment, they often have to **discard** many possessions.

get through with—finish

- They did not **get through with** the meeting until three in the morning.
- They did not **finish** the meeting until three in the morning.

put up with—tolerate

- The citizens of the town decided that they could no longer **put up with** motorists speeding through the downtown area.
- The citizens of the town decided that they could no longer **tolerate** motorists speeding through the downtown area.

think back on—remember

- When she **thinks back on** her days living in Africa, she becomes emotional and nostalgic.
- When she **remembers** her days living in Africa, she becomes emotional and nostalgic.

自動詞句

come back—return

- The man **came back** to his little village after many years abroad.
- The man **returned** to his little village after many years abroad.

come over—visit

- My grandfather would come over every Sunday afternoon.
- My grandfather would visit us every Sunday afternoon.

show up—arrive

- The manager asked us to **show up** to work early.
- The manager asked us to **arrive** to work early.

> **TIP** 以下のようなスラングや非常にカジュアルな言い回し、手紙や電子メール
> で使うような言葉、絵文字、不適切な表現は避けましょう。

alright	brilliant	ha ha	OMG	suck
awesome	BTW	hippy	piece of cake	tacky
babe	bum	hyper	pig	take it easy
bad	chap	icky	quack	thing
bananas	chicken	jerk	retarded	vibe
barf	cool	jock	savvy	wicked
bash	cuz	junkie	scam	wimp
beer belly	expat	LOL	screw up	wow
big deal!	fancy	looker	screwed	wuss
big time	fatso	neat	shut up!	yeah
blow away	feds	nerd	slob	yuck
blow it	go bust	newbie	sort of	yucky
boozer	goofy	Oh man!	stuff	zit

　受動態の文を使いすぎないようにしましょう。受動態は、適切に使用すれば効果的ですが、使い
すぎると、文章が退屈で面白みに欠ける読みづらいものになります。能動態の文の方が一般的に読
みやすくなります。ある専門家は、良い文章の目安として、受動態の文が占める割合を5%程度と
する人もいます。とはいえ、受動態を使うべきではない、ということではありません。このセクシ
ョンでは、受動態の最適な使い方を説明します。まずは、以下の2つの文を見てください。最初の
文は受動態です。2つ目の文は能動態で、こちらの方が適切です。

受動態

The speech was heard on the radio by millions of people.

能動態

Millions of people heard the speech on the radio.

1. 行為そのものが行為の主体よりも重要な場合は、受動態を使います。

　The restaurant was closed because of the poor sanitary conditions.

　The sign was taken down after the neighbors complained about it.

2. 行為の主体よりも行為の対象となる人や物の方が重要な場合は、受動態を使います。

   The applications were sent to 200 candidates.

   The statues were found in an old museum warehouse.

文章を洗練させる

　基本を押さえたところで、今度は細かい部分を見ていきましょう。よりフォーマルな文体を使って書くことで、ライティング・セクションのスコアを上げることができます。ただし、語句を正しく使うことが必要です。以下は、カジュアルな単語やフレーズと、それをフォーマルに言い換えた表現のリストです。適切な語句を選ぶことで、各例文のフォーマルさの程度が上がる点に注目してください。下記の例文では、スラッシュの右側にある単語やフレーズの方が左側のものよりもフォーマルです。

例文1　My friend was always able to run **a bit/a little** faster than me.

例文2　Writing good papers requires **a lot/a great** deal of time and effort.

例文3　It took him **about/approximately** five minutes to introduce the topic of the lecture.

例文4　She wrote to the hospital **about/concerning** the poor treatment her mother had received there.

例文5　He asked **about/inquired** on the cost of recording his new film.

例文6　He **asked for/requested** a raise, but his supervisor told him it was not possible.

例文7　Crime is a **big/major** problem in most American cities.

例文8　Crime is a **big/major** problem in most American cities, but many believe that the **bigger/greater** problem is the lack of economic development.

例文9　Crime is a major problem in most American cities. **But/However**, many believe that the greater problem is the lack of economic development.

例文10　For example, most families **buy/purchase** food in large quantities rather than in small packages.

例文11　When given an option, children will always **choose/select** the snack that has more sugar and calories.

例文12　The course was very useful because I **got/obtained** practical information by taking it.

例文13　Most companies project that profits will **get smaller/decrease** in the next quarter.

例文14　Many drivers stopped to **help/assist** the accident victims.

例文15　Offering a good benefits package will help companies **keep/retain** talented workers.

例文16 Good parents do not **let/permit** their children (to) participate in activities that are overly dangerous.

例文17 For example, my mother would always **make sure/ensure** that my siblings and I had a balanced breakfast before going to school.

例文18 The professor gave us **many/numerous** examples of how forests serve to keep the environment free of pollutants.

まとまりと一貫性

一貫性とは？

良い文章を書くために必要なもう一つの鍵は「一貫性」です。段落や文章に一貫性があれば、読み手は容易に内容を理解できます。文章中の要素は違いに関連があり、文章全体を通じて１つの論旨にはっきり焦点が当たっているものです。一貫性を保つことが非常に重要なのは、iTEP のライティング・パート２でも同様です。採点者には、あなたのエッセイを読むことに膨大な時間をかける余裕はないのです。あなたの文章中の主張の流れについて、採点者が少しでも疑問を抱いたり混乱をきたしたりすれば、おそらく減点してしまうでしょう。

まとまりと一貫性の違いとは？

まとまりと一貫性は、明確に理解できる文章を書くために必要な要素、という点で似ています。しかし、まとまりは、書き手の語句の使い方に関連して用いられる言葉で、これには、キーワードやフレーズ、代名詞、修飾語、つなぎ言葉などの使い方が含まれます。一方、一貫性とは、一つ一つの文に込められたアイデアに関連して用いられる言葉です。まとまりのある文章のアイデアやコンセプトは、明確で、焦点が絞られており、直接的です。簡単に言えば、「まとまり」は文章作成のテクニックに、「一貫性」は文章中のアイデアに関係しています。

まとまりはあるが、一貫性がない文章はありえるか？

ありえます。まとまりを作る言葉をたくさん使っていても、一貫性のない書き方になってしまうことがあります。下の文章を見てみましょう。書き手は文章を一つの段落にまとめる方法を分かっているのに、段落の中の主張に一貫性がありません。トピックから読んでみましょう。

Topic: What factor is most important in business—profitability or stability? State your opinion with detailed examples as support.

First, stability is one of the most valuable things that a company can provide to its workers, suppliers, and customers. Indeed, firms achieve that stability by working closely with suppliers to make sure that a high degree of quality is maintained. For example, if a company's products lose their quality, the reputation

of the business will suffer. Companies like Toyota and Apple are known for making products that meet the needs of customers. If a company fulfills its customer's needs completely, it will surely make a profit and achieve stability.

　最初、採点者は、この文章を安定について述べているものだと思うでしょう。冒頭の文は素晴らしく、提示されたトピックにうまく対応しているように見えます。しかし、この後に一貫性がなくなっていきます。焦点は、安定から品質へ、そして品質から評判へと移り始めます。また、評判から顧客のニーズへと焦点が変わります。結局、書き手は段落の最後にビジネスの安定と利益に言及することで論点を再設定しようとするものの、すでに遅く、文章全体の一貫性は失われてしまっています。書き手はまとまりを作る言葉をふんだんに使用していますが、そうした言葉は残念ながら、散らかっているアイデアをまとめられるものではありません。

一貫性はあるが、まとまりがない文章はありえるか？
　ありえます。下記がその例です。

　　　First, stability is one of the most valuable things that a company can provide to its workers, suppliers, and customers. Companies achieve stability by consistently making a profit. Ten years ago, banks in my country lost a great deal of money because they were lending money to people and companies that could not pay the banks back. The profits of the banks fell, and they stopped lending money. The banks fired many workers. If the banks had not lost money and maintained their profits, the economy in my country would have been more stable and many workers could have kept their jobs.

　では、まとまりと一貫性の両方を兼ね備えた文章を読んでみましょう。まとまりを作り出す言葉を太字で強調してあります。

　　　First, stability is one of the most valuable features that a company can provide to its workers, suppliers, and customers. **Firms** achieve **this stability** by consistently making a profit. **A good example of this** is the banking **institutions** in my country. Ten years ago, **these banks** lost a great deal of money because **they** were lending money to people and **businesses** that could not pay **them** back. The profits of **these banks** fell, and **they** stopped lending money. They also had to fire many workers. If **these banks** had not lost money and maintained **their profits**, my country's economy would have been more **stable**, and **many people** could have kept their jobs.

まとまりと一貫性のどちらが重要か？

　もちろん、文章にまとまりと一貫性の両方があることが望ましいのですが、パート2の文章では一貫性のほうがより重要です。もし文章中にまとまりを作り出す言葉がなくても、文章全体に一貫性があれば高いスコアが得られるはずです。しかし文章に一貫性がないと、すぐに減点されてしまいます。そのため、まずは論旨と冒頭の一文に集中することです。首尾一貫したまとまりのある文章は、4から5の範囲でスコアが与えられるでしょうが、そうでない文章には2または3程度しか与えられないかもしれません。

Chapter 8 実践練習

ここでは、フォーマルな文章を書く練習を行います。［正解はp. 290］

問題1

各文中の句動詞を、以下のリストから適切な動詞を選び、置き換えてください。同じ時制を使うことを忘れずに。

fluctuate	investigate	eliminate
raise	propose	intervene
establish	reduce	

1. Researchers have been looking into the problem for 15 years.

_____

_____

_____

2. This issue was brought up during the seminar.

_____

_____

_____

3. It is assumed that the management knows what is happening and will step in if there is a problem.

_____

_____

_____

4. Schools cannot altogether get rid of the problem of truancy.

Grammar

Listening

Reading

Writing

Speaking

Appendix

5. The number of staff has been cut down recently.

6. It was very difficult to find out exactly what happened.

7. House prices have a tendency to go up and down.

8. A potential solution was put forward two years ago.

問題2

以下の文中の句動詞を、よりフォーマルな単語に置き換えてください。

9. The locals could not **put up with** the visitors from the city.

10. The decline was **brought about** by cheap imports.

_____

11. The university is **thinking about** installing CCTV.

_____

12. Sales are likely to **drop off** in the third quarter.

_____

13. He **went on** speaking for over an hour.

_____

14. The meeting was **put off** until December.

_____

15. The cinema was **pulled down** 10 years ago.

_____

16. People have **cut down** their consumption of beef.

_____

問題3

文中で太字で示されている2つの語句うち、どちらがアカデミックライティングに適していますか？

17. The government has made **considerable/great** progress in solving the problem.

18. We **got/obtained** excellent results in the experiment.

19. The results of **lots of/numerous** tests have been pretty **good/encouraging**.

20. A loss of jobs is one of the **consequences/things** that will happen if the process is automated.

21. The relationship between the management and workers is **extremely/really** important.

22. Some suggestions **springing up/arising** from the study will be presented.

問題4

次の太字の語句を、よりフォーマルな語句に置き換えてください。

23. The reaction of the officials was **sort of** negative.

_____

24. The economic outlook is **nice**.

_____

25. Car manufacturers are planning a **get together** to discuss their strategy.

_____

26. The resulting competition between countries is **good**.

_____

27. The economy is affected by things that happen **outside the country**.

_____

28. She was **given the sack** because of her poor record.

_____

29. The examination results were **super**.

_____

Chapter 9 実践問題

　次の4つの小テストは、ライティング・パート1と2と同じように時間が設定されており、iTEPテストと同じようなプロンプトが使用されています。

以下のことを忘れない注意して実践問題にトライしてみてください。

▶ 時間を計って問題を解く
▶ パソコンで解答を入力する
▶ メモを取る
▶ 適切な論文を作成する
▶ 2〜3分おいて、自分の書いたものを確認する

問題1

Part 1—You have **five minutes** to write a response to the following prompt:

Topic: Write a letter to a friend about your favorite subject at school and explain why you like it.

Part 2—You have **20 minutes** to write a response to the following prompt:

Topic: Do you believe people learn more by doing or reading? Compare and contrast the knowledge learned from books with hands-on experience. Which learning experience is most valuable in your opinion?

Notes:

_____

_____

_____

_____

_____

Grammar

Listening

Reading

Writing

Speaking

Appendix

_____

_____

_____

_____

_____

_____

問題2

Part 1—You have **five minutes** to write a response to the following prompt:

Topic: Write a letter explaining who your favorite person is. Explain why.

Part 2—You have **20 minutes** to write a response to the following prompt:

Topic: Do teenagers learn the most from parents or teachers? Use detailed examples to support your opinion.

Notes:

_____

_____

_____

_____

_____

_____

_____

_____

_____

_____

問題3

Part 1—You have **five minutes** to write a response to the following prompt:

Topic: What is your favorite activity in your free time? Why is it your favorite activity?

Part 2—You have **20 minutes** to write a response to the following prompt:

Topic: People enroll in higher education with various goals and objectives in mind. In your opinion, why do most adults continue their education at a university or college?

Notes:

_____

_____

_____

_____

_____

_____

_____

_____

_____

問題4

Part 1—You have **five minutes** to write a response to the following prompt:

Topic: Who is your least favorite person? Explain what makes him/her your least favorite person.

Part 2—You have **20 minutes** to write a response to the following prompt:

Topic: Do you agree or disagree with the following statement? Children raised in urban environments grow up with more opportunities than children raised in rural environments. Use specific examples to show whether a city or a country environment is better for children.

Notes:

_____

_____

_____

_____

_____

_____

_____

_____

_____

Grammar

Listening

Reading

Writing

Speaking

Appendix

UNIT 5
SPEAKING

Introduction to SPEAKING

スピーキングは、iTEPで課される2つ目の実技試験です。iTEPのスピーキングでは、ライティングと同様に、自分の意見や見解を英語で表現する実践的なスキルが求められます。さまざまな意味で、スピーキングは英語力を測る最大の要素と考えられており、ビジネスの場でも、教室でも、英語を話す人たちと交流を持つ場面では自分の考えを言葉で伝えなければなりません。ライティングで特定の実践力が求められるのと同様に、スピーキングでも以下のような技能が求められます。

▶ 質問に対して適切に返答すること
▶ 高い語彙力を持ち、実際に使用すること
▶ 単語やフレーズを明確に発音すること

出題構成

試験時間：**5分間**

レベル：**CEFR A〜C**

パート1
CEFR A1-B2

低・中級レベルの問題を聞いて読む
30秒解答を準備する時間が与えられた後、45秒で解答

パート2
CEFR B1-C2

上級レベル。ある論点と、それに対する2つの見解が提示される
45秒解答を準備する時間が与えられた後、60秒で解答

TIP ▶ 課題に対する自分の意見を述べるという点において、スピーキングとライティングは似ていますが、根本的な違いが1つあります。問題文を聞いた後、メモを準備して解答するところは同じですが、スピーキングの場合、適切な語句を選び正確な文章を構成するだけでなく、発音にも注意し、できるだけ明確に解答を伝えなくてはなりません。
まずは、このテストに慣れることから始めましょう。

出題形式
スピーキングパート1、2ともに問題文は音声で流れると同時に、スクリーンにも表示されます。パート1は30秒で解答を準備し、45秒で解答を話す必要があります。

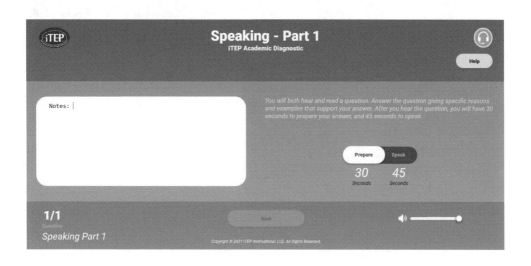

スピーキングのパート２では、ある論点とそれに対する２つの異なる見解が音声で流れます。

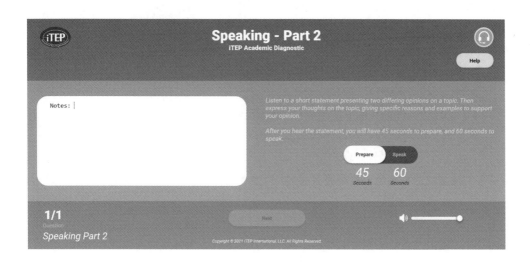

　パート２では、45秒で課題に対する自分の意見を準備し、60秒以内で話すことになります。いずれの問題でも、前の質問に戻ったり、録音のやり直しを行うことはできません。

Grammar

Listening

Reading

Writing

Speaking

Appendix

> **TIP** ▶ スピーキングでは、解答の明瞭さにスコアが大きく影響します。始める前に、ヘッドフォンを調整し、マイクが適切な位置にあることを確認し、自分の解答を明瞭に録音できるようにしましょう。

Speaking

Chapter 1　スピーキングの基本的なスキル

スピーキングのスキルを高めよう

　スピーキングのスコアは、質問に対してどれだけ明確かつ効果的に解答したかによって決まります。まず、解答は課題に関連したものでなければなりません。例えば、歴史上の重要人物について話すように指示されているのに、自分の好きなデザートについて話した場合、例えそのデザートについて多くの啓発的で有益なことを話したとしても、間違った解答であるとして減点されてしまいます。

　ですから、重要なのは質問に正確に答えることです。有名人について話す課題であれば、有名人について話し、家族の誰かについて話す課題であれば、両親やいとこなどの身近な人について話すようにしましょう。学校についての質問があった場合は、学校での経験について話す必要があります。課題に対して忠実に解答を行いましょう。

高スコアを出すための4つのポイント

- ▶ Key #1：課題に対して忠実に解答する
- ▶ Key #2：正確に、正しく話す
- ▶ Key #3：詳細や例を挙げて主張を補足する
- ▶ Key #4：話す内容の正誤は気にしない

Key #1：課題に対して忠実に解答する：上で述べたように、必ず問題文に沿った解答を行うようにしましょう。

Key #2：正確に、正しく話す：スピーキングでは文法や構文が厳密に評価されるわけではありませんが、構成がしっかりしていれば解答の質が高まり、印象も良くなりますので、正しい文法で話すように心がけましょう。

Key #3：詳細や例を挙げて主張を補足する：話し上手になる秘訣の一つは、明確な発信を行うことです。聞き手に話を理解してもらうためには、まず自分自身がその話を理解していなければなりません。決められた時間内に十分なメモを用意し、答えを準備しておくことで、自信を持って話すことができます。

Key #4：話す内容の正誤は気にしない： このセクションでは、課題に対する意見を求められますが、最終的な評価はあなたの意見がどのようなものかではなく、あくまでどのように表現したかで決定されます。臆することなく、自信を持って話してください。

> **TIP**　もう一つ大事なことは、解答するよう指示があったら、すぐに発言を始めることです。第一印象を良くするには、しっかりとしたスタートを切りましょう。

準備はできましたか？　さっそく始めましょう！

Speaking

Chapter 2 スピーキング・パート1

　スピーキングのパート1では、カジュアルなトピックについて簡単な内容で話すことを求められます。好きな食べ物、行ってみたい国、会ってみたい人など、内容は比較的身近なものになるでしょう。繰り返しになりますが、内容に正解・不正解はないので、正直に話しましょう。

　次のページに、パート1で出題される例題を載せています（例題1）。30秒で解答を準備し、45秒で解答を話します。解答の準備にメモを取ってもかまいません。実際のテストでは、メモは画面上に直接入力することができます。45秒以内で、できるだけ長く解答するようにしましょう。そのためには、30秒を有効に使って、トピックに即した解答を準備するようにしてください。

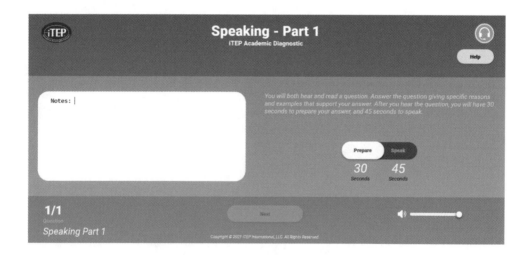

高スコアを出すには、質の高い準備が必要

　解答への準備がしっかりできていればいるほど、よりスムーズに話すことができることを覚えておいてください。正式なスピーチではないので、言うことをすべて書き留めておく必要はありませんが、自信を持って話すために、必ずメモを取るようにしましょう。それでは、例題を見てみましょう。

例題1

> Think of ONE person from history whom you would like to meet. Who is that one person and what would you ask him or her?

解答を考える前に、まずは前述した4つのポイントのうち **Key #1** を思い出しましょう。

▶ Key #1：課題に対して忠実に解答する

頭を働かせて、話題に挙げやすい人を思い浮かべてみましょう。

例として、19世紀の歴史上の重要人物であるトーマス・エジソンを考えてみましょう。

次に、話すときに使用するメモを用意します。このメモを完全な文章や、一字一句読むための台本にする必要はありません。

Why might someone like to meet Thomas Edison?

ここでは、解答の際に必ず触れておきたいポイントをいくつか紹介します。

    1. 発明家
    2. 電気を使う方法を発見した
    3. 発明と発見で世界を変えた

次に、残りの時間で、なぜこの話題にエジソンを選んだのかを考えてみましょう。個人的に何かつながりがありますか？ それは学校で彼について学んだことですか？ 本で読んだり、映画で見たりしたものですか？ 今、日常で目にしている何かについて、彼に質問してみたいことはありますか？

    1. 学校で彼について学んだ
    2. 彼の献身的な姿勢に感銘を受けた
    3. 今日の世界の技術についてどう思うか聞いてみたい

これで、6つの話す材料の準備ができました。これらをまとめていくのですが、まずは解答をどのように始めるかを考えましょう。最初にあなたが質問を理解し、適切な解答ができることを、明確に示すことが重要です。そのためには、課題文を解答に組み込んでしまうことです。例えば、次のような解答が望ましいものです。

If I could meet one person from history, the person I would choose is Thomas Edison.

Speaking

これは良い始め方です。正確で長すぎず、採点者に自分が良い解答を準備し、この後も解答を続ける準備ができていることを示せています。

次に、メモを見ながら、それを明確で首尾一貫した文章にまとめましょう。最初の3つのメモについて考えてみます。

　　　1. 発明者
　　　2. 電気を使う方法を発見した
　　　3. 発明と発見で世界を変えた

これらをまとめると、以下のようになります。

パート1解答例

Thomas Edison was an incredible inventor who invented many things that changed the world. He was the first person to make electricity available for people to use in their homes. He also invented the telephone and the record player.

次に、残りの時間で、残っているメモを使ってさらに充実した解答になるようにしましょう。それができるとスコアをさらに向上させることができます。

　　　1. 学校で彼について学んだ
　　　2. 彼の献身的な姿勢に感銘を受けた
　　　3. 今日の世界の技術についてどう思うか聞いてみたい

I enjoyed learning about Edison in school, hearing about how hard he worked; he barely slept at all! I would like to ask him what he thinks of the technology in the world today and if he ever thought his inventions would still be around today.

情報が豊富であるにもかかわらず、自然な構成となっています。また、**he barely slept at all**のような、ちょっとした言い回しを入れることで、単なるスピーチではなく、考えながら話していることをアピールするとよいでしょう。

では、これまで学んだことをおさらいしてみましょう。まず、再度例題を見てみましょう。

例題1

Think of ONE person from history whom you would like to meet. Who is that one person and what would you ask him or her?

そして、下記がトーマス・エジソンについて作成したメモです。

1. 発明家
2. 電気を使う方法を発見した
3. 発明と発見で世界を変えた
4. 学校で彼について学んだ
5. 彼の献身的な姿勢に感銘を受けた
6. 今日の世界の技術についてどう思うか聞いてみたい

その結果、以下のような解答例を作ることができます。

If I could meet one person from history, the person I would choose is Thomas Edison. Thomas Edison was a great inventor who invented so many things that changed the world. He was the first person to make electricity available for people to use in their homes. He also invented the telephone and the record player. I enjoyed learning about Edison in school, hearing about how hard he worked; he barely slept at all! I would like to ask him what he thinks of the technology in the world today and if he ever thought his inventions would still be around today.

その調子です！

 TIP ▶ スピーキングは、「実際に話す」ことなしには上達しません。話す練習ができる場所で、この解答を声に出して練習してみてください。さらに、自分の声を録音すれば、自分の声を聞くことができますし、自分の良いところや改善できるところを発見することができます。

ここまで、iTEPスピーキングのパート1で高得点を取るために必要な基本的なスキルを学んできました。次は、パート2を見てみましょう。

Speaking

Chapter 3 スピーキング・パート2

出題形式

　スピーキングのパート2では、提示されたある課題と、それについての2つの異なる意見について話すことを求められます。

　解答を準備する時間は45秒、発言時間は60秒です。残り時間が画面に表示されます。

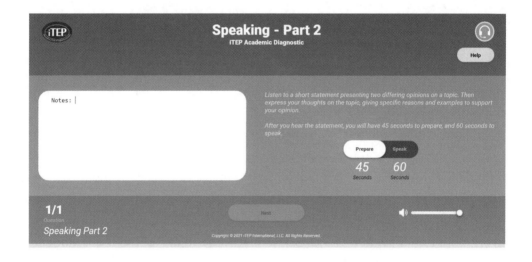

　問題文は画面と音声の両方で確認できます。問題を見てしっかりとメモを取ることが重要です。問題文の音声が終了したら、さらに45秒間、解答を準備する時間が与えられます。解答を準備するためのメモは画面に直接入力します。また、自分の意見を裏付ける理由や例を示す必要があるので、そのことにも注意してメモを取りましょう。音声がしっかり録音できているかどうかがスコアに直接影響するため、ヘッドフォンがしっかりと固定されていること、マイクが口から適切な距離にあることも確認してください。

　以下は、このセクションで出題される問題の例です。解答を準備するためにメモを取ってください。45秒でそのトピックについての解答を準備し、60秒で発言します。

例題1

Many works of art from the past, such as paintings and sculptures, have been taken from the countries that produced them and put on display in museums in other countries. Some people say that these works of art should be returned to the countries that produced them.

Other people say that the works of art should remain in the museums where they are now because they are safe and can be viewed and appreciated by more people.

What are your thoughts on this topic?

パート1と同様に、パート2でもメモを準備することから始めましょう。課題がパート1とは異なるため、メモの内容も少し異なることを念頭に置いておきましょう。一つのアプローチは、自分が選んだ考え方の利点を列挙することです。例えば、「美術品は返還されるべきだ」という意見を選んだ場合、下記のような文で解答を始めることができます。

I believe that art should be returned to the country that produced it.

意見が決まれば、メモを作成することができます。そのためには、質問を考えます。ここでは、「芸術作品がその作品を生み出した国のものであるべき理由は何か」という質問がよいでしょう。

例として、以下のようなメモを作ることができます。
1. 芸術作品はその国のアイデンティティーの一部である。
2. 芸術作品はその国のものである。
3. 人々が芸術作品を見たいと思えば、その作品が帰属する国を訪れればよい。
4. 芸術作品は、それが帰属する国の人々にインスピレーションを与える。

答えを準備するときには、採点ポイントを意識しましょう。

高スコアを出すための4つのポイント
- ▶Key #1：課題に対して忠実に解答する
- ▶Key #2：正確に、正しく話す
- ▶Key #3：詳細や例を挙げて主張を補足する

Speaking

▶Key #4：話す内容の正誤は気にしない

したがって、メモを参考にして、以下のような答えを作成することができます。

パート２解答例

　　　　Key #1 I believe that art should be returned to the country that produced it. **Key #2** Art is an important part of a country's identity. **Key #3** For example, when people think of Italy, they think of seeing Michelangelo's sculptures in Florence. **Key #3** On my school trip to London, we learned a lot about British history by visiting the National Portrait Museum. **Key #4** If I were from Italy, I would not want to leave the country and travel to another part of the world to see some of my country's culture. I think I would feel more patriotic and excited about my country if I could show visitors some of the best art made by my country's artists. For these reasons, I think that art belongs in the same country as the artists who make it.

　　問題文を再掲します。

> Many works of art from the past, such as paintings and sculptures, have been taken from the countries that produced them and put on display in museums in other countries. Some people say that these works of art should be returned to the countries that produced them.
>
> Other people say that the works of art should remain in the museums where they are now because they are safe and can be viewed and appreciated by more people.
>
> What are your thoughts on this topic?

メモは以下のとおりです。
1. 芸術作品はその国のアイデンティティーの一部である。
2. 芸術作品はその国のものである。
3. 人々が芸術作品を見たいと思えば、その作品が帰属する国を訪れればよい。
4. 芸術作品は、それが帰属する国の人々にインスピレーションを与える。

　　先に進む前に、パート２の解答例をよく見て、さらに良くするためのポイントを身につけましょう。記入欄にあなたの考えを書いてみてください。

1. 解答の良い点はどこですか？

_____

_____

_____

　次に、高得点を取るためのポイントに沿って解答を検証しましょう。

2. 解答では、立場をはっきりと選んでいますか？　解答の冒頭部分で明確に述べていますか？

_____

_____

_____

_____

3. 解答では、自分の立場を裏付けるためにいくつかのポイントを挙げていますか？　言葉の使い方は正確ですか？

_____

_____

_____

_____

4. これが説得力のある解答であるかどうか、自問自答してください。なぜ説得力のある解答なのでしょうか？　あるいは、なぜ説得力のある解答ではないのでしょうか？　前ページのヒントに照らして、話し手は、効果的な解答を作るためのガイドラインを守っていたでしょうか？　この解答を改善するには、どのような方法が考えられますか？

_____

_____

_____

_____

　次の章では、解答をいっそう説得力あるものにし、スコアをいっそう高くするための、さらなるスキルを学習します。

Speaking

Chapter 4　高度なスピーキング スキル

スピーキング・パート2における、高度な課題と解答の例

　ここまで、効果的なスピーキングの解答を作成するための、4つのポイントについて学習してきました。あらためて、この4つのポイントを以下に挙げます。

高スコアを出すための4つのポイント

▸ Key #1：課題に対して忠実に解答する
▸ Key #2：正確に、正しく話す
▸ Key #3：詳細や例を挙げて主張を補足する
▸ Key #4：話す内容の正誤は気にしない

　作成した2つの解答例を検討する際に、解答をより良くするための他の要素に気づいたかもしれません。ここでは、さらにスコアを伸ばすための4つのポイントを紹介します。

スピーキングの高度なポイント

▸ Key #1A：語彙や文体に幅を持たせる
▸ Key #2A：自然な会話の流れを作る
▸ Key #3A：話しながら文法を修正する
▸ Key #4A：強く締めくくる

1. 語彙や文体に幅を持たせる——多様なフレーズや表現、単語を容易に使いこなせるようになると、解答がより良くなります。
2. 自然な会話の流れを作る——解答の中で複数のアイデアを比較したり対比したりするときには、それらのアイデアを明確に伝えるために正確な切り替えのフレーズを使います。
3. 話しながら文法を修正する——動詞の形を間違えるなど、誤りを犯した場合には、ためらわずにすぐに修正して次に進みましょう。訂正することで、採点者に自分の誤りを修正する能力があることを示すことができます。
4. 強く締めくくる——解答の最後に、自分の考えを簡潔にまとめた強い結論の文を置くことにより、自分の考えを簡潔にまとめて、採点者に強い印象を与えることができます。

　それでは、以前に作成した解答を検討して、4つの高度なポイントがどこで使われているかを見てみましょう。

> 　　　I believe that art should be returned to the country that produced it. Art is an important part of a country's identity. **Key#2A** For example, when people think of Italy, they think of seeing Michelangelo's sculptures in Florence. On my school trip to London, we learned a lot about British history by visiting the National Portrait Museum. **Key#4A** If I were from Italy, I would not want to leave the country and travel to another part of the world to see some of my country's culture. I think I would feel more **Key#1A** patriotic and excited about my country if I could show visitors some of the best art made by my country's artists. **Key#2/4A** For these reasons, I think that art belongs in the same country as the artists who make it.

1. 語彙や文体に幅を持たせる——patrioticやexcitedといった単語を使っているのが良く、またこの解答は、長く複雑な文構造を用いています。
2. 自然な会話の流れを作る——for exampleやfor these reasonsといった、会話の流れを作るフレーズを巧みに用いています。
3. 話しながら文法を修正する——明らかな誤りがないため、修正すべき点はほとんどありません。
4. 強く締めくくる——最後の文はもっと強めることができますが、適切な流れをつくるフレーズが含まれており、課題における問題に関する立場を明確に再提示しています。

　それでは、別の解答例を見てみましょう。

> **例題2**
>
> The Internet and cell phones have revolutionized how people communicate with each other. But some people say that even though the technology has changed, the communication is the same.
>
> Do you agree or disagree that communication between people has fundamentally changed?

解答例

> 　　　It's true, I do believe that today with Internet, with SMS, with text messaging, with cell phones, and with emails, people do have a quicker way of communicating

Speaking

with each other. Actually, it was my birthday recently, and I was quite surprised to see how many people left birthday wishes for me on my Facebook—people who otherwise wouldn't have sent me a postcard or a letter. And I also feel that this has changed how people communicate with each other. In some ways they are more friendly; they are happy to wish everyone a happy birthday. But, they also don't know people very well because they know—or think they know—so many people. I guess it is a question of quality and quantity. With that in mind, I would say that technology has certainly changed how people communicate with each other.

それでは、この解答について検討しましょう。

1. この解答の良い点は何ですか？

　トピックを直接扱い、自分の発言の裏付けとなる具体的な情報を用いています。

次に、この解答が点数アップのポイントを用いているかどうかを見てみましょう。

2. 解答は明確な立場を選択していますか？　その立場は解答の中で明確に述べられていますか？

　はい、最初と最後に述べられています。

3. 解答は、立場を裏づけるポイントを複数用いていますか？　言葉使いは正確ですか？

　はい、otherwiseやactuallyといった言葉が効果的に用いられています。

4. これが説得力のある解答かどうかを考えてみましょう。その理由は何でしょうか？

5. この解答をより良くする方法として、どのようなものが考えられますか？

Speaking

Chapter 5 練習問題

　ここまで、iTEPのスピーキングテストの解答をどのように準備するか、また、高得点を取るためのポイントや4つの高度なポイントなど、説得力のある解答を生み出す要素について学んできました。それでは、これまでの学習の成果を試してみましょう。皆さんが、実際のiTEPのスピーキング用課題を使って練習を始める番です。

　ここで重要なヒントがありますので、よく肝に銘じておきましょう。

> **TIP**　　　**声を出してスピーキングの解答を練習しなければなりません。**

　先に述べたように、iTEPのライティングとスピーキングの根本的な違いは、「話すこと」です。黙って心の中で答えを言っているだけでは、スピーキングの練習にはなりません。効果的に練習し、上達を実感するには、声に出して話さなければなりません。また、自分の解答から学び、より良いものにするためには、自分の解答を録音して聞くようにしましょう。

　ここでは、iTEPのスピーキングの練習のための簡単な4つのステップを紹介します。

P - P - R - R
Prep, Practice, Review, Repeat
（準備、練習、レビュー、反復）

Prep（準備）　　　――　課題を読み、課題について自分用の個人メモを作成します。

Practice（練習）　――　解答を口に出し、できれば自分の声を録音します。

Review（レビュー）――　自分の解答を聞き、どのくらい上手に言えたか、どこを改善できるかをメモします。

Repeat（反復）　　――　もう一度やってみましょう！　英語を話すことについては、練習こそが上達の鍵です。反復と十分な練習ほどスキルを上げてくれるものはありません。

　もう一度、iTEPのスピーキングで高スコアを取るための4つのポイントを振り返ってみましょう。

高スコアを出すための 4 つのポイント

▶ Key #1：課題に対して忠実に解答する
▶ Key #2：正確に、正しく話す
▶ Key #3：詳細や例を挙げて主張を補足する
▶ Key #4：話す内容の正誤は気にしない

練習問題 1

準備時間：30秒
話す時間：45秒

Some people work for one company for most of their lives. Other people work for several different companies. Which do you think is better?

Talk about which you think is better and why you think so.

準備時間：30秒

メモ：

_____

_____

_____

_____

_____

話す時間：45秒　始めましょう！

解答をレビューする

良い点：

_____

_____

_____

Speaking

改善すべき点:

練習問題2

準備時間：30秒
話す時間：45秒

> Some people use the Internet for finding important information while others use it to connect to people. What is one way that you use the Internet? How does it help you?
>
> Talk about one way that you use the Internet that is helpful to you.

準備時間：30秒

メモ：

話す時間：45秒　始めましょう！

解答をレビューする

良い点:

_____

_____

_____

_____

_____

改善すべき点:

_____

_____

_____

_____

_____

さらにスコアを伸ばすための4つのポイント

　次の3つの課題はパート2のためのもので、より長い解答が要求されます。解答に、スピーキングの高度なポイントを含めるようにしましょう。

スピーキングの高度なポイント
- ▶ Key #1A：語彙や文体の幅を持たせる
- ▶ Key #2A：自然な会話の流れを作る
- ▶ Key #3A：話しながら文法を修正する
- ▶ Key #4A：強く締めくくる

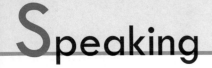

Speaking

練習問題3

準備時間：45秒
話す時間：60秒

> Many countries are very concerned about saving the environment and have very restrictive laws to limit pollution. They insist that other nations follow these laws and restrictions as well. Some other nations say they have other priorities and can't afford to follow such restrictions. They say each nation should have the right to choose for itself. What do you think? Should all nations agree to the same laws about the environment, or should each country have the right to choose for itself?
>
> Talk about which you think is better and why you think so.

準備時間：45秒

メモ：

_____

_____

_____

_____

_____

_____

話す時間：60秒　始めましょう！

解答をレビューする

良い点：

_____

_____

_____

_____

_____

改善すべき点：

_____

_____

_____

_____

_____

練習問題 4

準備時間：45秒
話す時間：60秒

In many countries, lawmakers fund public projects by increasing taxes on all items that are sold. These items are called purchased goods. Opponents to these plans say that it would be fairer to tax based on income instead of sales. Which is a better solution? Should taxes be based on the sale of goods or on people's incomes?

Talk about which you think is better and why you think so.

準備時間：45秒

メモ：

_____

_____

_____

_____

_____

_____

話す時間：60秒　始めましょう！

Speaking

解答をレビューする

良い点：

_____

_____

_____

_____

_____

改善すべき点：

_____

_____

_____

_____

_____

練習問題 5

準備時間：45秒
話す時間：60秒

Certain schools restrict students' access to cell phones and mobile devices, saying that students' use of these devices distracts from learning in the classroom. Some students' parents insist that it is important for their children to have their phones at all times in case of emergencies. What are your thoughts on this question? Should schools be allowed to restrict students' use of cell phones and mobile devices?

Talk about which position is better and why you think so.

準備時間：45秒

メモ：

_____

_____

_____

_____

_____

話す時間：60秒　始めましょう！

解答をレビューする

良い点：

_____

_____

_____

_____

改善すべき点：

_____

_____

_____

_____

_____

Grammar

Listening

Reading

Writing

Speaking

Appendix

Speaking

まとめ

● iTEPのスピーキングテストには、準備と練習が要求されます。
● 準備：アイデアを検討して、自分用のメモを書きます。
● 練習：声を出し、練習を録音します。
● 聞く：自分の解答を聞いて、再度やってみましょう。

1. できるだけ多く英語で話す練習をしましょう。
2. 英語のネイティブスピーカーに話しかけて、自分の発音が正しいかどうか聞いてみましょう。インターネットを活用して、英語のネイティブスピーカーの話を聞きましょう。
3. レコーダーに向かって話す練習をした後、自分の解答を聞いて、より明瞭な話し方を身につけましょう。事前に指示や質問の種類を把握しておきましょう。
4. テストを受ける前に、スピーキングのポイントについて準備しましょう。解答のアイデアを考えましょう。準備時間を利用して、スピーチのポイントを考えておきましょう。
5. 長い解答(パート2)に対処するには、準備時間を利用してメモを作りましょう。制限時間内に質問に完全に答えるようにしましょう。
6. 流れを作る表現を使って、スピーチの趣旨とその裏付けとなるポイントを明確にしましょう。趣旨を裏付けて展開するために、具体的な詳細や例を挙げましょう。
7. 言葉を正確に使い、落ち着いて話しましょう。
8. 友好的な聞き手に向かっているつもりで話しましょう。友達や先生に向かって話していることを想像するとよいでしょう。
9. 録音した自分の解答を聞きながら、長い母音や、子音の組み合わせなど、難しいと感じる特定の音がないか確認しましょう。あらゆる言語は、特定の音素（その言語に共通する音の単位）によって識別されます。英語の中に、これまであなたが聞いたことのない音素があるかもしれません。そのような音を見つけたら、口に出す練習をしてみましょう。

   練習、練習、練習！　反復練習が大切です。

Appendix

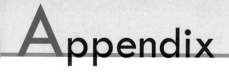

Appendix

正解

Unit 1 Grammar

Chapter 1	
Part 1	
1	A
2	B
3	A
4	C
5	A
6	B
7	A
Part 2	
8	B
9	D
10	A
11	B
12	A
13	D
14	D
15	B
Chapter 2	
Part 1	
1	A
2	C
3	A
4	C
5	D
6	C
7	D
8	C
Part 2	
9	B
10	A
11	C
12	B
13	C
14	B
15	A

Chapter 3	
Part 1	
1	B
2	B
3	C
4	C
5	D
6	D
7	B
8	B
Part 2	
9	B
10	A
11	D
12	A
13	B
14	A
Chapter 4	
Part 1	
1	A
2	B
3	C
4	C
5	A
6	D
7	D
8	B
Part 2	
9	A
10	C
11	B
12	C
13	B
Chapter 5	
Part 1	
1	A

2	C
3	A
4	C
5	B
6	A
7	A
Part 2	
8	B
9	D
10	D
11	C
12	C
13	D
14	C
15	C
Chapter 6	
Part 1	
1	B
2	A
3	D
4	C
5	D
6	B
7	B
Part 2	
8	D
9	B
10	A
11	B
12	B
13	C
Chapter 7	
Part 1	
1	C
2	A
3	B

4	D
5	B
6	D
7	B
8	B
Part 2	
9	B
10	B
11	D
12	C
13	D
14	D
Chapter 8	
Part 1	
1	C
2	D
3	B
4	A
5	B
6	A
7	A
Part 2	
8	A
9	D
10	D
11	A
12	D
13	D
14	A
Chapter 9	
Part 1	
1	C
2	A
3	D
4	B
5	C

6	D
7	C
8	B
Part 2	
9	C
10	C
11	D
12	A
13	D
14	A
Chapter 10	
Part 1	
1	C
2	B
3	D
4	A
5	B
6	B
7	C
8	B
Part 2	
9	A
10	A
11	A
12	A
13	B
14	C
15	A
Chapter 11	
Part 1	
1	C
2	D
3	A
4	D
5	D
6	B

7	C
Part 2	
8	C
9	D
10	D
11	C

12	C
13	A
Chapter 12	
Part 1	
1	D
2	B

3	D
4	D
5	B
6	A
7	A
8	B

Part 2	
9	B
10	B
11	C
12	A
13	C

14	C
15	A

Unit 2 Listening

SLATE	
Part 1	
1	C
2	C
3	D
4	D
Part 2	
5	B

6	D
7	D
8	C
Part 3	
9	C
10	A
11	D
12	C

13	C
14	D
Academic	
Part 1	
1	A
2	D
3	C
4	A

Part 2	
5	C
6	A
7	D
8	A
Part 3	
9	A
10	C

11	D
12	A
13	A
14	C

Unit 3 Reading

SLATE	
Part 1	
1	C
2	D
Part 2	
1	C

2	D
3	B
4	D
5	A
6	B
7	A

Academic	
Part 1	
1	D
2	C
3	B
4	C

5	B
6	C
7	A
8	C
Part 2	
1	C

2	C
3	C
4	D
5	A
6	D
7	B,C,D

Unit 4 Writing

Chapter 2
Examples 1 & 2

Example 2 is the stronger essay. The writer of example 2 forms more developed paragraphs and demonstrates control of more complex sentence structures and vocabulary. For example, the author of example 1 writes, "When they become scarce the costs will go up and this will hurt poor countries and poor people." The example 2 author writes, "Scarcity will cause prices to go up, hurting poor countries and poor people." This sentence shows an example of a reduced causative clause connector. The use of "scarcity" shows an advanced vocabulary and usage.

Examples 3 & 4

Example 3 is the stronger essay for one simple reason. The author of example 3 maintains the same unifying topic throughout the whole essay. The author of example 4 jumps from one topic to another and therefore does not

Grammar Listening Reading Writing Speaking Appendix

Appendix

answer the question properly. The prompt asks for "one charitable cause," but the example 4 author gives three.

Chapter 4
Thesis Statements
1. weak
2. weak
3. weak
4. strong
5. strong
6. weak
7. weak
8. weak
9. weak
10. weak
11. weak
12. strong

Chapter 8
Practice Exercises
Exercise 1
1. looking into = investigating
2. brought up = raised
3. step in = intervene
4. get rid of = eliminate
5. cut down = reduced
6. find out = establish
7. go up and down = fluctuate
8. put forward = proposed

Exercise 2 (possible answers)
9. tolerate, handle
10. started, created
11. debating
12. decline, fall, decrease, shrink
13. continued
14. postponed
15. demolished
16. reduced

Exercise 3
17. considerable
18. obtained
19. numerous / encouraging
20. consequences
21. extremely
22. arising

Exercise 4 (possible answers)
23. slightly
24. encouraging
25. meeting
26. beneficial
27. internationally, abroad
28. fired, terminated, dismissed
29. superior

SLATE リスニング・スクリプト

SLATE Part 1 (p. 99)

1. Schedule
Woman: So, have you gotten your schedule for next week?

Man: Yeah, my boss said I can have that Sunday off because I told him about our trip.

Woman: Perfect! This is going to be so much fun.

2. The Dance
Woman: Do you think you're going to ask her to the dance this weekend?

Man: Well, I don't know yet. I am mostly just afraid that she is going to say no.

Woman: You just have to see for yourself. You'll never know until you try!

3. The Paper
Woman: Did you finish the paper that I assigned?

Man: Yes, I finished it last night. Would you like me to email it to you, or should I bring in a paper copy?

Woman: It's best if you email it.

4. Would It Be Okay?
Boy: Would it be okay for me to go meet up with some friends before the football game?

Woman: That's fine, as long as you finished picking up the clothes in your room.

Boy: Shoot! I haven't done that yet. I'll go do it right now so that I can go.

SLATE Part 2 (p. 99)

Too Much Homework

Man: Mrs. Jones, do you have a minute to talk to me about the homework that you assigned?

Woman: Sure, David. Are you having a problem understanding the material?

Man: No, it's not that. I like the way that you explained how to figure out these math problems. I actually enjoy this type of math.

Woman: Well, thank you. I'm glad that you are enjoying the material. But what is it that you want to talk about?

Man: Actually, I just don't feel it is fair to expect us to do this much homework. You know that this isn't my only class. I have a project that I am working on for my history class and I have a paper that is due tomorrow for my literature class.

Woman: Oh, well I appreciate you coming to me with your concern. But tonight's assigned homework should only take you about 30 minutes to complete.

Man: Are you serious? I could see it taking me three hours or more.

Woman: Three hours? I'm only asking that you complete the assignment at the end of the third chapter.

Man: But doesn't that include doing all of the practice quizzes in the third chapter and the practice test at the end?

Woman: No, you don't have to do those. All I'm asking for you to complete is the assignment that is printed on the last page of the chapter. It is the section that comes before the practice test.

Man: Oh, I am so sorry, Mrs. Jones. I thought for sure that you meant for us to complete all of the questions that are included throughout the third chapter. And I took that to mean that we also had to do all of the practice quizzes and the practice test.

Woman: I'm sorry, David. I can see how you could have been confused by the way that I explained the assignment. I definitely could have done a better job at giving the instructions for tonight's homework.

Man: Oh, it's okay. But Mrs. Jones, I don't think I am the only student who was confused.

Woman: Why do you say that?

Man: Because I heard Josh and Jake complaining about the number of hours of homework that they think you assigned for us to do. I'm pretty sure that they also think we have to complete all of the practice quizzes and the practice test.

Woman: Well, if I have confused multiple students, then it was definitely my fault for not doing a better job of explaining the assignment.

Man: I'm just afraid that Josh and Jake are going to stress themselves out tonight.

Woman: I don't want them to stress out because I made a mistake.

Man: They are already on the bus. But I could call them when I get home and let them know that all we have to do is the short assignment.

Woman: That would be awesome if you would do that for me. Thank you so much, David.

SLATE Part 3 (p. 100)

Lecture—Pavlov's Dog Experiment

Alright everyone, sit down and take out a piece of paper and a pencil. We're going to talk about one of the experiments you read about in your textbook last night—Ivan Pavlov's famous dog experiment. I know the reading assigned last night about the experiment was a little hard to understand. I promise you, though, that this is actually a very simple experiment and a very important one, too. I'll simplify it for you. The reading talked a bit about the scientist in charge of this experiment, right? His name was Ivan Pavlov. He lived during the 1800s in Russia and was a very smart and well-respected man. He's most well-known for his dog experiment, the one you read about last night, but he also researched human anatomy, too.

Right, so like I said, I know the reading about the experiment was kind of hard to understand. Really, Pavlov's experiment was very simple and actually, that's the way it is with most experiments in psychology. The experiments are really simple but the results are important. Pavlov conducted his experiment at a medical school in the 1890s. He started his experiment by stating, "There are some things a dog doesn't have to learn." That's true, right?

A dog doesn't have to learn to blink or breathe or salivate, which is just when they create saliva (or spit) in their mouths. And neither do we, right? No one taught you any of those things. That's because all of those actions are instincts. We are born knowing how to do these things; they happen automatically. Pavlov took his idea that there are some things dogs don't have to learn how to do such as to salivate, or create saliva, and he created an entire experiment around it.

Pavlov said that the actions dogs don't have to learn how to do, such as creating saliva, are reflexes, or unconditioned responses. No one had to condition—or teach—the dog how to create saliva. Pavlov tested that idea a little bit. He took some dogs and he set food in front of them. The dogs saw and smelled that food and they started to drool, of course, because they wanted to eat the food. And Pavlov wondered if he could train—or condition—the dogs to drool when he didn't set any food in front of them. Could he make them automatically create saliva? Pavlov decided that he was going to use a bell. He called the bell a neutral stimulus, which basically just means the bell had nothing to do with the dogs or their food; if Pavlov rang the bell it wouldn't make the dogs automatically do anything. Pavlov went back to his dogs and he put the food in front of them except this time, when he put the food in front of them, he rang the bell. And he did this over and over and over again.

Give the dog food; ring the bell. Give the dog food; ring the bell. Eventually, after he did this enough times, he rang the bell but he didn't give the dogs any food. And even though he didn't give the dogs any food, the dogs began to salivate when they heard him ring the bell. He called their response, how they began to drool when there was no food and just a bell, he called that a conditioned response because he conditioned, or taught them, to do that automatically. And he called the bell, which used to be a neutral stimulus, a conditioned stimulus because now, when he rang it, the dogs automatically did something. And that's the whole experiment. It's pretty simple, right?

It's just some dogs, some food, a bell, and saliva. But this experiment actually was a major breakthrough back then and is considered to be one of the most important experiments in psychology.

And if you think about it, you might even kind of see Pavlov's experiment at work in your own life with your own dog. For example, your dog's leash is really just a piece of fabric, right? But when you pick up your dog's leash your dog probably gets really excited and starts jumping around because he has learned that the leash means he gets to go on a walk. The leash was a neutral stimulus, but now it's a conditioned stimulus. Your dog getting excited was an unconditioned response, but now it's a conditioned response. Pavlov's findings are at work in your own life!

Academic リスニング・スクリプト

Academic Part 1 (p. 101)

1. 82nd Street

Woman: Excuse me, does this bus go to 82nd Street?

Man: This bus goes to 82nd Street and Main Street, but if you want to get to 82nd and Broad Street, you'll have to wait for the next bus.

Woman: I need to go to Broad Street, so I'll wait for the next bus.

2. Dishes

Man: There are a lot of dishes in the sink, and I think it's your turn to wash them.

Woman: I think it's you turn, actually. I just washed them yesterday.

Man: Oh, I forgot. I will get started on them in a few minutes.

3. The Last Question

Woman: I'm worried that my answer for the last one on our homework assignment is incorrect.

Man: I left my assignment at home, and I don't remember what I wrote. Maybe I can call you when I get back, and we can compare our answers.

Woman: That would be good. I should be home by 8 p.m.

4. Presentation

Man: I'm scheduled to give a presentation in class next Tuesday, but I will be out of town.

Woman: I guess we will have to reschedule your presentation. Are any of your classmates willing to switch days?

Man: I will ask a few people and see what they say.

Academic Part 2 (p. 101)

Applying for Loans

Man: Still searching for scholarships on the web?

Woman: Yeah, I've found a few I want to apply to. A couple are asking me to fill out a form.

Man: The government loan? Yeah, it's online. Go to studentloans.ed.gov and complete it.

Woman: I really don't have time today.

Man: It took me only about fifteen minutes.

Woman: Okay, but I don't have a job or good credit history.

Man: That doesn't matter. They ask you about your parents' income, but only if you depend on them for money. They'll also ask about which school you're attending, what year you are in school and when you intend to graduate.

Woman: Sounds pretty easy. So I really need to fill it out if I want scholarship money?

Man: You won't need it to apply for every scholarship, but based on their determination, you may qualify for government loans, grants, and maybe federal work study.

Woman: How much did you pay for the application fee?

Man: Nothing. It's free. Just go to the home page and click the tab that says, "Free Application."

Woman: Wow. Sounds too good to be true.

Man: It really isn't. And you can fill it out on your own time. If you start the application and have to stop in the middle, save it under your account.

Woman: I have to set up an account? Ugh! Sounds tiresome.

Man: It's not tiresome. You just need to create a user name and password. It's similar to setting up an email account. Once you have your email and password, begin the application. And like I said, you don't have to fill out the entire form in one sitting. You can always save it and go back to it. Just remember to get it done by the deadline.

Woman: There's a deadline?

Man: I think the deadline is June 30th for the upcoming school year. Check the website to make sure, though.

Woman: What happens after I fill out the application?

Man: Usually within a few days you get a report back. Your report will tell you which types of aid you qualify for.

Woman: Did you qualify for any financial aid?

Man: Yes. My family is low-income, so I got a grant. I'm supposed to get a few thousand dollars from it when school starts back in the fall. I don't anticipate taking any loans, but if I need them, they're available.

Woman: I'll fill out the government loan application right now. Thanks!

Academic Part 3 (p. 102)

Epigenetics—How Our Lifestyle Determines Which Genes Get Turned On

Most of the things that we call chronic diseases are related to lifestyle and environment. What you eat, the people you are socially connected with, your spiritual life, and your general mood all factor into your overall health. But your daily habits also determine which of your genes get turned on. The study of gene expression over the lifetime of a person is known as epigenetics. OK, so what is epigenetics? Epigenetics is basically the study of which genes get turned on and off.

If a doctor says to you that you have the gene that makes you more prone to be fat, or I should use the medical term "obese," then you still have a say in whether or not that gene gets expressed, or turned on. I know that if I had that gene, I'm not going to eat junk food. I'm going to start eating green leafy vegetables and nuts. I'm probably also going to watch my sugar intake. And I'm going to go out and exercise because I do not want that obesity gene to express.

It can be useful to think of epigenetics in terms of an analogy. Our genes can be thought of as a series of light switches. Imagine the genes that you inherit from your parents as the light switches in a house. Now imagine that each room in the house has one or more light switches. Depending on where you spend your time in the house, some of those light switches will be turned on more often than others. This is the basis of epigenetics. Even though you inherit a set of genes from your parents, the genes will get turned on and off based on the life that you live.

OK, you might be asking how epigenetic theories can be tested. Well one of the most fascinating ways is to study identical twins. Identical twins look the same genetically when they are born. But if you were to genetically test the twins when they turn 50, you would probably see two very different people. They've each turned different genes on and off depending on their lifestyle choices. Populations with similar genetic traits are also interesting to study for tracing gene expression. Researchers have studied why an Amish community, who happens to carry the obesity gene, does not get obese. It's because the Amish are very active people who walk and exercise as part of their daily routine. The research showed that the obesity gene stayed dormant because of the physical activity.

What if we taught people to follow a vegan diet and to start exercising more? We could teach healthy activities like doing yoga, learning to meditate and participating in an active social life. Doesn't that sound like a good prescription to fight against any disease? It turns out that just as genes get turned on, certain genes can be turned off if we adopt healthy habits. Even dangerous cancer genes can be turned off with lifestyle changes. In this way, it turns out that lifestyle change is one of the most powerful forms of medicine.

When we think about the origins of medical problems, we have to take toxin exposure into consideration. Cardiologists who work with heart patients understand that over-exposure to mercury is linked to coronary heart disease. Researchers also know that the cadmium mineral is linked to kidney disease. The children in Flint, Michigan, who were exposed to lead-tainted water might suffer from developmental disabilities. The potential impact of toxins is not just in heavy metals, but it's also in the air we breathe. It's also in the water that we drink, which might contain BPA that has leached out of plastic bottles.

Genetic information is even used by doctors to guide them on what drugs work best for their patients. But it's also true that we can't just take pills and think that medicine alone will cure us. I think the approach of taking a pill and thinking that it's going to cure everything is very limiting. We are each responsible for our own health, and we can all take steps to improve our daily lives in ways that make us less likely to get sick. For most people, that means eating a diet rich in vegetables, getting daily exercise, and allowing plenty of time to laugh with friends.

パートナー校一覧

iTEPで留学できる大学一覧

＊2021年7月時点のリストです。随時変更がありますので、最新情報は必ず https://www.itepexam.com/academic-partner-schools でご確認ください。

School	Score
United States of America	
Alabama	
Auburn Global	None
Auburn University at Montgomery	Graduate: 3.7
	Undergraduate: 3.7
Jacksonville State University	Undergraduate: 4.5
South University, Montgomery	Associate: 4.0
	Graduate: 4.5
	Undergraduate: 4.0
Troy University	Graduate: 4.0
	Undergraduate: 3.5
University of South Alabama	Graduate: 3.7
	Undergraduate: 3.6
Arizona	
Embry-Riddle	English Language Program: 4.0
Keller Graduate School of Management Glendale Center	Graduate: 4.5
Keller Graduate School of Management Mesa Center	Graduate: 4.5
Pima Community College	Associate: 3.5
Arkansas	
Arkansas State University	Graduate: 4.5
	Undergraduate: 4.0
University of Arkansas	Undergraduate: 3.9
California	
American English College - Monterey Park	None
American English College - Rowland Heights	None
American English Institute California State University, Fresno	Undergraduate: 3.6
Anaheim University	Associate: 4.0
	Undergraduate: 4.0
Bakersfield College	Associate: 3.0
Berkeley City College	Undergraduate: 4.0
California Institute of Advanced Management	Graduate: 3.8
California International Business University	Graduate: 6.0
	Undergraduate: 4.5
California State University, Fresno	Graduate: 4.5
	Undergraduate: 3.6
California State University, Northridge	Undergraduate: 5.0
California State University, Sacramento	English Language Program: 3.0
	Graduate: 5.0
	Undergraduate: 4.2

School	Score
California State University, San Bernardino, International Extension Programs	None
Cerritos College	None
Chabot College International Student Program	Undergraduate: 4.0
Charleston Southern University	Graduate: 3.7
	Undergraduate: 3.7
Citrus College	Associate: 3.5
Cogswell Polytechnical College	Undergraduate: 4.5
College of Alameda	Associate: 4.0
College Of The Canyons	Associate: 2.0
College of the Desert	Associate: 3.0
	Undergraduate: 3.0
Contra Costa College	None
CSU Channel Islands Semester for CI Program	None
Cypress College	Undergraduate: 5.0
De Anza College	Undergraduate: 4.0
Diablo Valley College	Undergraduate: 3.5
East Los Angeles College	Associate: 3.5
El Camino College	Undergraduate: 3.1
Evergreen Valley College	Undergraduate: 3.7
Foothill College	Undergraduate: 4.0
Fremont College	Undergraduate: 4.0
Fullerton College	Undergraduate: 3.5
Gemological Institute of America	Undergraduate: 3.5
Golden West College	Associate: 5.0
Horizon Institute	Graduate: 5.5
	Undergraduate: 5.0
Humboldt State University	Graduate: 4.5
	Undergraduate: 3.7
International American University	Associate: 3.5
	Graduate: 3.7
	Undergraduate: 3.5
Irvine Valley College	Associate: 3.5
	Undergraduate: 3.5
Keck Graduate Institute of Applied Life Sciences	Graduate: 5.0
Keller Graduate School of Management Elk Grove (Sacramento)	Graduate: 4.5
La Sierra University	None
Lake Tahoe Community College	Associate: 3.4
Laney College	Associate: 4.0
Las Positas College	Associate: 4.0
Loma Linda University	Associate: 3.5
	Graduate: 3.5
	Undergraduate: 3.5

Long Beach City College	Associate: 3.5	UCLA Extension - Study Abroad	Study Abroad at UCLA Program: 5.0
	Undergraduate: 3.5	UCLA Summer Sessions	Undergraduate: 4.0
Los Angeles City College (LACC)	Undergraduate: 4.0	UCSC Extension	Extension: 3.7
Los Angeles Harbor College	Associate: 3.5	University of California Irvine - Summer Session	English Language Program: 0
Los Angeles Pierce College	Undergraduate: 4.0		Associate: 3.5
Los Angeles Trade-Technical College	Associate: 3.4		Graduate: 4.0
Los Medanos College	None		Undergraduate: 3.5
Menlo College	Undergraduate: 4.5	University of California Santa Cruz Extension	Graduate: 3.7
Merritt College	Undergraduate: 4.0	University of Redlands	None
Moorpark College	Undergraduate: 3.0	USC School of Pharmacy	None
Mount St. Mary's University	Graduate: 5.5	West Hills Community College	Associate: 3.5
	Undergraduate: 3.8	West Los Angeles College	None
Mt Sierra College	Undergraduate: 3.0	Westcliff University	Graduate: 3.5
National University, Los Angeles Campus	None		Undergraduate: 2.5
National University, San Diego	None	Whittier College	Undergraduate: 4.0
Newport International University	Graduate: 3.8	Woodbury University	Graduate: 5.0
	Undergraduate: 3.5		Undergraduate: 4.0
Notre Dame De Namur University	Graduate: 4.5	**Colorado**	
	Undergraduate: 4.5	Northeastern Junior College	Remedial English Coursework: 3.0
Orange Coast College	Associate: 3.5	**Connecticut**	
Pacific Union College	Associate: 3.5	Sacred Heart University	Undergraduate: 5.0
	Undergraduate: 3.5	University of New Haven	Associate: 3.7
Palomar College	None		Graduate: 3.7
Pasadena City College	Undergraduate: 3.0		Undergraduate: 3.7
Peralta Community College District	Associate: 4.0	**Delaware**	
Rio Hondo College	Associate: 3.0	University of Delaware	Graduate: 3.9
Riverside Community College	Undergraduate: 3.5	**District of Columbia**	
Saddleback College	Associate: 4.0	American International Accelerator	None
Saint Mary's College of California	Undergraduate: 3.8	Potomac College	Undergraduate: 4.0
San Francisco State University	Semester and Summer Programs: 4.0	University of The District of Columbia	Graduate: 5.0
	Undergraduate Certificates: 4.0		Undergraduate: 5.0
Santa Barbara Business College	Associate: 5.0	**Florida**	
	Graduate: 5.0	Broward College	None
	Undergraduate: 5.0	Hillsborough Community College	Undergraduate: 4.0
Santa Clara University	Graduate: 4.5	Keller School of Management Orlando Center	Graduate: 4.5
	Undergraduate: 4.5	Miami International University of Art & Design	Undergraduate: 4.5
Santa Monica College	Undergraduate: 3	Nova Southeastern University	None
Santa Rosa Junior College	Associate: 4.0	SAE Institute	None
Santiago Canyon College	Associate: 3.0	South University, Tampa	Associate: 4.0
School of Audio Engineering (SAE)	Associate: 5.0		Graduate: 4.5
Solano Community College	Associate: 3.5		Undergraduate: 4.0
Southern California Institute of Technology	Associate: 3.5	South University, West Palm Beach	Associate: 4.0
	Undergraduate: 3.5		Graduate: 4.5
The Young Americans College of the Performing Arts	Two-Year Associate Studies: 3.7		Undergraduate: 4.0
UC Berkeley Summer Sessions	Undergraduate: 5.0	**Georgia**	
UCLA Extension - Certificates Programs	None	Keller Graduate School of Management Atlanta Buckhead	Graduate: 4.5

Keller Graduate School of Management Atlanta Perimeter	Graduate: 4.5
Point University	Undergraduate: 4.0
Shorter University	Graduate: 3.5
	Undergraduate: 3.0
South University, Atlanta	Associate: 4.0
	Graduate: 4.5
	Undergraduate: 4.0
South University, Savannah	Associate: 4.0
	Graduate: 4.5
	Undergraduate: 4.0

Hawaii

Hawaii Pacific University	Remedial English Coursework: 3.0
	Undergraduate: 3.7

Idaho

Boise State University	Undergraduate: 3.7

Illinois

DePaul University	Graduate: 3.0
	Undergraduate: 3.0
Eastern Illinois University	Graduate: 5.0
	Undergraduate: 4.5
Joliet Junior College	Undergraduate: 3.7
Keller Graduate School of Management Lincolnshire Center	Graduate: 4.5
Keller Graduate School of Management Online MBA & Graduate Programs	Graduate: 4.5
Keller Graduate School of Management Schaumburg Center	Graduate: 4.5
Lake Land College	Associate: 4.0
Southern Illinois University, Carbondale	Associate: 3.8
	Graduate: 5.0
	Undergraduate: 3.8
Tribeca Flashpoint College	Associate: 4.5
	Undergraduate: 4.5
University of Illinois, Springfield	Undergraduate: 4.5
University of St. Francis	Graduate: 3.5
	Undergraduate: 3.5
Western Illinois University, Macomb Campus	English Language Program: 3.7
	Graduate: 3.7
	Undergraduate: 3.7

Indiana

American Honors - Ivy Tech Community College of Indiana - Ft. Wayne	Associate: 4.5
	Undergraduate: 4.5
American Honors - Ivy Tech Community College of Indiana - Lafayette	Associate: 4.5
	Undergraduate: 4.5
Butler University	Undergraduate: 3.8
Valparaiso University	Undergraduate: 5.0

Iowa

Buena Vista University	Remedial English Coursework: 3.0
	Undergraduate: 3.5
Cornell College	Undergraduate: 3.8
Grand View University	Undergraduate: 3.4

Kansas

Benedictine College	Graduate: 5.5
	Undergraduate: 5.0
Butler Community College	None
Fort Hays State University	Graduate: 3.9
	Undergraduate: 3.6
Hesston College	Undergraduate: 4.0
International KU	None

Kentucky

Georgetown College	Graduate: 4.5
	Undergraduate: 4.5
Sullivan University	Graduate: 5.0
	Undergraduate: 4.0
Sullivan University (Lexington)	None
Sullivan University (Louisville)	None
Sullivan University Online	Graduate: 5.0
	Undergraduate: 4.0
University of the Cumberlands	English Language Program: 3.0
	Graduate: 4.0
	Undergraduate: 3.8

Maine

Husson University	Associate: 5.0
	Graduate: 5.0
	Undergraduate: 5.0

Maryland

Frostburg State University	Graduate: 4.5
	Undergraduate: 3.6
Frostburg State University Exchange Program	Undergraduate: 3.5

Massachusetts

Assumption College	Undergraduate: 3.7
Bay State College	Associate: 4.0
	Undergraduate: 4.0
Becker College	None
Benjamin Franklin Institute of Technology	Undergraduate: 3.6
Bunker Hill Community College	Associate: 3.0
Fisher College	English Language Program: 2.0
	Associate: 3.5
	Undergraduate: 3.5
Karen Pryor Academy for Animal Training and Behavior - Dog Trainer Professional Program	iTEP Academic: 3.0

Appendix

MCPHS University School of Pharmacy	Bridge Admission: 3.7
	Graduate Admission (lab-based programs): 4.5
	Graduate Admission (non-lab-based programs): 4.0
	Undergraduate: 4.0
Western New England University	None
Worcester State University	Graduate: 3.5
	Undergraduate: 3.5
Michigan	
Ferris State University	Graduate: 4.0
	Undergraduate: 4.0
Great Lakes Christian College	Undergraduate: 4.5
Northern Michigan University	Undergraduate: 3.7
Saginaw Valley State University	Graduate: 3.4
	Undergraduate: 3.3
	Undergraduate: 3.5
University of Michigan-Flint	Undergraduate: 4.5
Western Michigan Christian High School	None
Minnesota	
Concordia University, St. Paul	Graduate: 3.7
	Undergraduate: 3.5
Saint Mary's University of Minnesota	Graduate: 4.0
Mississippi	
University of Southern Mississippi	Undergraduate: 4.0
Missouri	
Columbia College of Missouri	None
Cottey College	Associate: 3.7
	Undergraduate: 3.7
Culver- Stockton College	Graduate: 4.0
	Undergraduate: 4.0
Maryville University of St. Louis	Remedial English Coursework: 3.3
	Graduate: 3.9
	Undergraduate: 3.6
Missouri Southern State University	English Language Program: 0
	Undergraduate: 3.7
Missouri Western State University	None
Park University	Graduate: 3.7
	Undergraduate: 3.5
Rockhurst University	Graduate: 3.9
	Undergraduate: 3.9
Southeast Missouri State University	Graduate: 3.9
	Undergraduate: 3.7
Stephens College	Graduate: 3.7
Truman State University	Graduate: 3.8
	Undergraduate: 3.8

Webster University	Graduate: 3.9
	Undergraduate: 3.7
William Woods University	Graduate: 4.0
	Undergraduate: 4.0
Montana	
Carroll College	Undergraduate: 4.5
Montana State University	Undergraduate: 3.7
Montana State University Billings	Associate: 3.5
	Graduate: 3.5
	Undergraduate: 3.5
University of Montana	None
Nebraska	
Bellevue University	None
Nevada	
College of Southern Nevada	Associate: 4.0
Truckee Meadows Community College	Undergraduate: 3.7
New Hampshire	
Southern New Hampshire University	Graduate: 4.2
	Undergraduate: 3.8
New Jersey	
American Honors - Mercer County Community College (West Windsor, NJ)	Associate: 4.5
	Undergraduate: 4.5
Felician University	English Language Program: None
Rider University	Undergraduate: 3.5
New York	
Adelphi International	None
Berkeley College	Undergraduate: 5.0
Concordia College - New York	Undergraduate: 3.5
Erie Community College - SUNY	Associate: 3.3
Fulton-Montgomery Community College	Associate: 3.5
Gemological Institute of America	Undergraduate: 4.0
Hofstra University	Graduate: 4.0
Manhattan Institute of Management	Graduate: 5.0
	Undergraduate: 5.0
Medaille College	Undergraduate: 3.5
Mohawk Valley Community College (SUNY)	Associate: 3.4
Monroe College	English Language Program: 3.0
	Associate: 3.5
	Graduate: 4.5
	Undergraduate: 4.0
Nassau Community College - SUNY	Associate: 3.4
New York Conservatory for Dramatic Arts	Associate: 3.7
New York University	Undergraduate: 4.5
New York University Stern School of Business	Graduate: 4.5
Russell Sage College For Women	Undergraduate: 5.0
Sage College of Albany	Undergraduate: 5.0
St. Francis College	None

State University of New York at Geneseo	None		Sinclair Community College	Associate: 4.0
State University of New York at Oswego (SUNY)	Graduate: 4.0		The University of Toledo	None
	Undergraduate: 4.0		Tiffin University	Graduate: 3.9
SUNY Broome	Associate: 3.5			Undergraduate: 3.4
SUNY Buffalo State	Undergraduate: 3.5		**Oregon**	
SUNY Canton	Associate: 3.5		George Fox University	Graduate: 3.9
	Undergraduate: 3.5			Undergraduate: 2.9
SUNY Cobleskill	Undergraduate: 4.0		**Pennsylvania**	
SUNY College at Old Westbury	Graduate: 4.0		Arcadia University	Graduate: 5.0
	Undergraduate: 3.5			Undergraduate: 4.5
SUNY Cortland	Graduate: 3.9		California University of Pennsylvania	English Language Program: 0
	Undergraduate: 3.5			Associate: 3.5
SUNY Delhi	Undergraduate: 3.5			Graduate: 4.0
SUNY Farmingdale State College	Undergraduate: 3.5			Undergraduate: 3.5
SUNY Fredonia	Graduate: 3.0		Chatham University	None
	Undergraduate: 3.0		Edinboro University	None
SUNY Geneseo	Undergraduate: 3.7		Global TEFL Academy	Undergraduate: 3.8
SUNY Morrisville State College	International Pathway Program (IPP): 3.3		Lock Haven University of Pennsylvania	Undergraduate: 3.7
	Undergraduate: 3.5		Millersville University of Pennsylvania	Graduate: 4.5
SUNY Oneonta	Undergraduate: 3.5			Undergraduate: 4.0
SUNY Polytechnic Institute	Graduate: 4.4		Moravian College	None
	Undergraduate: 4.4		Robert Morris University	Undergraduate: 5.0
SUNY Potsdam	Undergraduate: 3.5		Saint Francis University	Graduate: 4.0
SUNY Purchase College	Graduate: 3.7			Undergraduate: 4.0
	Undergraduate: 3.7		Temple University	Undergraduate: 3.9
SUNY Sullivan	Associate: 3.1		**South Carolina**	
Westchester Community College (SUNY)	Associate: 3.3		Anderson University	Undergraduate: 3.7
North Carolina			College of Charleston	Undergraduate: 3.8
Appalachian State University	Undergraduate: 3.8		South University, Columbia	Associate: 4.0
Durham Technical Community College	Two-Year Associate Studies: 3.0			Graduate: 4.5
Gardner-Webb University	Undergraduate: 3.5			Undergraduate: 4.0
Greensboro College - Master of Arts in TESOL	Graduate: 3.9		**South Dakota**	
High Point University	None		Black Hills State University	Undergraduate: 3.6
Montreat College	Undergraduate: 3.5		South Dakota State University	Graduate: 3.7
University of North Carolina at Greensboro	Undergraduate: 3.8			Undergraduate: 3.6
William Peace University	Undergraduate: 4.0		**Tennessee**	
North Dakota			Bethel University	Undergraduate: 3.6
Minot State University	Graduate: 5.0		Maryville College	Undergraduate: 3.9
Ohio			Middle Tennessee State University	Undergraduate: 3.6
Cleveland State University	Graduate: 5.0		Tennessee Tech University	Undergraduate: 4.5
	Undergraduate: 5.0		Tusculum College	None
Lorain County Community College	Associate: 3.5		Union University	Undergraduate: 3.9
Miami University Middletown - English Language Center	None		**Texas**	
			Alamo Colleges District	None
Ohio Wesleyan University	Undergraduate: 3.8		Dallas Baptist University	Graduate: 3.9
Shawnee State University	Associate: 4.0			Undergraduate: 3.7
	Graduate: 4.0		Jacksonville College	Associate: 3.5
	Undergraduate: 4.0		Midwestern State University	None

Panola College	Associate: 3.5
Southwestern Adventist University	English Language Program: 3.0
	Graduate: 5.0
	Undergraduate: 3.9
Sul Ross State University	Graduate: 3.5
	Undergraduate: 3.5
Tarleton State University	Graduate: 3.9
	Undergraduate: 3.5
Texas Wesleyan University	Graduate: 5.0
	Undergraduate: 4.0
The Art Institute of Dallas	Undergraduate: 4.5
The Art Institute of Houston	Undergraduate: 4.5
The University of Texas at San Antonio	Undergraduate: 3.8
University of Dallas- Satish and Yasmin Gupta College of Business	Business Studies: 3.9
University of Houston-Victoria	Graduate: 3.5
	Undergraduate: 3.5
University of Mary Hardin Baylor	Undergraduate: 5.0
Utah	
Southern Utah University	None
Westminster College	None
Vermont	
Saint Michael's College	English Language Program: 4.0
	Remedial English Coursework: 4.5
	Undergraduate: 5.0
Virginia	
California University of Management and Sciences	Associate: 3.5
	Exit Test: 3.5
	Graduate: 4.0
	Undergraduate: 3.5
IGlobal University	None
Liberty University	Associate: 4.0
	Graduate: 4.5
	Undergraduate: 4.0
University of North America	Graduate: 3.5
	Undergraduate: 3.5
Virginia International University	Graduate: 5.0
	Undergraduate: 5
Washington	
American Honors - Community Colleges of Spokane (Spokane, WA)	Associate: 4.5
	Undergraduate: 4.5
American Honors - Pierce College (Lakewood, WA)	Associate: 4.5
	Undergraduate: 4.5
Cascadia College	Associate: 4.0
	Undergraduate: 4.0

City University of Seattle	Graduate: 4.5
	Undergraduate: 3.5
Green River College	Undergraduate: 5.0
Lake Washington Institute of Technology	Associate: 4.5
Olympic College	Undergraduate: 4.5
Peninsula College	Associate: 4.5
Pierce College	Associate: 4.0
South Seattle Community College	Associate: 4.5
Spokane Community College	Undergraduate: 4.0
Spokane Falls Community College	Undergraduate: 4.0
University of Washington Bothell	Undergraduate: 3.7
	Undergraduate: 3.9
Walla Walla University	Associate: 3.9
	Graduate: 3.9
	Undergraduate: 3.9
Wisconsin	
University of Wisconsin - Madison Visiting International Student Program (VISP)	English Language Program: 3.8
University of Wisconsin- Baraboo/ Sauk County	Associate: 4.0
University of Wisconsin- Barron County	Associate: 4.0
University of Wisconsin- Fond du Lac	Associate: 4.0
University of Wisconsin- Fox Valley	Associate: 4.0
University of Wisconsin- Manitowoc	Associate: 4.0
University of Wisconsin- Marathon County	Associate: 4.0
University of Wisconsin- Marinette	Associate: 4.0
University of Wisconsin- Marshfield/ Wood County	Associate: 4.0
University of Wisconsin- Richland	Associate: 4.0
University of Wisconsin- Rock County	Associate: 4.0
University of Wisconsin- Sheboygan	Associate: 4.0
University of Wisconsin- Superior	Undergraduate: 4.0
University of Wisconsin- Washington County	Associate: 4.0
University of Wisconsin- Waukesha	Associate: 4.0
University of Wisconsin- Whitewater	Undergraduate: 3.7
University of Wisconsin-Madison	Undergraduate: 3.8
Wyoming	
Northwest College	Undergraduate: 5.0
None	
ACEI - Academic Credentials Evaluation Institute	None
DeVry University	Associate: 4.0
	Undergraduate: 4.0
Canada	
Alberta	
DeVry University Canada	Associate: 4.0
	Undergraduate: 4.0
British Columbia	
Coast Mountain College	None
College of New Caledonia	None

Focus College	Undergraduate: 3.6

Ontario

Biztech College of Health Sciences, Business & Technology	English Language Program: 3.4
	Remedial English Coursework: 3.4
	Associate: 3.5
	Graduate: 3.5
	Undergraduate: 3.5
Canadian Technical And Management College	Undergraduate: 3.5
Centennial College	Undergraduate: 3.7
Mohawk College	Undergraduate: 3.5
Sault College	None
Sheridan College	Undergraduate: 3.6

United Kingdom

England

Newbold College of Higher Education	Graduate: 4.0
	Undergraduate: 3.5
Richmond the American International University in London (EU nationals only)	Graduate: 5.0
	Undergraduate: 4.5

Mexico

Playa del Carmen

Universidad Tecnlógica de la Riviera Maya	Remedial English Coursework: 2.0
	English Language Program: 2.5
	Undergraduate: 3.4

Iraq

Sulaimaniyah

Interchange Institute	None

Sulaymania

American University of Iraq, Sulaymania	Undergraduate: 3.9

Iran

Tehran

Shahid Beheshti University (SBU)	Ph.D Program: 3.5

France

Paris

American Business School Paris	None

Ecuador

Quevedo

World English Institute Ec	English Language Program: None

Colombia

Bogota

Fundacion Universidad de America	Graduate: 3.5

Colombia

Universidad Cooperitiva de Colombia	Graduate: 3.5
Universidad de La Sabana	Undergraduate: 5.0
Universidad del Bosque	Undergraduate: 4.0
Universidad del Norte	Graduate: 3.5
Universidad del Rosario	Graduate: 4.0
Universidad Militar Nueva Granada	Graduate: 3.5
Universidad Nacional Abierta y a Distancia Colombia	Graduate: 3.5
Universidad Pedagogica y Tecnologica	None

China

Beijing

BELA Education International (Beijing Foreign Studies University)	English Language Program: 3.0
	Associate: 3.5

アイテップ
iTEP公認 プラクティスガイド

2021 年 8 月 12 日　第 1 刷 発行

著　　者　　iTEP International

発 行 者　　浦　晋亮

発 行 所　　IBC パブリッシング株式会社

　　　　　　〒 162-0804 東京都新宿区中里町 29 番 3 号 菱秀神楽坂ビル 9F
　　　　　　Tel. 03-3513-4511　Fax. 03-3513-4512
　　　　　　www.ibcpub.co.jp

印 刷 所　　株式会社シナノパブリッシングプレス

落丁本・乱丁本は、小社宛にお送りください。送料小社負担にてお取り替えいたします。

Printed in Japan

ISBN978-4-7946-0670-9

装幀　　　　岩目地英樹 (コムデザイン)
翻訳　　　　English-i
編集協力　　オフィス LEPS、iTEP Japan